AMERICAN
GAME
COOKING

AMERICAN GAME COOKING

A Contemporary Guide to Preparing Farm-Raised Game Birds and Meats

John Ash & Sid Goldstein

Produced in association with Fetzer Vineyards

ARIS BOOKS

Addison-Wesley Publishing Company, Inc.

Reading, Massachusetts   Menlo Park, California   New York
Don Mills, Ontario   Wokingham, England   Amsterdam   Bonn
Sydney   Singapore   Tokyo   Madrid   San Juan
Paris   Seoul   Milan   Mexico City   Taipei

Many of the designations used by manufacturers and sellers to distinguish their products are claimed as trademarks. Where those designations appear in this book and Addison-Wesley was aware of a trademark claim, the designations have been printed in initial capital letters (e.g., Cry-ovac).

Library of Congress Cataloging-in-Publication Data
Ash, John, 1942–
   American game cooking / John Ash & Sid Goldstein.
      p.   cm.
   "Produced in association with Fetzer Vineyards."
   "Aris books."
   Includes bibliographical references.
   ISBN 0-201-57005-X
   1. Cookery (Game)   I. Goldstein, Sid. II. Title.
TX751.A79   1991
641.6'91—dc20

91-8040
CIP

Portions of some of the recipes in this book appeared, in somewhat different form, in other publications:

The recipes on pages 155 and 230 are reprinted with the permission of Mark Miller and are from the book *Coyote Cafe,* published by Ten Speed Press, 1989. All rights reserved.

The recipe on page 112 is reprinted with the permission of Susan Feniger and Mary Sue Milliken from the book *City Cuisine,* published by William Morrow and Co., 1989. All rights reserved.

The recipe on page 199 is reprinted with the permission of John Folse from the book *The Evolution of Cajun & Creole Cuisine,* published by Wimmer Brothers, Inc. 1989. All rights reserved.

The recipe on page 111 is reprinted with the permission of Anne Rosenzweig from the book *The Arcadia Seasonal Mural and Cookbook,* published by Harry N. Abrams, Inc., 1986. All rights reserved.

The recipe on page 211 is reprinted with the permission of Hugh Carpenter from the book *Pacific Flavors,* published by Stewart, Tabori, and Chang, 1988. All rights reserved.

Photography: Patrick Barta
Styling and Design: Inez McGowen, Imaginez
Jacket Design: Diana Coe
Text Design: Linda Dingler
Technical Illustrations: Claude Martinot
Set in 12-point Goudy Old Style by NK Graphics

 2 3 4 5 6 7 8 9-VB-95949392
First printing, September 1991

CONTENTS

II A COOK'S TOUR OF GAME BIRDS AND MEATS 167

ACKNOWLEDGMENTS

No book has ever been written without the assistance, advice, inspiration, love, and support of a lot of people. This one is certainly no exception. In particular, we'd like to shine a very bright light on the following beings who made this particular dream a reality.

From Sid: To Suzanne and Zachary Goldstein, my deepest love and thanks for all your patience, for the weekend days that Dad had to bang on the computer instead of "playing rough house," baseball, or bike ride with Zack, and to my true love, Suzanne, for your constant faith and support; to Mom, who gave me the genetic resources to inspire this effort and the passion for food and temperament in the kitchen to carry it out; to the Fetzer family, particularly Jim, Mary, Patti, and John, for your foresight and vision; to John Ash, my mentor, who has taught me a greater respect for food than I ever imagined learning; to Inez McGowen and Patrick Barta, for beautiful styling and photography; to John Law, for helping bring me to my place of destiny; to Dorothy Woll, for manuscript assistance; to Conrad Rogers and Apple Computer, for loan of "the machine"; to John Harris, our fearless editor, for his unending interest in this slow-to-unravel discourse, and to Greg Kaplan, for his technical recipe edit; to Gerald Prolman and Mark Stech-Novak, two incredibly experienced game runners whose early input helped get this project rolling; to Mitch at The Game Exchange, for great product with which to cook; to Tom Cole; to all of the chefs whose recipes helped to make this book complete; and to the many friends who so willingly gave of their appetites to experience these dishes. To all of you—go ahead—be game!

From John: To Sid, for his energy, patience, and daily reminders—the best "Jewish grandmother" I've ever had; to my own Grandmother, who started me cooking; to Jeff Madura, friend and chef at John Ash & Company, for his help and ideas with recipes; and, of course, to my collective kids—Nancy, John, Emily, and Tyler. Thanks for being here.

LIST OF RECIPES

Goose

Partridge & Grouse

Pheasant

Quail

Rabbit and Hare

Squab

Wild Turkey

Venison

Exotic Game Animals

ALLIGATOR

ESCARGOT

FROG'S LEGS

RATTLESNAKE

SQUIRREL

INTRODUCTION

*T*he world of game cooking is a gastronomic universe without peer, one that brings immense gratification to both the knowing cook and the appreciative diner. It is a world unexplored by many—a new frontier in contemporary gastronomy with enormous potential. Those of us who've dined on game often are captivated by its deep flavors and infinite flexibility. The smell of a marinated squab over an open wood fire tantalizes our senses and makes our mouths water, just as the savory flavors of a long-simmered rabbit stew, redolent of herbs, spices, and winter vegetables, is a reassurance of the blessings of another time and place.

As we enter the 1990s, it is ironic that game should be thought of as a new culinary trend since game dishes are the oldest legacy of our cooking heritage. Yet, for most of America over the past few decades, with the exception of the occasional Thanksgiving or Christmas bird, game has been all but nonexistent at the nation's table.

That we should be rediscovering this important food source at a time when medical authorities are alerting us to the many benefits of low-fat, low-cholesterol, high-protein foods is fatefully appropriate. Most game offers many health benefits in addition to incomparable flavor (see Nutritional Guidelines, page 263).

The current resurgence of interest in game comes at a time when American cuisine is being thoroughly redefined by contemporary chefs. For generations raised on more conventional meats, seafood, and poultry, the hearty, robust taste of venison, wild boar, buffalo, pheasant, rabbit, and small game birds provides welcome new flavor experiences that harken back almost subliminally to the cuisines of our forefathers. For many years, game has been thought of as exotic and strange, yet it has always been one of our basic, indigenous food sources.

We are not hunters. Therefore, this is *not* a book on how to shoot, skin, pluck, gut, or hang a wild animal. Hunters seeking such information can find those procedures well-documented in other excellent books on the subject. Nor will this book attempt

1

to be a complete dictionary on wild game animals; this too has been expansively treated in other volumes.

This *is*, however, a book that speaks directly to the home cook looking for new challenges and tastes. It deals primarily with farm-raised game—pheasant, squab, quail, and so on—which are raised on vast acreages where they are allowed to range freely. Most of these animals are reared totally free of hormones, antibiotics, and steroids, and they are state or federally inspected for quality and freedom from disease and parasites. Because of the availability of farm-raised animals year round, the recipes in this book reflect a wide range of outdoor spring and summer dishes as well as the more traditional fall and winter specialties. Game fortunately is no longer a one or two season phenomenon.

Most importantly, this "new breed" of game is increasingly stocked in mainstream butcher shops and supermarkets in a variety of familiar cuts. Our goal is to teach you how to purchase, prepare, and cook this game properly and how to recognize the types and cuts best suited to a particular cooking method. In the process, we also hope to introduce those who hunt wild game to some new cooking techniques and exciting flavor combinations.

The growth of the farm-raised game movement brings with it a torrent of discussion. Issues of ecological concern, animal rights, the comparative taste and flavor of farm- or ranch-raised game versus wild game, and health and nutritional value are increasingly debated as this new industry expands.

To those who support animal rights, we acknowledge that the farm raising of game will probably not please you any more than the farming of cattle, sheep, or poultry does. Clearly, the lack of standards of many of our food-processing industries in the past, as well as our astonishing insensitivity to certain scarce populations of creatures in the wild, is a cause for concern.

We see in the farm-raised game movement in America, however, a tremendous opportunity to correct many past mistakes. Most notably, the feverish decimation of the buffalo population in this country has almost singlehandedly been reversed by the conscientious farming of buffalo. Similar accomplishments can be found in the raising of many almost-extinct species of game birds, such as wild turkey.

The impact of farm-raised game on our land is significant as well. Studies have shown that game animals, principally venison, are more efficient land users than domesticated livestock. Venison and antelope graze randomly and obtain most of their water from plant vegetation; they are also able to conserve water naturally in their bodies. Cattle, in contrast, tend to stay near their watering hole. After some time, the land shows the natural effects of overgrazing, with a desertlike environment developing immediately around the watering area. Many game breeders feel that the overall environmental impact of these animals on the land is highly positive and that such farming will ultimately prove to be the most efficient use of marginal agricultural land in the United States.

Those involved in the farm-raised game industry can also make a virtually indisputable claim to the conscientious processing of their animals. It is a welcome and extraordinary achievement to offer the home cook and professional chef alike animals that have been raised in a simulated natural environment, totally free from the chemicals used in much of modern agribusiness. We applaud the foresight and dedication of many of these producers and can only hope that their sensitivity to the health and sanitation of their product continues.

Game is not difficult to cook. The procedures outlined in this book are straight-forward. The skills required of a true master of game cooking are experience and sensitivity. The ability to prepare properly the game at hand involves understanding such simple culinary principles as marinating and seasoning and then applying the appropriate cooking technique.

If there is one key lesson that runs through most of the recipes in this book, it is not to overcook game! Many cooks have somehow absorbed the mistaken notion that most game has to be cooked forever—somewhat like the famous spaghetti sauce that cooks on the back of the stove for days. Because in many such instances, clean, fresh flavors are lost almost entirely, our recipes emphasize the least amount of cooking time needed to arrive at a superb dish. As a case in point, in order to retain its natural juices, a tender loin of venison or fine cut of buffalo should never be cooked beyond medium rare.

We've also expended some effort to focus on recipes that stress the nutritious, low-fat, low-cholesterol nature of game. It would be counterproductive to do otherwise. We do admit to including some of our favorite recipes, such as Warm Duck Foie Grâs Salad with Blackberry Vinegar and Grilled Buffalo Steaks with Chili-Corn Sauce, that, although on the rich side, are simply too good not to share.

This book concentrates on the most widely available farm-raised game: venison, buffalo, wild boar, and rabbit from the hooved-animal family; and duck, goose, partridge, pheasant, quail, squab, and wild turkey from the game-bird clan. For each of these animals, we've presented a classic recipe that recalls the traditions of wild-game cooking, a heritage that plays a central part in our contemporary approach and without which no game book would be complete. We've included a brief section on some of the more exotic game animals—squirrel, rattlesnake, alligator—but with limited recipes since these animals aren't readily available to the consumer.

There are no recipes for free-range chicken, poussin, Cornish game hens, and capon since these are not game birds and fall more specifically into the poultry domain.

They can be substituted for pheasant, quail, and squab in many of the recipes in this book, however.

In addition to the featured game recipes, we've presented many appropriate side dishes. These should be considered highly transferable, which is to say that we encourage you to use your imagination to mix and match them with various game dishes in the book.

During the writing of this book, as the two of us have traveled the country cooking, teaching, interviewing chefs, and researching regional game dishes, we've encountered extraordinary talent. Both American and European chefs in our country's finest restaurants have developed a fondness for farm-raised game. We're pleased to be able to share their culinary revelations along with our own.

Cutting through the crosscurrents of American game cooking, we find some striking regional differences. Note, for instance, the disparity of ingredients between Nancy Oakes's decidedly Californian Grilled Quail Salad with Grilled Plums and Prosciutto with Black Muscat Vinaigrette (page 173) and Frank Stitt's southern-inspired Roast Quail Stuffed with Green Onion Cornbread and Pecans (page 179).

For those who have problems locating game, a list of suppliers, both wholesale and retail, is located at the back of the book. The best way to ensure a ready supply of the specific birds or meats you desire is to let your local supermarket and specialty poultry and butcher shops know of your serious interest in game and encourage them to stock the product. Only then will we see greater availability (and perhaps lower prices).

Perhaps in showing that game is not so exotic and strange, and that it is healthful, nutritious, delicious, and easy to prepare, we can establish the concept that domesticated game belongs in our contemporary kitchen as much as wild game did in the kitchen of our ancestors. It is our intention that as we lobby for this acceptance that we also avoid the abuse that has been so pervasive with some species of wild game in the past.

We hope that the information in this book will prove to be an unending source of inspiration and satisfaction, as it has been to us in collecting it. We've attempted to develop recipes that appeal to the home cook, knowing full well that any cookbook that doesn't winds up a forgotten item on the back shelf, or not on any shelf at all.

If we succeed in demystifying the preparation and cooking of game even a little, we'll feel a real sense of accomplishment. If our book inspires you to bring glorious, nutritious game dishes to your table with regularity, we'll be truly proud of our work.

I

THE
COMING OF
AGE OF
GAME
COOKING

THE COMING OF AGE
OF GAME COOKING

*I*t seems shortsighted to plunge into a cookbook on game in contemporary cuisine without first exploring its rich heritage. After all, it is those very traditions that make game an integral part of today's cooking palette. To our hunter-gatherer ancestors, game was not only food, but clothing and shelter as well. In a sense, we owe it to them not to pretend that game is a "new" food source.

Prior to the invention of agriculture, game was both the primary diet and the focus of battles in the fields. As he stumbled about in his cave, the job of the Neolithic cook was to recognize the good meat from the bad and to learn to extract the most from the best. Over the millenia, this task has remained much the same.

If we pass quickly over the culinary exploits of our Stone Age ancestors, we discover that the American Indians were the first avid practitioners of game cooking. About four hundred years ago, Captain John Smith, the famous British explorer, noted in his diary that the New World was filled with game and that the Indians dined extensively, if not exclusively, on elk, deer, wild birds, duck, rabbit, and squirrel.

The legendary hunting prowess of the Indian is well documented. Armed with bow and arrow, he ostensibly lived on the animals of the wild, as well as fish from the streams, native plants, herbs, nuts, and berries. The huge bison herds that roamed the plains were the Indian's biggest prize, with one buffalo providing a huge ration of meat for a very large tribe.

As the first European settlers migrated to America, they brought with them strong culinary traditions surrounding game. Brillat-Savarin, the eighteenth-century French gastronome and writer, said of game in his classic *Physiology of Taste:* "[It] is one of our favorite delicacies; it is a food at once healthy, warming, savorous, and stimulating to the taste, and is easily assimilated by anyone with a youthful digestive apparatus. . . . But game, under the command of the knowing chef, undergoes a great number of cunning modifications and transformations, and supplies the main body of those highly flavored dishes which make up truly gastronomical cookery." Game was clearly held in high esteem in the European kitchen.

By the mid-nineteenth century in America, game birds and venison were found in meat markets around the country. Early cookbooks unveiled a diverse collection of simple preparations for venison, quail, and pheasant, as well as jugged hare, potted pigeons, and partridge pie.

Game continued to make further inroads in the American kitchen. The dutiful housewife of the hunter learned to prepare savory game stews, roast quail and pheasant in brandy or apple cider, and to create simple, fruit-based sauces for duck. Not to be ignored are the culinary achievements of "campfire cuisine." The hunter didn't always bring home the bounty, often preferring to enjoy it simply in the male camaraderie of the hunt.

The passenger pigeon was possibly the most common bird ever to exist in the United States. In 1810 the ornithologist Alexander Wilson reported a flock a mile wide and 240 miles long. Through either our aggressiveness or for sport, the last one was shot in 1899. Flocks of as many as one hundred wild turkeys, each weighing up to forty pounds, abounded in the woods.

This magnificent abundance established one tradition that we are still struggling to overcome. Overeating by North Americans has been a problem since the arrival of the first colonists. As Benjamin Franklin observed in *Poor Richard's Almanac:* "I saw few die of starvation but hundreds [die] of eating and drinking."

With the dawn of the twentieth century, game started its dramatic fall from favor in the American kitchen. The once-plentiful buffalo and elk that roamed the prairie were decimated by the rifles of greedy hunters to whom killing was often more satisfying than eating. Populations of wild game ran for cover, and were subsequently replaced by domesticated livestock. It was the beginning—and end—of an era.

Urbanization, suburbanization, and modern agriculture have pushed game out of modern American life. As the country has progressed, people's lives have become more complex, and reliance on "instant," processed, microwavable, freeze-dried, and vacuum-packed foods has emerged. This realm of convenience eating has little affinity for the raw muscle of game. Although the United States boasts some twenty-five million hunters, game has remained a rarity in most homes.

In order to protect the diminishing herds, laws were established to control the hunting and sale of wild game. Subsequently, in America, one of our greatest culinary traditions was temporarily abandoned, and game was relegated to the tables of sheiks, princes, and ambassadors of international domains.

The often-misunderstood laws regarding game are a result, in part, of conflicts between state and federal laws regarding its sale in this country. In general, state law governs the inspection of game in America, usually in conjunction with United States Department of Agriculture (USDA) inspection standards. The Food and Drug Administration becomes involved because their charter is to be responsible for food items that don't fall under the direct authority of other federal agencies. However, it does little from a practical standpoint because it has no inspection capability.

In contrast to Europe, where hunted game can be sold to restaurants, it is strictly prohibited to sell native deer and antelope in America. According to federal law, any game sold through commercial channels must now be raised on a farm or ranch and must be inspected by either the USDA or a state or local authority. It must also be sold through a licensed distributor in order to assure absolute conformity to health and sanitation regulations and to protect the consumer from improper handling and possible bacterial contamination.

The trendy, food-conscious decade of the 1980s was a springboard for rediscovering many of our lost culinary traditions. We learned to grow numerous varieties of fresh herbs and vegetables in our home gardens and experienced the joy of making preserves and chutneys with fruit from our orchards. Specialty farmstead cheese-making and olive oil and vinegar production are on the rise. In short, we're becoming a nation of flavor fanatics, seeking new culinary thrills and adventures with ribald enthusiasm combined with righteous awareness of health and ecological issues. With this evolution in our national food awareness, we are reconnecting with our culinary past, including the rich heritage of game cookery.

This revival of game in America is a relatively recent phenomenon. In 1979 the late cooking teacher–philosopher James Beard wrote about game that "most of the population will encounter nothing during their lifetime except frozen Long Island duckling," a gloomy prophecy that, fortunately, appears to be incorrect, as this book attests.

Farm-Raised Game: A New Beginning

The resurgence in game cooking in America would not be possible were it not for the recent availability of conscientiously processed, farm-raised game birds and meats from quality-oriented purveyors, both in America and abroad. These newly domesticated animals offer a wealth of versatile foods for the jaded American palate. Having lurched trendily through the culinary eighties, we may now be discovering something more substantial and enduring in game.

Whether it be buffalo steaks from Wyoming; ducks, pheasant, and squab from Sonoma County in Northern California; antelope and deer from the Texas hill country;

Australian boar; Scottish red deer; or imported New Zealand venison; Americans are starting to explore game as a nutritious, "new" food product.

The success of many top European and European-trained chefs in America is another factor in game's resurgence. Those chefs, to whom game is an integral part of a classical menu, have brought the traditions of their respective cuisines to the American table, and the impact has been tremendous. Restaurants across the country are now offering a wide variety of classic and innovative game dishes. Likewise, a new generation of young American chefs, curious about tradition and titillated by the taste of game, is reveling in game's potential for gustatory pleasure. To these chefs, who've long felt limited by the "palette of colors" available to them, game offers an exciting opportunity for creativity—an undiscovered gastronomic realm in which to experiment.

As these young chefs increase their understanding of how to prepare this new, farm-raised product properly, many age-old misconceptions are being eliminated in the process. Game is no longer hung for long periods to develop a strong, gamy flavor, tastes (and hygiene) have evolved, and the preference is for cleaner, fresher flavors in all foods. Brillat-Savarin describes the tradition of hanging game birds wonderfully when he talks about pheasant: "Pheasant, when eaten three days after its death, has nothing distinguishing about it. It is neither as delicate as a pullet nor as savorous as a quail. At its peak of ripeness, however, its flesh is tender, highly flavored, and sublime."

Farm-raised game is harvested when it is young and tender but not before it has developed full flavor. It is not restrained in overly crowded quarters, as animal-rights activists justifiably abhor; yet it does offer a unique, rich taste that is not as gamy as that of older hunted animals.

Some differentiation should be made between farm-raised and ranch-raised game. Ranched animals eat a more widely varied diet because they range freely over a very large enclosed area with no physical handling, whereas farmed game has a more restricted diet and is herded with some regularity.

Propelled by the increasing interest among both consumers and chefs, the farm-raised game industry is burgeoning. Small and large breeders have sprung up worldwide, anxious to cash in on escalating demand. Wholesalers in different parts of the country provide the important connection between the farmer-breeder and restaurants or markets. Improved techniques in icing and packing game, as well as development of reliable air express services, have also been instrumental in nurturing the growth of this important new industry.

The revived interest in game also has helped upgrade the industry tremendously, since suppliers have had to conform to rigid health standards. Ongoing communication between chefs and suppliers means that the exacting requirements of the restaurant kitchen are being better understood by suppliers, some of whom had previously raised their animals for gun clubs.

Success Stories: Venison from New Zealand, Texas, and New York

In the late 1800s and early 1900s, deer were brought to New Zealand from English parks and Scottish highlands to provide game for English sportsmen who settled there. The multiplying herds created a population boom that became a problem, so professional hunters were enlisted to shoot the deer to help stabilize the population.

Many years later—in the 1960s—a few entrepreneurs started exporting deer to Europe, where venison had long been a favored dish. Shooting took place largely from helicopters. The animals were packed in sacks, frozen, and immediately shipped. This unsportsmanlike style of hunting became lucrative as export tonnages increased.

By 1970 the New Zealand government had started licensing deer farms so that venison could be farm raised and bred, rather than shot in the wild. Six-foot-high fences were erected to provide a spatial limit to the animals' territory, but acreages were still large enough to allow some free-range capability.

Today there are 1.3 million New Zealand deer, a breed of Scottish red deer, on approximately fifty-five hundred farms. Exports of New Zealand venison to the United States have increased to close to 1.2 million pounds per year, with world-wide exports now reaching 10 million pounds per year. These deer are grass-fed; growth hormones or other chemical additives are not used. The animals are slaughtered in clean, highly regulated environments, where they are then skinned and desinewed for easier preparation. Following inspection by a government authority, they are chill-packed in Cryovac packages to ensure freshness.

The boom areas are not only international. In this country, the plains states and the Southwest are fertile areas for a wide variety of game breeding. One of the top entrepreneurs is Mike Hughes, whose Texas Wild Game Cooperative, founded in 1983 in Ingram, Texas, one hundred miles west of Austin in the Texas Hill Country, is an active wholesaler of game to top restaurants around the country.

Hughes's activity started in 1975 when he bought three large Texas ranches totaling seven thousand acres. Some years later, in 1983, sensing an opportunity at hand, Hughes made arrangements with eighty Texas ranchers, whose livestock trade was dwindling, to raise non-native breeds of antelope and venison, such as the tender, succulent axis deer, black buck and nilgai antelope from India, sika deer from the Orient, and fallow deer from Europe. These rare, imported breeds had previously been a source for year-round hunting, dating back to the 1930s when Eddie Rickenbacker, the famed World War II flying ace, and others brought a wide variety of these animals to Texas for recreational hunting.

Axis, sika, and fallow deer and nilgai and black buck antelope are raised by Hughes to one to two years old before they are harvested. They roam freely on large preserves and feed largely on grass, but their diet also includes scrub cedar, prickly pear cactus, nuts, herbs, and juniper berries. These varied dietary ingredients play a role in the development of more complex flavor in the meat of the animals, although it is said that the non-native breeds have a milder flavor and less fibrous muscle than the native American white-tailed deer. The whitetail feeds on leaves, acorns, and weeds, and exhibits a muskier, wilder flavor and a more sinewy texture.

Under the name Broken Arrow Ranch, Hughes's Texas Wild Game Cooperative sells over one hundred thousand pounds (approximately two thousand animals) a year of exotic, non-native game, which is raised and harvested the year around on private land. If Hughes's activities sound a bit cold and sterile, it should be noted that the success of his operation has prompted a virtual revolution in ranching in Texas, Colorado, and Wyoming. Deer and buffalo have proven to be more profitable for many ranchers than cattle, with estimates ranging as much as twice the profit per acre. The success of operations like the Texas Wild Game Cooperative has also precipitated a previously unfound interest in breeding and raising game, thus assuring the perpetuation of different species.

Equally promising is the venture of Baron von Kerckerinck, a West German native who settled in the United States in 1978. Von Kerckerinck, sensing an opportunity at hand, established a forty-five-hundred-acre preserve on a former dairy ranch in Chaumont, New York, and began by raising fifty fallow deer, which he purchased from game parks.

The fallow deer were a natural extension of von Kerckerinck's heritage, as they were the species in northern Europe since Roman times. They are still an important part of agribusiness in England, and particularly in Germany, where approximately fifteen hundred deer farms exist.

Today, the Lucky Star Ranch has a herd that ranges from eighteen hundred to twenty-five hundred fallow deer, and von Kerckerinck is further promoting the farm raising of deer through a book, a video, and an association (the North American Deer Farmers' Association) that helps other farmers convert their land to this more efficient, more profitable business. Partly through von Kerckerinck's efforts, over forty states have created legislation governing the farming of deer.

California Duck Farms

In the 1870s, approximately three dozen Pekin ducks sailed into San Francisco Bay on a clipper ship from China. Two dozen of the birds were sent off to Long Island where their descendants have been marketed ever since as Long Island ducks; the other dozen seem to have been mysteriously sidetracked to a small farm in Petaluma in Northern California owned by the Reichardt family. Today, the Reichardt duck farm is run under the watchful eye of Jim Reichardt, great grandson of the original founder.

Approximately one million ducks a year are bred, raised, and processed on a self-contained duck farm that is the epitome of contemporary technology. Much care is given to starting with a clean egg. The eggs are placed in incubators set at 98° to 99°F, and the eggs are periodically rocked gently to simulate the wild conditions of a mother hen sitting on her nest.

At any one time there are 180,000 ducks on the Reichardt farm. Ducklings are raised in large, covered wire pens under low light, where they are fed corn crumble when they are one to two weeks old. They're later moved to outdoor pens and raised on a diet of corn and supplemental grains.

Slaughtering takes place at forty-five to fifty-two days old in a controlled environment under the supervision of the USDA. The ducks are then processed through a scalder and picker to loosen their feathers; subsequently, they pass through wax tanks and an ice chill to assure final removal of all pinfeathers. Every phase of the process is designed to control potential bacterial problems, right down to a final chill bath at 40°F before packing.

Selective breeding from carefully chosen stock has developed a bird that has the most desirable traits for the market: a succulent, tasty duck with well-developed breasts and an adequate layer of fat. One of the successes of the Reichardt project is that no new blood lines have been introduced for more than fifty years, so there has been virtually no disease, and subsequently no need for antibiotics. The result is a healthy, clean, extremely uniform bird.

Reichardt is currently experimenting with free-range ducks, which are raised in an open field bordered by nearby trees to provide shade. These birds are given one hundred square feet per bird of space, similar to the European method, with the goal of developing more lean muscle and wild flavor than their domestic counterparts.

Clearly, we are dealing with an industry that is very much in its embryonic stage. These few examples of the burgeoning movement toward farm-raised game are only a hint of how extensive game could become in our diets in the twenty-first century. The prospects are intriguing, indeed!

A FIRST "HUNT" IN THE TEXAS HILL COUNTRY

BY SID GOLDSTEIN

*I*t's a late March afternoon in the tiny Texas town of Ingram in the hill country near Austin. Mike Hughes, the portly, genial owner of the Texas Wild Game Cooperative, eyeballs me with the glare of a Marine drill sergeant looking over a new crop of bootcampers. He sees a slightly intimidated kid from the streets of San Francisco, a pure, out-and-out virgin when it comes to big game hunting and creatures of the wild.

I'm in Ingram on a journalistic mission, seeking to discover more about new ways of raising deer on vast preserves that attempt to simulate a natural environment. Hughes has kindly offered to take me along on a hunting expedition with his well-seasoned crew of sharpshooters, skinners, and the state health inspector.

We tour the refrigeration rooms of his Ingram facility, where various large cuts of axis, sika, and fallow deer are intermingled with nilgai and black buck antelope. All are being cold-aged in Cryo-vac wrapping, awaiting dispensation to the best kitchens in America. At a stop in a room full of deer hides, I'm educated in the subtleties of deer skin quality.

Hughes then shows me his mobile slaughtering facility, which has been built in close cooperation with the Texas Department of Health to exacting standards. The refrigerated truck includes a walk-in cooler with capacity for storage of as many as fifty deer carcasses, self-contained electricity, and a propane-powered water heater. This, I'm told, is where we'll process our catch from the evening's hunt.

It's getting toward dusk as we drive in Hughes's truck across vast expanses of rolling hills to the far reaches of the Broken Arrow Ranch where the hunt will commence. Engulfed in mental controversy about the coming few hours, I begin to envision myself looking down the barrel of a long rifle and pulling the trigger for the first time ever on a beautiful animal of the wild. Shocked by the mere thought, I suddenly feel strangely benign toward the animals that I love so dearly to eat. Yet, I'm strangely excited about the hunt, wearing my machismo boldly and momentarily envisioning the antlers above my mantle.

We bounce along the backroads leading up to Hughes's ranch. The gnarly Texas scrub provides a vivid counterpoint to the fading sunlight. We meet up with the crew and the mobile slaughtering facility. Parked in the middle of this beautiful, natural terrain, it looks cold and menacing. Rifles are unpacked and ammunition is handed out. Hughes exchanges a few words with the crew about where we'll hunt.

I find out quickly that the closest to hunting I'll be doing on this quiet Texas evening will be to drive the truck for Hughes so that he can look for deer. As we bounce up a hill, in and out of potholes, and over the grassy terrain, Hughes lays out the plan for me.

"You're going to be my driver," he says with a grin.

"An accomplice," I think to myself with a sigh of relief, "but not the killer."

Patiently, he explains how we sight the deer. We are to cruise slowly over these rocky hillsides with high-powered spotlights beaming into the dense brush. The deer will respond to the light and turn to look. We'll see the light reflected in their eyes. My job will be to place the truck at an angle so that Hughes can position his .30mm Steyr Mannlicher rifle with a twenty-inch silencer for a clean, quick head shot, before the animal is startled and runs away. This reduces the surge of adrenalin common in wild, hunted animals and produces a better quality of meat.

My heart is bounding with excitement. All at once, my fear, apprehension, and curiosity begin a dizzying dance.

"Right," I say, not quite sure if I'm ready to sink or swim.

As we begin to drive, Hughes explains that we can only shoot male axis deer, since the females are used for breeding stock. The first task is to sight the deer, then determine the species and gender. White-tailed deer, by law, cannot be shot, so we must be sure of what we see before he pulls the trigger.

We bump over hill and dale, in and out of shrubs and brush that Hughes seems to know like the palm of his hand. It's totally dark now. I can see nothing, but I'm following orders and driving . . . slowly. A few moments later, Hughes taps me.

"Stop!" he says. "What have we got here?"

About a hundred yards away, I see the bright reflection of our spotlight in the eyes of a deer frozen in time and space. My adrenalin surge could service the needs of West Texas for a week. Hughes pulls up his rifle and looks down the long barrel.

"It's an axis alright," he says calmly, "but I can't tell if it's a female or a male. Pull up a little."

My foot can't decide if I want to re-create the Indy 500 or follow orders. I follow orders. . . . After a few more seconds, which feel like a fortnight, he advises that it's a female. I inhale a deep breath. We continue on. And on.

Over the next couple of hours, the sightings continue, with almost mystical similarity. Each sighting results in the discovery of either a female axis or white-tailed deer. We radio to the rest of the crew and get similar reports.

"Must be one helluva stag party going on somewhere on this property," Hughes laughs.

The Texas sky is beginning to resemble a sixties acid flashback. Lightning bolts about a hundred miles away are sending out cracks into the sky of awesome proportion. Thunder rockets off in the distance. The breeze is picking up.

While frustration has yet to sink in, Hughes explains that the usual haul for an evening's hunt is at least three deer. He tells me that only a couple of times a year will they strike out completely. I'm beginning to get the message. The evening is not looking good for venison stew. But we continue our mission as the night begins to chill and the sky explodes in the distance.

It's almost ten o'clock; we've been hunting for three and a half hours. We've spotted probably forty deer, all females, or whitetail. I'm craving venison now, not having eaten much but a bag of pretzels before we started, and thinking about all the great venison dishes I've ever cooked or tasted. I'm feeling like my ambivalence about the hunt is perhaps an omen for its lack of success. Hughes finally suggests we call it a night.

"The wind's up and they're all lying down now," Hughes explains. "They lose their keen sense of smell and direction when the wind picks up like this. They tend to feel more vulnerable, so they get close to the ground. We won't have much chance now."

My inner confusion continues. I realize I'm relieved. I won't have to actually see the animal killed, field dressed, skinned in the portable facility, and eviscerated under the careful supervision of the state inspector. But this is what I came for, dammit! And God, I'm hungry. I can taste the rich meat of venison studded with ripe apples and sweet Texas onions.

As we congregate back at the slaughtering facility and pack up for the evening, I confess to Hughes that I hope I didn't bring him bad luck.

"It's okay, pal. There'll be other nights," he says reassuringly. "Care for some greasy fried chicken? My wife made it today in case we got hungry."

It's the most delicious thing I've ever tasted in my life.

A GAME COOK'S REPERTOIRE: TECHNIQUES AND BASIC RECIPES, STOCKS AND SAUCES, AND SPECIAL INGREDIENTS

Techniques and Basic Recipes

It might seem a bit odd to have a whole subchapter devoted to techniques. After all, cooking is cooking. Yet the subtleties of game cooking are such that a better understanding of a few specialized techniques will help immeasurably in the preparation of the recipes in this book.

This section, arranged alphabetically, will also differentiate between the techniques used for wild and for farm-raised game. Many of the methods traditionally used in cooking game are unnecessary when preparing domestic game because of the significantly different diet and habitat of the animals.

BARDING

Certain cuts of wild boar and venison, such as the leg, round, bottom round, and eye, as well as most wild game birds, call for barding to maintain moisture while cooking. Barding is achieved by wrapping thin sheets of pork fat or bacon around these meats and then slowly roasting them so that the heat renders the fat, creating a basting layer on the skin of the bird or on the meat. This adds moisture and encourages a more tender result.

Barding is seldom necessary with farm-raised game birds and only occasionally appropriate with game meats, such as tougher cuts of venison and boar.

Surround meat with thin sheets of fat and tie into place before roasting.

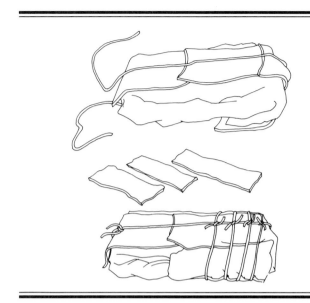

BASTING

Most grilling enthusiasts understand the importance of basting to both moisten and flavor meat. Basting game with fat rendered from the meat, an oil-based marinade, or butter also helps to prevent unbarded roasts from drying out. Brushing such liquids onto the meat creates a crust that helps to tenderize it. When roasting lean meats and small game birds, basting is essential to maintain moisture.

We recommend using basting brushes with natural boar bristles; don't use cheap plastic brushes because they tend to melt in the heat. We also like to use branches of fresh herbs such as thyme, rosemary, and tarragon when they are available.

BASIC BASTE FOR GAME BIRDS OR MEATS

MAKES ABOUT 1½ CUPS

This simple baste can be made in larger quantities and stored in the refrigerator for a couple of weeks.

1 cup white or red wine
½ cup Basic Game Bird Stock (page 40) or Basic Game Meat Stock (page 40)
¼ cup soy sauce
3 tablespoons roasted garlic purée (page 31)
1 teaspoon minced fresh ginger

Place all ingredients in a small saucepan and simmer gently for 10 minutes to reduce slightly.

BONING

With boning knife, cut down middle of back and carefully scrape meat away from bone, following down along the rib-cage. Be careful not to tear the skin.

Scrape meat away from around thigh bone.

Scrape meat away from leg bone and remove bones.

Bird completely boned, ready for grilling or stuffing.

Confit

The word *confit* (pronounced con-fee) comes from the French *confire*, "to preserve." In short, this is a time-honored method of preserving, or potting as it is sometimes called, meats in their rendered fat. The technique typically utilizes the leg and thigh pieces of duck, goose, small game birds, and turkey.

Paula Wolfert, the noted culinary authority, relates an expression commonly heard in the southwest of France: "A Gascon will fall to his knees for a good *confit*." Thus, it's not surprising that *confit*, which embraces the notions of thrift and preservation exquisitely, is the soul and foundation for much of that region's cooking.

In the vigorous, hearty cooking of southwest France, *confit* is ultimately put to use in the preparation of cassoulets and in the regional dish called *garbure*, a soup containing cabbage, beans, salt pork, and a healthy dose of *confit*. Salads with mixed greens and top-quality olive oil or walnut oil can also be greatly enhanced by *confit*. Many gourmets favor the use of *confit* with lentils or fava bean dishes as well.

Despite the substantial use of fat in the cooking and preservation of *confit*, the finished meat is extremely smooth, delicate, and savory, and, surprisingly, does not contain a significant amount of fat. A method practiced by Paula Wolfert when making *confit* involves slowly raising the temperature of the fat along with the meat to let the *confit* cook evenly, and then slowly cooling the meat in the fat.

In France, *confits* are typically preserved in a cool cellar or pantry where they are stored in heavy stoneware jars. Storage in such jars permits an interaction of the meat with the fat and the salt, which acts as a preservative. The fat seals the meat and protects it from oxidation, creating what some have called an aging or mellowing effect. In order to accomplish this result, however, the *confit* must be put up for at least a week; a longer period—up to three or four months—is recommended.

Confits are an important part of any serious game cook's repertoire. While they take some advance planning and time to prepare, the pleasure derived from lifting the savory, utterly sensuous meat out of its storage jar and preparing a simple, quick meal around it months later provides more than equitable reward. A popular contemporary use calls for grilling *confit* and using it in composed salads, or frying it in its own fat until browned.

When you read through the lore of game cooking, you will find many references to "potted" or "jugged" meats. We consider these to be in the same category as *confit*. Potted game is, as the name implies, game that has been cooked until very tender, then shredded or puréed and sealed with fat in a small pot.

It's quite an English tradition and the simplest recipe we know is one of Elizabeth David's that takes three parts game bird meat to one part good, fatty ham, which is then pureed with sweet butter and seasoned with cayenne pepper and fresh lemon juice. It's then sealed with a layer of melted butter, chilled, and served with hot, thin, crisped toasts.

BASIC *CONFIT* OF GOOSE OR DUCK

SERVES 6 TO 8 IF USING GOOSE,
3 TO 4 IF USING DUCK

Perusing other cookbooks, you may find more complex *confit* recipes, but this one is an excellent starting point to which other ingredients, such as dried herbs, garlic, or mixed peppercorns, may be added, if desired, for additional flavoring. *Confit* is typically used more as an ingredient in other dishes rather than served by itself.

1 goose (about 8 pounds), or 1 duck (about 4 pounds)
2 bay leaves
1 cup dry white wine
3 tablespoons kosher salt if using goose, or 1 tablespoon kosher salt if using duck
12 black peppercorns

Cut goose or duck into quarters and place in a large, heavy-bottomed pot. Add all remaining ingredients and simmer over low heat for 2 hours. Remove from heat and let cool.

When fat has settled but before it has set, spoon some of it off into a sealable, airtight glass jar to form a ½-inch-thick layer. Lay a goose or duck quarter on the fat, cover with more fat, top with another quarter, and so on, ending with a ½-inch-thick layer of fat that completely covers the top piece of goose or duck. Be careful not to use any of the meat juices, only the fat. Let the fat cool completely and cover the jar tightly. Keep refrigerated for 3 to 4 months before using.

CUTTING

Large bird cut into six serving pieces, plus carcass for making stock.

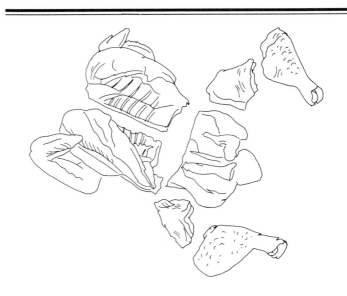

Rabbit cut into six serving pieces.

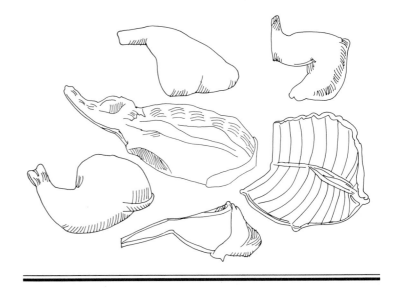

GRILLING

Grilling is our oldest cooking technique, even though it certainly was not called that when early man first started roasting game over an open fire.

In recent years, grilling has become quite fashionable, both for the flavor that it renders and because of health concerns. Grilling has two key advantages: It is an extremely fast way to cook, and it imparts a distinctive flavor as a result of the smoke that is created from the fat of the bird or meat hitting the hot coals or wood. Grilling's health dividend is that it renders fat from the meat.

There are four ways of flavoring meat: wet marinades, which are used to flavor the meat in liquid before grilling; dry marinades and rubs, which are usually patted on the meat at least 30 minutes before it's grilled; bastes, or mops as they are called in the South, which are brushed on the meat while it's cooking; and sauces, which are placed on the meat just as it comes off the grill. Some of these may be used in combination when grilling meat or game birds.

A few grilling tips:

- Bring meat to room temperature before grilling.
- Make sure the grill rack is clean. Bits of food left on the grill will scorch, burn, and become bitter when they are reheated.
- The best time to clean the grill is while it is still hot. Keep a wire brush handy for this purpose and rub down the grill after finishing your cooking.
- To prevent sticking, always heat the grill rack and rub it with oil before placing foods on it.
- If meat has been marinated, pat it dry with paper towels before grilling.
- Always start cooking meat with the fat or skin side down. As the meat begins to firm from cooking, it will be less likely to stick to the grill.
- Try not to pierce the meat when moving it on the grill, or juices will be lost. Use tongs instead of a fork.
- If using wooden skewers, soak them in water for at least 30 minutes before using to prevent them from burning on the grill. We like to have wine handy for keeping skewers moist; it's also a good excuse for having a glass to sip while grilling!
- Make sure that if you are using a combination of rubs, marinades, bastes, and sauces that the flavors are complementary. Using an Asian-style marinade and finishing with a Latin-inspired sauce doesn't make culinary sense.
- Never, ever use charcoal lighter to start coals. The petroleum fumes take a long time to burn off, and it's an ecologically unsound method for igniting a fire. Electric lighters or charcoal chimneys with newspaper are the preferred methods.
- To add a smoke flavor to your coals, add soaked wood chips, such as alderwood, cherrywood, walnut, or applewood, on top of the coals just prior to grilling. We have also had great success with grapevine cuttings and herb sprigs, such as basil and thyme.

BASIC BARBECUE SAUCE

MAKES ABOUT 2 CUPS

This sauce should be used on meat once it is grilled; it will burn if you put it on the meat while it is still on the grill. It is particularly good on buffalo and boar.

¼ cup minced shallots or green onion
1 tablespoon minced garlic
5 tablespoons tomato paste
1½ cups apple cider
1 tablespoon soy sauce
3 tablespoons cider vinegar
2 tablespoons brown sugar
½ teaspoon salt
Tabasco sauce to taste

Combine all ingredients, except Tabasco sauce, in a saucepan and simmer for 20 minutes, or until the sauce is reduced and fairly thick. Add Tabasco.

LARDING

By its very nature, wild game meat is quite lean. Larding, a technique commonly used on wild game, bastes the meat with just enough pork fat or bacon to prevent it from drying out. This is done by rolling thin strips of pork fat in herbs, garlic, and pepper and then inserting the strips into the meat by means of a larding needle. The pork fat bastes the interior of the meat during cooking. Larding slows the cooking process, however, since the fat heats more slowly than the muscle tissue. It is rarely necessary to lard farm-raised game, since the meat is seldom as lean as its wild counterpart.

Larding needles are a specialty item. They can be found in many gourmet stores or can be purchased through mail-order houses, such as Williams-Sonoma and restaurant-supply houses.

Place fat strip in larding needle and push through meat, turning gently from side to side. Hold end of fat strip with tip of knife or finger.

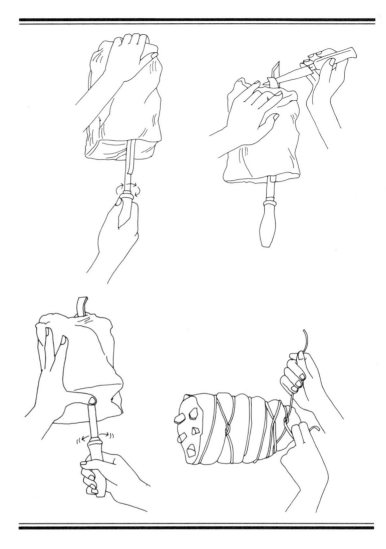

Carefully remove larding needle with a gentle rotating motion. Tie meat if desired.

Marinades and Rubs

The use of marinades is traditional in game cooking, but the role of marinades differs significantly between wild and domestic game. Most wild game is shot while "under stress" (running or flying from the threat of man); the surge of adrenalin that comes with this state contributes to the tightening of the animal's muscles. Marinating the meat to "ease" some of this muscle tightening is almost always required to help break down the tissues.

Because most farm-raised game is not killed while under stress, marinating to achieve tenderness is typically unnecessary. Marinating these meats is more of a creative flavoring technique, and one we endorse with great enthusiasm, particularly when the game is going to be grilled.

Marinating can be accomplished with simple mixtures of oil, salt, pepper, and herbs, or with more complex blends involving an acid element—typically wine, vinegar, or citrus juices—and a variety of seasonings and spices. The acid helps tenderize the meat. The more tender cuts, such as roasts, loins, and steaks, are best served by a dry or wet marinade of short duration; the tougher ones may need a longer liquid marinade to help tenderize them.

Marinades that contain acids must be used judiciously. An overmarinated piece of meat will turn gray and develop a flabby texture. While there is no firm rule, it can generally be stated that marinades should be used anywhere from a few hours to a couple of days, depending on the cut and age of the meat. The key is in the cooking; no amount of marinating will tenderize a tough cut of meat.

In the old days it was not uncommon to marinate certain game meats for as long as 10 days to help tone down some of the gaminess. This is virtually never done nowadays, and is not recommended.

Traditional marinades for game include wine and herbs, but milk, cream, and yogurt were (and still are) used because their neutrality helps to extract harsher gamy flavors.

When marinating game, we like to place all the ingredients in a large, sealable plastic bag and let the meat rest in the refrigerator. By turning the bag occasionally, all of the meat will receive good exposure to the marinade. Keep acid-based marinades out of aluminum pans; they will adversely react with the metal.

Before cooking, the meat should be patted dry. If you're going to use the marinade again within the next few days, bring it to a boil for five minutes, cool, and store in the refrigerator for up to five days, or freeze for use at a later date.

Some common ingredients for marinades are red and white wine, vermouth, port, sherry, brandy, Armagnac, Cognac, cassis, citrus fruits (orange, lemon, and lime), red and white vinegar, fresh and dry herbs (parsley, bay leaf, thyme, basil, oregano, rosemary, sage, and tarragon), onions, garlic, shallots, leeks, chives, juniper berries, and black, green, and white peppercorns.

BASIC LIQUID GAME MARINADE

MAKES ABOUT 1 QUART

This is a great all-purpose marinade for many of the game meat and bird dishes found in this book, such as Venison with Juniper Berry Sauce (page 243) and Marinated Loin of Venison Roasted in Mustard (page 250). It can also be used with domestic pork to make it taste more like wild boar.

2 medium carrots, peeled and chopped
½ large yellow onion, chopped
1 shallot, chopped
1 large clove garlic, chopped
1 tablespoon olive oil
2½ cups hearty red wine
¼ cup red wine vinegar
2 bay leaves
3 sprigs fresh parsley
8 juniper berries
1 teaspoon sea salt or kosher salt
6 black peppercorns

In a nonreactive pan, sauté carrots, onion, shallot, and garlic in oil until lightly browned. Add all remaining ingredients and bring to a boil. Reduce heat and simmer for 10 minutes. Let cool before using. Place meat or game birds in marinade and refrigerate for 4 to 6 hours or overnight.

BASIC YOGURT MARINADE

MAKES ABOUT 2½ CUPS

Use marinade on delicate cuts of meat, such as loin of venison and most game birds.

2 teaspoons yellow mustard seeds, lightly toasted and crushed
1½ tablespoons minced garlic
1 teaspoon freshly ground black pepper
½ cup minced shallots or green onion
2 cups low-fat plain yogurt
2 tablespoons fresh lemon juice
2 teaspoons kosher salt

Combine all ingredients and place meat or game birds in marinade. Refrigerate for 4 to 6 hours or overnight. Wipe off excess marinade before cooking.

ASSYRIAN POMEGRANATE MARINADE FOR GAME MEATS

MAKES ABOUT 2 CUPS

Narsai David, a San Francisco Bay Area chef *par excellence*, contributed this flavorful marinade, which he primarily uses on lamb. We like to marinate boar chops, venison roasts or loins, and buffalo steaks or chops in it.

2 large quartered onions
2 cloves garlic
½ lemon, unpeeled
½ teaspoon freshly ground black pepper
1 cup pomegranate juice
1 teaspoon kosher salt
½ cup red wine
2 teaspoons dried basil

Place all ingredients in a blender or food processor and purée until smooth. Rub marinade into meat and refrigerate for 6 to 8 hours or overnight.

BASIC DRY GAME MARINADE

MAKES ABOUT ½ CUP

Small game birds such as quail, squab, and partridge are enhanced by this marinade.

1 teaspoon kosher salt
1 tablespoon white peppercorns, crushed
1 teaspoon dry mustard
1 teaspoon dried thyme
1 teaspoon dried oregano
1 teaspoon ground ginger
1 teaspoon freshly grated nutmeg
½ teaspoon ground cloves
¼ teaspoon ground allspice
½ teaspoon cayenne pepper
¾ teaspoon juniper berries
1 bay leaf

Combine all ingredients and crush thoroughly in a mortar with a pestle or with a spice grinder. Rub on birds at least 30 minutes prior to cooking.

LAVENDER-PEPPER RUB

MAKES ABOUT 3 TABLESPOONS

Try this unusual rub on venison, boar, or buffalo that is going to be grilled or sautéed.

2 teaspoons coarse sea salt or kosher salt
2 teaspoons black peppercorns
2 teaspoons fennel seed
1 teaspoon white peppercorns
2 teaspoons dried lavender blossoms (see Note)

Combine all ingredients and crush thoroughly in a mortar with a pestle or spice grinder. Rub on meats at least 30 minutes prior to cooking.

NOTE: Dried lavender blossoms can be found at natural-food stores.

CURRY-PEPPER RUB

MAKES ABOUT ¼ CUP

Similar to the Lavender-Pepper Rub, this spicy mixture is suitable for venison, boar, and buffalo, but it is also very nice on small game birds.

2 jalapeño chili peppers, chopped, or ½ teaspoon red-pepper flakes
1 teaspoon chopped garlic
1 tablespoon chopped red onion
1 teaspoon ground coriander, lightly toasted
1 teaspoon ground cumin, lightly toasted
1 teaspoon ground turmeric
2 teaspoons peanut oil
1 teaspoon kosher salt

Combine all ingredients and rub on meat at least 30 minutes prior to cooking.

PÂTÉS AND TERRINES

Volumes have been written about the making of pâtés and similar "meat loaves." We've included a basic pâté recipe made with either game birds or meats.

Today the terms *pâté* and *terrine* are used interchangeably. Originally a pâté was a meat mixture baked in a pastry crust. Pâté now describes meat loaves that are prepared with and without a crust. Terrine basically describes the dish in which the loaf is baked and served, but can also be used to describe the food itself. The word *terrine* is derived from *terra* ("earth"); typically the dish is earthenware.

BASIC GAME PÂTÉ

MAKES 1 PÂTÉ, ABOUT 20 SLICES

Unfortunately, the key to a good pâté is fat. Fat is what gives pâté its unctuous, rich flavor and texture, and despite every effort to find an alternative, there simply isn't any. If you are on a fat-free diet, pâtés aren't for you. They are, however, another one of life's great culinary pleasures and should be enjoyed in moderation.

A good pâté should contain at least one-third fat; otherwise it tends to be dry and tough. Fresh pork fat cut from the back or belly works best. You'll also need thin sheets of fat to line the terrine. As an alternative, use the skin of a boned bird for a goose or duck pâté; the skin contains a great deal of fat.

Pâtés taste better after they have aged for 1 or 2 days in the refrigerator. Serve pâté with cornichons, coarse-grain mustard, chutney, and crusty French bread.

½ to ¾ pound fresh pork fat or game fat, fully chopped
¾ cup minced yellow onion
1½ pounds game meat, finely ground
2 tablespoons roasted garlic purée (see Note)
¼ cup Cognac or other brandy
1 tablespoon salt, plus salt to taste
½ teaspoon freshly ground black pepper
2 teaspoons fresh thyme, or 1 teaspoon dried thyme leaves
½ teaspoon minced fresh sage, or ¼ teaspoon dried sage
½ teaspoon ground allspice
⅓ cup rolled oats
2 large eggs
About 1 pound pork fat sheets (or blanched bacon or salt pork), cut about ⅛ inch thick
½ pound game meat, livers, and/or smoked ham, cut into ¼ inch square strips
Boiling water, as needed
Freshly ground black pepper to taste

In a skillet over medium-high heat, render about 2 tablespoons of the fat. Add the onion and sauté until soft but not browned. Let cool. In a large bowl, combine onion, the remaining chopped fat, ground meat, garlic purée, Cognac, 1 tablespoon salt, pepper, herbs, allspice, rolled oats, and eggs and mix thoroughly. Sauté a bit of the mixture to taste for seasoning and then adjust seasonings.

Preheat oven to 350°F. Line a 2-quart terrine with pork fat sheets and fill it half full with meat mixture. Cover with meat strips and pack remaining meat mixture on top, leaving ½ inch between meat and terrine rim. Cover top completely with the fat sheets.

Cover terrine tightly with aluminum foil or a lid and set in a roasting pan. Fill pan with boiling water to come two-thirds up sides of terrine. Place in preheated oven and bake for 2 hours. Pâté is done when meat begins to shrink from the sides of pan and a thermometer registers 165° to 170°F.

Remove terrine from oven, loosen foil around edges, and place terrine in a larger pan. Put a weight (a brick or canned goods) in a smaller loaf pan and place on top of terrine. This will press out excess fat and make pâté firmer for slicing. Don't pour off juices. When cool, refrigerate overnight with weight still on.

At this point, the pâté can either be unmolded from the terrine or served from it. Wipe off all excess fat and slice thinly to serve.

NOTE: To roast garlic, cut off top quarter of a whole head of garlic. Drizzle with a tablespoon or so of olive oil and season with salt and freshly ground black pepper. Wrap in foil and bake in a 350°F oven until garlic is very soft and sweet, about 1 hour. Squeeze garlic out of husk to use. To store roasted garlic, place in a small jar, cover with olive oil, seal with a lid, and store at room temperature for up to 2 weeks.

ROASTING

One of the purest gustatory pleasures is the flavor of a slowly roasted game bird or meat that has developed a crisply textured skin and succulent, moist flesh. Over the years, the oven has become both friend and enemy to the game cook; many a fine bird has been roasted into oblivion behind its closed doors.

Typically, cookbooks have used "minutes per pound" to gauge cooking time. This can be helpful, but it's not accurate enough. We strongly recommend the use of an instant read thermometer to determine doneness more accurately. These handy little devices can be inserted into the thickest part of the meat, usually the leg-thigh section, to give you an instant internal temperature reading. Most of the recipes in this book will give an internal temperature recommendation rather than a minutes-per-pound guideline.

SAUSAGES

Like pâtés, there are as many versions of sausages as there are cooks who make them. The secret of making good sausages is a well-balanced mixture of one part high-quality fatback to two parts lean game meat, along with the seasonings and spices you prefer. Many sausage afficionados prefer an even higher ratio of fatback to meat.

You can obtain sausage casings and caul fat from most good butcher shops, but you will need to order them in advance. If you plan on making sausages in casings, you need a sausage horn in your kitchen arsenal; this will allow you to pack the meat firmly into the casing with the right amount of density and without air. Mixers, such as Kitchen Aid, offer this as an optional attachment.

BASIC GAME MEAT SAUSAGES

MAKES ABOUT 16 SAUSAGES

2 pounds lean game meat, well trimmed
1 pound high-quality fatback
1½ tablespoons kosher salt
1½ tablespoons freshly ground black pepper
¼ teaspoon ground nutmeg
¼ teaspoon ground ginger
¼ teaspoon ground cloves
¼ cup good brandy or Cognac
Sausage casings or caul fat

Mix all ingredients together and grind in a meat grinder or in a food processor, using short bursts. Stuff the mixture into casings with a sausage horn; or wrap in caul fat to form a *crepinette;* or wrap in plastic wrap with tightly closed, tied ends; or simply form into patties.

Cook using desired method (saute, grill, broil, or poach) until done, depending on the thickness of the sausage.

SMOKING

The smoking of game has a long culinary history. Prehistoric man discovered that exposing meat to smoke was a natural preservation technique that rewarded him with an extended bounty. This tradition continued throughout Europe and in America until the early 19th century, when the modern refrigerator had its birth and assumed many of the preservation duties previously performed with smoking.

The preservation capabilities of smoking are no longer as vital as they once were, so nowadays smoking is being explored as a creative means of flavoring meats. Smoking is actually a two-phase process, with the first involving the exposing of the meat to either a wet or dry brine to flavor and help preserve it.

A dry brine is a seasoned salt mixture; a wet brine is traditionally an 80 percent salt solution. In the recipes that follow, the percentage of salt has been lowered for health reasons. In both cases, the salt inhibits bacterial growth in the meat.

With most game, wet brining is employed. Some cooks, however, prefer dry brines for duck breasts, boar and venison legs, or older loins. To counteract the saltiness of the brine and the subsequent effect of dehydrating the meat, a contrasting sweet element—sugar, honey, molasses, or pure maple syrup—can be added. Brining times vary from a minimum of 4 hours for duck breasts, small birds, and buffalo or boar chops, to 8 hours for whole ducks, and up to 2 or 3 days for whole turkeys or geese. Meats should be refrigerated while being brined. Always pat game dry with paper towels before smoking.

The second phase of the process is the smoking itself. The two easiest methods of home smoking involve either the covered kettle-style grill or an enclosed electric smoker with wire racks and a heat source at the bottom. Of these, the standard kettle-style grill is the most common, although electric smokers are becoming more readily available. Of the electric varieties, we like the moderately priced Luhr-Jensen "Little Chef" from Oregon, which is inexpensive and works extremely well.

There is much debate on the proper fuel sources for smoking. Some swear by charcoal briquettes or mesquite charcoal. Most real smoking enthusiasts, however, prefer wood chips from hickory, applewood, alderwood, cherry, or walnut trees, or even corn cobs on top of the coals. In the Northern California wine country at harvest time, we favor soaked grapevines added to the coals for our fuel source. We also like to use large bunches of basil and other fresh herbs, which impart a unique flavor of their own.

Any type of untreated, nonresinous hardwood may be used for fuel; pine and redwood are resinous types that should be avoided. Regardless of origin, these wood chips must be soaked in water for about 30 minutes and then drained before using so that they smolder rather than burn. The indirect-heat method, with the coals to the sides of the grill and a drip pan positioned beneath the meat, is most suitable for large whole game birds and meats. Water should be added to the drip pan to help keep some moisture in the kettle.

The primary effect of smoking is to caramelize the exterior of the meat and cook the interior just enough to impede bacterial growth. This typically requires about 3 to 4 hours, depending on the specific meat, using lower cooking temperatures and wood chips that are constantly moistened. If the smoked meat is later going to be reheated, then the smoking process should be terminated when the meat is rare, or the subsequent cooking process will overcook it.

Because smoking is a time-consuming process (although it does not require constant attention), many people smoke a number of meats or birds in succession, much in the same way that cooks preserve quantities of fruits and vegetables in large batches. This ensures a ready supply for a few weeks without having to repeat the process.

A final word on brines: Many enthusiasts of smoking have their own favorite brines and accompanying ideas on how long they want to keep their game in the brine. Ultimately, it all comes down to personal taste. The following recipes might serve as a useful starting point for those who want to try smoking game.

BASIC WET BRINE FOR GAME BIRDS

MAKES ABOUT 3½ CUPS

This basic brine for smoking can be used on meats and birds alike. It renders a particularly pleasing quality to quail, squab, and pheasant. The amount is sufficient for 8 small birds, 2 ducks, 2 pheasants, 2 rabbits, or 1 goose.

1½ cups water
½ cup fresh orange juice, apple juice, or cranberry juice
½ cup dry white wine or sherry
¾ cup soy sauce
¼ cup kosher salt
¼ cup firmly packed dark brown sugar, honey, or molasses
1 teaspoon onion powder
2 tablespoons ground ginger
1 tablespoon dried rosemary
1 tablespoon dried basil

Combine all ingredients and mix thoroughly. If brining fatty birds such as goose and duck, puncture skin lightly with a fork. Brine small birds or rabbit for 4 to 6 hours; larger birds for 8 to 12 hours refrigerated. Make sure the bird or birds are fully submerged in the brine. Remove bird(s) from brine and allow to sit for about 45 minutes before smoking. Pat dry with paper towels before smoking. Brine may be re-used. Boil for 5 minutes and use within a week or two.

BASIC WET BRINE FOR GAME MEATS

MAKES ABOUT 7 CUPS

Smoked Saddle of Wild Boar with Currant Sauce (page 75) calls for this highly versatile brine. The amount is sufficient for 8 chops or 1 loin.

2 cups cider vinegar
4 cups water
1 cup kosher salt
1 tablespoon black peppercorns
1 teaspoon juniper berries, crushed
½ cup firmly packed dark brown sugar
1 bay leaf
4 whole cloves
2 teaspoons grated orange zest
2 tablespoons chopped fresh parsley
1 medium yellow onion, chopped
1 shallot, chopped
1 clove garlic, halved
1 medium carrot, peeled and sliced
1 medium celery stalk, sliced
1 cup dry red wine

Combine all ingredients, except wine, in a large, nonreactive saucepan and bring to a boil. Reduce heat and simmer for 30 minutes. Strain into a large container, making sure to press all liquid free from solids; add red wine. Brine venison, boar, buffalo, or other large game meats for 3 to 4 days in refrigerator, or as directed in recipe, turning meat often. Make sure meat is fully submerged in brine. Remove meat from brine and allow to sit for about 45 minutes before smoking.

BASIC DRY BRINE FOR GAME

MAKES ABOUT ½ CUP

Game bird recipes, such as Smoked Duck Breasts with Persimmon, Kiwifruit, and Tropical Fruit Sauce (page 103), are complemented by this brine. The amount is sufficient for 4 small birds or 1 duck.

¼ cup regular salt
¼ cup firmly packed dark brown sugar
⅛ teaspoon freshly ground white pepper
¼ teaspoon dried thyme
¼ teaspoon dried sage

In a small bowl, mix together all ingredients thoroughly. Rub birds or meat well on all sides with mixture, cover with plastic wrap, and refrigerate for 1 to 2 hours, or as directed in recipe. Remove from refrigerator and let sit for about 45 minutes before smoking.

STEAMING GOOSE OR DUCK TO RENDER FAT

Both duck and goose have a fairly thick layer of fat beneath their skin that protects them from cold weather. Their meat is actually quite lean; the trick in cooking either is to try to render as much of the fat as possible without overcooking and drying out the meat.

It should be noted that the rendered fat of duck and goose has traditionally been savored by the French and others for sautéing other foods, especially potatoes and eggs. Currently, however, with concerns about saturated fats, we recommend that you moderate your intake of it despite the wonderful flavor it imparts.

A simple way of rendering some of the fat of ducks and geese is to steam the bird for about 30 minutes before proceeding with a recipe. Gently pierce the skin of the bird in several places with a sharp knife, being careful not to pierce the meat itself. Place a rack in a pot holding 1 to 2 inches of gently simmering water. Place the bird on the rack (it should not touch the water), cover, and steam for approximately 30 minutes. This will liquify and reduce the fat considerably. Reduce the cooking time in the recipe by 30 minutes.

TRUSSING

Thread trussing needle and pierce body just under thigh. Push through body to other side.

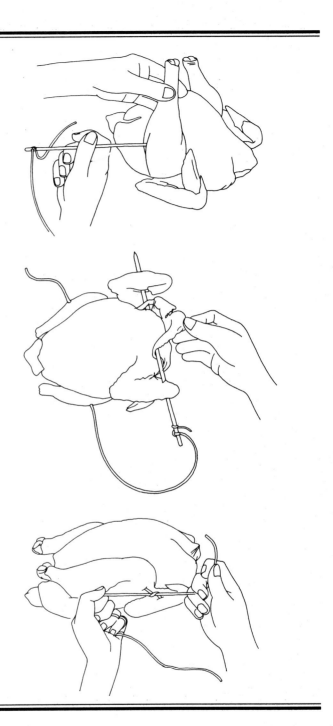

Push needle through first wing joint and body, and exit through opposite wing.

Pull string tight and tie bird into compact shape.

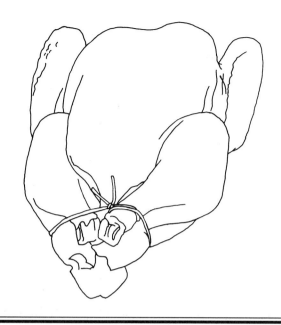

Loop string around tail (pope's nose) and then around legs. Pull tight and tie.

Stocks and Sauces

Suffice to say, volumes have been written on stocks and sauces. French masters Escoffier, Carême, and others have given us countless worthwhile interpretations that fill our libraries. Our goal here is not to write another treatise, but simply to suggest how well-made stocks and sauces play a pivotal role in game cooking, and to offer some quick tips on how to make them.

STOCKS

Good stocks are essential to good sauces, soups, and to flavorful cooking in general. This chapter includes recipes for basic game bird and meat stocks that are not difficult to make, but that do require quality ingredients and time on the stove. When making stocks, always make more than what is needed for the dish at hand, as they can be frozen quite successfully for a few months, if they are well sealed, or refrigerated prior to use for up to two weeks. Before using the stock, remove the fat that has risen to the surface.

Frozen Commercial Stocks: A number of small specialty-food manufacturers have begun to offer ready-made frozen stocks and *glaces* (stocks that have been reduced and concentrated so that they are almost solid). Many of these are quite good, but they are also expensive. If you are absolutely without a stock and need one, one of these, or a canned, low-salt chicken or beef consommé, will do. The main drawback to many of these products is that they tend to be too salty, especially for reductions. They also don't echo the flavor of the bird or meat with which they're being combined. However, sometimes we simply must do with what we've got.

Salt in Stocks: Fresh stocks should be made without salt. If you use a salted stock and then reduce and concentrate it, you also concentrate the salt, and once the salt is there, it is impossible to remove. A good practice is to salt only at the end of a recipe. Interestingly, we've found that if you do this, you tend to use less salt to achieve the desired results—a worthwhile goal these days.

***Demi-Glace* and *Glace de Viande*:** In Western cooking, the French have established the standards for stock and sauce making. As a result, even in American kitchens, we tend to use French terminology to describe stocks. This might, in part, explain the resistance many home cooks have to making fresh stocks. The recipes sound intimidating, but in fact they're extremely simple.

Occasionally, a recipe contains a reference to a *demi-glace* ("half glaze"). This traditionally refers to a rich meat stock that is simmered with caramelized aromatic vegetables (onions, carrots, and celery), wine, and a bit of *roux* (fat and flour that have been cooked together to form a paste), and then reduced by half, strained, and refrigerated or frozen. A full *glace de viande*, or "meat glaze," is made by reducing a rich stock to a concentrated, syrupy stage, which, when cooked, is a solid, rubberlike mass. This concentrated essence, an essential ingredient in many restaurant kitchens, is then used to add flavor and body to simpler stocks and sauces. It can easily be frozen in a small container and reserved for sauces that require it.

A final note: Do not heavily boil stocks. This produces a cloudy result that, although it still tastes good, makes sauces less attractive than when they are made with a clear stock. If stocks need to be further reduced because of storage limitations, continue cooking at a gentle simmer. Keep your eye on them so that they don't scorch or burn.

Bouillon cubes, which are, in theory, a kind of *glace*, are highly salted and lack any kind of real meat flavor. We recommend against using them if flavor and health are your goals.

Obtaining Game Bones for Making Stock: There are two ways to accumulate enough bones for making good stocks: Save the carcasses from boning that you do at home and freeze them in airtight plastic bags, or let your local butcher or game supplier know that you require bones, and have him or her save them for you. (Typically they will charge a small amount for these bones.)

BASIC GAME BIRD STOCK

MAKES ABOUT 2 QUARTS

Although this stock can be made with the bones of any game bird or poultry, it is best when made with the bones of the bird that is being used in the recipe itself. We also use this stock in rabbit dishes. It supplies a great backbone for Coffee-and-Spice-Rubbed Quail with Vanilla-Scented Sauce (page 168).

2 medium onions, sliced
2 medium carrots, peeled and sliced
3 stalks celery, chopped
2 tablespoons butter or vegetable oil
4 to 5 pounds wings, backs, necks, and trimmings of duck, goose, or small game birds, or bones and carcass from rabbit
1 large bay leaf
2 teaspoons fresh thyme leaves, or 1 teaspoon dried thyme leaves
3 sprigs fresh parsley
2 whole cloves
6 black peppercorns
4 quarts water

In a heavy-bottomed stockpot, sauté onions, carrots, and celery in butter or oil until just beginning to brown. Add bones, bay leaf, thyme, parsley, cloves, peppercorns, and water and bring just to a boil. Reduce heat and simmer slowly, uncovered, for 2 to 3 hours, skimming any scum that rises to surface. When stock is reduced and full of flavor, strain carefully, let cool, and store.

BASIC GAME MEAT STOCK

MAKES ABOUT 2 QUARTS

Meat stocks are essential to the intense sauces commonly found in game cooking. Roasted Venison with Sweet Onion Sauce (page 245) is a classic example.

3 pounds game meat trimmings, cut into 1-inch cubes
2 to 3 pounds game bones
2 medium onions, unpeeled and roughly chopped
3 large cloves garlic, chopped

2 medium carrots, chopped
2 celery stalks, chopped
2 large bay leaves
1 tablespoon fresh thyme leaves, or 1½ teaspoons dried thyme leaves
4 sprigs fresh parsley
8 juniper berries, crushed
2 teaspoons minced sage, or 1 teaspoon dried sage
2 cups hearty red wine
3 tablespoons tomato paste
5 quarts cold water

Preheat oven to 425°F. Place meat, bones, onions, garlic, carrots, and celery in a large roasting pan. Roast in preheated oven for 15 to 20 minutes, or until well browned. Turn occasionally and watch carefully so that mixture doesn't burn.

Transfer browned mixture to a heavy-bottomed stockpot and add all remaining ingredients. Bring slowly to a boil, reduce heat, and simmer slowly, uncovered, for 4 to 5 hours, skimming any scum that rises to surface. When stock is reduced and full of flavor, strain carefully, let cool, and store.

SAUCES

The trend today is toward lighter, fresher sauces that emphasize the flavor of the meat without the addition of a lot of butter or cream. A number of chefs now rely on reduction sauces, flavorful stocks to which herbs, spices, wines, and/or fruits are added and then reduced to thicken slightly and concentrate flavor. They are preferable to many sauces traditionally thickened with *roux* or other starches.

In this book, any sauce that is called for in a recipe is included with it. There are, however, some classic sauces that have traditionally been used with game in Europe. They are all fairly similar and usually use good vinegar and wine as major components. These acid ingredients are often used to "soften" the strong flavors of wild game. We've included two variations on classic sauces because we find them interesting and because they tend to heighten the unique flavor of simply cooked roasted or grilled game.

FRENCH CHARCUTIÈRE SAUCE

MAKES ABOUT ¼ CUP

Use with grilled steaks or chops.

3 tablespoons minced shallots
2 tablespoons butter
2 teaspoons flour
¼ cup red wine vinegar or raspberry vinegar
½ cup hearty red wine (Cabernet, Zinfandel, or Petite Sirah)
1 large bay leaf
½ teaspoon fresh thyme leaves
1½ cups Basic Game Meat Stock (page 40)
1 tablespoon tomato paste
1 teaspoon brown sugar
2 teaspoons Dijon-style mustard
¼ cup cornichon pickles, thinly sliced
1 tablespoon minced fresh parsley
1 tablespoon minced fresh chives
Salt and freshly ground black pepper to taste

In a small skillet over medium heat, sauté shallots in butter until soft and very lightly browned. Add flour and cook 2 minutes longer, stirring occasionally. Add vinegar and boil until most of the liquid has evaporated. Add wine, bay leaf, thyme, stock, tomato paste, and brown sugar and simmer until reduced to a light sauce consistency. Strain, return to pan, and whisk in the mustard, pickles, parsley, and chives. Season with salt and pepper. Keep warm until served.

ITALIAN CACCIAGIONE SAUCE

MAKES ABOUT 1½ CUPS

Use with roasted young birds or toss with pasta and a game meat.

2 tablespoons minced garlic
¼ pound prosciutto, finely diced
⅓ cup olive oil
2½ cups hearty red wine or white wine
Juice of 1 large lemon
2 teaspoons minced fresh sage, or ¾ teaspoon dried sage
1 teaspoon minced fresh rosemary, or ¼ teaspoon dried rosemary
6 juniper berries, crushed
3 ounces chicken livers, cut into ¼-inch dice
¼ cup minced fresh parsley (preferably flat-leaf variety)
Salt and freshly ground white pepper to taste

In a skillet over medium heat, sauté garlic and prosciutto

in oil until lightly colored. Add wine, lemon juice, sage, rosemary, and juniper berries and reduce over moderately high heat to a light sauce consistency, about 30 to 40 minutes.

Strain sauce, return to pan, and add chicken livers and parsley. Simmer until livers are just cooked through, 3 to 4 minutes. Season with salt and pepper and serve immediately.

TRADITIONAL CUMBERLAND SAUCE

MAKES ABOUT 1½ CUPS

Cumberland sauce has been used in game cooking for so many years that it is now considered a universal game sauce. This version was provided by our dear New York friend Fayal Greene, who is truly an expert on all things gamy. Serve hot or cold as a condiment to small game birds, pheasant, or meat dishes.

1 orange
1 lemon
Boiling water, as needed
3 shallots, chopped, or 1 small yellow onion, chopped
½ cup currant jelly
¼ cup port
½ teaspoon ground ginger
Pinch cayenne pepper
1 teaspoon Dijon-style mustard

Remove zest from orange and lemon; avoid the bitter white pith. Chop zest and blanch in boiling water to cover for 5 minutes. Drain and set aside.

Blanch shallots in boiling water to cover for 1 minute. Drain and set aside.

Squeeze juice from orange and half of the lemon. Strain juices into a saucepan and add jelly, wine, ginger, cayenne, and mustard. Heat gently until jelly melts. Add reserved zest and shallots and mix thoroughly.

Special Ingredients

In addition to a basic technical comprehension of game cooking, perfecting the art involves an understanding of certain ingredients. Whether using wild or farm-raised meat, the traditions of game cooking have relied on these ingredients to enhance the natural flavor of the game itself. Some of these ingredients are indeed special, such as juniper berries, truffles, and wild mushrooms, and include those that animals forage on in the wild. In the case of others, such as fruits, salt, and pepper, they have simply stood the test of time by contributing to the balance of flavors and textures in artful game cooking.

This is a selection of some of our favorite special ingredients, not a comprehensive listing of all ingredients. They are used throughout the book in chutneys and relishes, as flavorings for sauces, and in side dishes. Experiment with these ingredients and develop your own applications. When added to your culinary arsenal, they will enhance your game preparations immensely.

APPLES

When Eve took her fateful first bite of apple, the glorious fruit was immortalized as a symbol of temptation and instigation. The apple tree is native to Europe and Southwest Asia and started rapidly gaining popularity in North America in the 17th century. There are about 7,000 varieties of apples known to man, but only about 100 are grown commercially.

Apples (and apple cider) have played a key role in game cooking for many years. Because apples are a traditional fall and winter ingredient and game is often associated with the same time of year, the two have a seasonal as well as textural and flavor affinity. Apples are a superb addition to many braised dishes, relishes, and compotes, and are an excellent garnish for grilled game bird salads.

Many new apple varieties—actually "old" varieties that are being rediscovered—are making their way to market. The following are a few of the standouts that are more readily available.

Empire: Developed in the 1960s in New York. A Red Delicious–McIntosh cross with lovely aromatic qualities. Dark red yellow skin.

Gala: Yellow skin with bright red stripes. Quite sweet, intensely flavorful, and thoroughly delicious. An apple to watch for in the market, although it is often more expensive than other varieties.

Granny Smith: A popular apple that originated in Australia. Grass green skinned. Crisp and tart. Good in game bird salads.

Golden Delicious: Originated in West Virginia in the early 1900s. Greenish yellow to bright yellow skin and firm flesh. Juicy and sweet.

Gravenstein: Developed in the early 1800s in Germany and Sweden, but is now favored in Sonoma County in Northern California. Greenish yellow to orange yellow with light red stripes. Aromatic and crisp with a juicy flesh.

Jonathan: A classic apple variety with very bright, shiny red skin and crisp, spicy flesh. Good in sauces.

McIntosh: A Canadian variety from the late 1800s. Greenish red skin. Juicy, crisp, tender flesh and highly aromatic.

Newton Pippin: Originated in Long Island, New York, in the early 1700s. The first American apple to gain popularity in Europe. Green or yellow skin with pinkish blue base. Fine-grained, juicy flesh.

Berries

Picking and eating wild berries in mid-summer is sheer joy. With fingers stained and mouths puckered and purple, our memories of indulgently consuming these succulent fruits are almost sinful. According to Indian legend, berries grow by the heavenly road—a wonderfully stained and thorny road it must be!

In addition to the bevy of wild berries available in many regions, many fine supermarkets and specialty-produce stores are beginning to carry a wider array of berries during the height of the season. The best way to store fresh berries is unwashed, in an open or perforated basket in the refrigerator. The basket allows the berries to breathe and thus prevents molding. If you are buying frozen berries, try to find packages marked "individually quick frozen" without sugar added.

While the obvious use of berries is for pies, cobblers, ice creams, sherbets, and mousses, they can also be used in relishes and sauces for game meats and birds to add a complementary sweet-tart tang.

Blackberry: There are many regional blackberry varieties. Most are medium-sized to large with a deep maroon or purple black color. They are usually found in large clusters on canes, protected by intimidating thorns that seem to say, "Dare to pick me." Boysenberries are similar to blackberries and are favored in game sauces; others, such as the evergreen blackberry, are slightly lower in acid.

The loganberry, a cross between the blackberry and the red raspberry, was developed in California in the late 1800s. Loganberries display a purplish dark red color. Their flavor is slightly tart and very distinctive, which makes them useful for wine-making. They are often combined with other sweet berries.

Difficult to find outside of the Pacific Northwest, marionberries are a real delight when they can be located. A cross between blackberries, red raspberries, and loganberries, they have a dark color, ravishing aroma, lovely texture, and superb acid balance, which makes them particularly succulent with venison. Marionberries freeze well and can sometimes be found in frozen-food sections.

Blueberry: Considered indigenous to America, blueberries were one of the first fruits discovered by early settlers in the country. The small, round, dark blue skin invites instant eating, and the fruit is amazingly versatile on the table. Blueberries are particularly enjoyable when combined with other berries, and they are quite plentiful in the United States.

Huckleberries are virtually indistinguishable from wild blueberries. They are known for their intensity of flavor and crunchy, edible seeds, but they typically must be gathered in the wild. Henry David Thoreau wrote of their abundance on Fair Haven Hill: "If you would know the flavor of huckleberries, ask the cowboy or the partridge . . . as long as Eternal Justice reigns, not one innocent huckleberry can be transported thither from the country's hills." Huckleberries make great sauces, but are equally irresistible all by themselves.

Cranberry: The American Indians invented the first cranberry sauce, sweetening the berries with maple syrup or honey to offset their natural tartness. The Indians ate cranberries along with buffalo jerky, a combination of flavors that is not difficult to imagine today.

Currant: This native Scandinavian fruit was first cultivated in the 16th century, and has often been associated with game. Both red and black currants now exist in the United States, where they can be found fresh much more readily than in years past.

Red currants, known for their immediate burst of flavor, are the primary ones found on the table. They are quite tart and usually need to be combined with other sweeter berries or balanced with some sugar or honey. Currants are particularly excellent in sauces, relishes, and chutneys for game meats, and can replace vinegar or lemon juice in recipes because of their acidity.

Gooseberry: Favored mostly by the British, who've grown them for 400 years, gooseberries have never gained much popularity in America. There are as many as 1,000 varieties available for cultivation in Britain; in the United States there are but a few. Gooseberries are related to currants, which they resemble mostly in their acidic structure, and they're used much in the same way.

Lingonberry: Highly prized in Scandinavia, lingonberries bear considerable resemblance to cranberries, which explains why they have been inappropriately named lowbush cranberries in America.

Raspberry: Thought almost surely to have come from Asia, raspberries have a musky, spicy bouquet that certainly echoes that heritage. Red, golden, and black raspberries (called black caps) are now found with some regularity; the black variety from Oregon displays the most intense flavor, but is the most difficult to locate. Black raspberries were used at one time by the government to make stamping ink, but they are no longer wasted in this manner. Red raspberries have a recorded history in America dating back to 1607.

The relatively new golden variety offers a distinctive amber golden hue, but it is relatively similar in flavor to the traditional red variety. About 90 percent of the nation's raspberry supply is raised in the Pacific Northwest and is available from mid-June to mid-August only. Raspberries are extremely perishable, but they freeze very well.

BLOOD ORANGES

Citrus fruit plays an extremely important role in game cookery, largely through its contribution of an acid base to marinades and sauces. One of the most interesting and unusual of the citrus varieties is the blood orange.

This relatively new orange to America has been favored throughout Europe and North Africa for years. The outer skin is highlighted by reddish purple flecks; the seedless, inner pulp is a radiant garnet-burgundy color. The season for blood oranges is from December through early spring, and they are primarily raised in Sicily, Spain, California, and Florida.

Of the few varieties available, the Moro and Ruby Blood are considered the best. The sweet-tart, raspberry-tinged flavor and reddish juice of the blood orange can intensify many sauces and marinades that call for a citric base.

CHESTNUTS

If one surveys the evolution of game cooking over the past few centuries, chestnuts surely stand out as an essential accompaniment. Typically prepared as a purée to accompany venison, boar, and many of the game birds, chestnuts offer a nutty complement to the deep, rich flavor of game meat, an affinity quite likely based on the fact that many animals in the wild forage for these nuts when they fall from the trees.

Chestnuts are found fresh in the market in late fall and early winter, making their seasonal timing one reason they are so prized with game. In order to use them, however, they require a rather tedious peeling process. To do this, the *L. L. Bean Game & Fish Cookbook* first recommends freezing them and then making a pair of sharp, shallow cuts on the flat side of the outer shell, placing the nuts in a preheated 400°F oven for 8 to 10 minutes, and then peeling off the outer shells and inner skins while the nuts are still hot. Alternatively, you can place the frozen, cut nuts in boiling water and then slowly return the water to a boil. Turn off the heat and let the chestnuts rest in the water as you take them out one at a time and peel off the shell and membrane. Chestnuts containing any mold at all should be discarded.

In the Dordogne region of France, where they have long been considered a staple, chestnuts play a prominent culinary role. In the poor region of the Cevennes, the chestnut tree was called *l'arbre à pain,* since the daily bread of the region was made from chestnut flour. The people there were said to "live on chestnuts and water." It's not surprising that duck, geese, and other game were all prized in this region as well.

The most common chestnut found in America is called the European chestnut, which is known for its size and sweetness. It was introduced in the 19th century on both coasts of the United States.

Peeled chestnuts from Italy can often be found frozen in specialty stores and gourmet sections of better supermarkets. Canned puréed chestnuts can also be located with some regularity and certainly offer the easiest (but not necessarily best) route to using chestnuts in your cooking. The following recipe is a good all-purpose chestnut purée.

CHESTNUT PURÉE

SERVES 4 TO 6

This recipe is an excellent accompaniment to many game meats, but we particularly like it with Venison with Juniper Berry Sauce with Chestnut and Celery Root Purées (page 243). The purée can be prepared in advance, covered, and refrigerated for 1 to 2 days. Reheat before serving.

1 pound chestnuts, peeled
1½ cups chicken stock, or as needed
2½ tablespoons Madeira, Marsala, or sweet sherry
2 tablespoons cream or half-and-half
2 tablespoons butter, at room temperature
¼ teaspoon freshly grated nutmeg
¼ teaspoon ground cinnamon
⅛ teaspoon ground allspice
Salt and freshly ground white pepper to taste

In a large saucepan, combine chestnuts, 1½ cups stock, and Madeira. Cover, bring to a boil, reduce heat, and simmer until nuts are soft when pierced with a knife, 35 to 45 minutes. Transfer chestnuts and remaining liquid to a food processor or blender. Add cream and process until smooth. Add butter, nutmeg, cinnamon, and allspice and blend well. Thin with chicken stock, if necessary, for proper texture. Season with salt and pepper.

CHILI PEPPERS

Chilies are native to the New World, and Columbus is credited with bringing them to the rest of the world's attention. Chilies, including bell peppers, are incorrectly called "peppers"; they actually belong to the *capsicum* genus and are not related to peppercorns at all. Botanically, they are closely related to tomatoes, nightshades, potatoes, and tobacco. Chilies are high in vitamins, especially vitamin C, and there is substantial evidence that they both aid digestion and clear up bronchial congestion.

Buying chilies can be confusing. The same chili is often called by several different names, depending on whether it is fresh, dried, or powdered. Even the spelling is controversial: Some swear by "chiles"; others by "chilies." The chilies most commonly used in this book are described here.

Fresh Chilies

Anaheim: A long, green, mild chili used in sauces and in chili rellenos.

Ancho: A richly flavored, mild chili known as ancho whether fresh or dried.

Cayenne: A fiery, intense, red chili that is known as cayenne pepper when dried and ground.

Jalapeño: The most widely available hot chili, jalapeños can be either green or red. They are also available pickled in cans.

Pimiento: Looks like a regular red bell pepper, but with a pointed base. Usually more flavorful than red bell peppers, pimientos offer a hint of heat. Pimientos become paprika when dried and finely ground.

Poblano: A dark green chili, similar in shape to pimiento, with a rich, mildly hot flavor. Green bell peppers are not a substitute.

Serrano: A small chili, one to two inches long, either red or green, and very hot.

Dried Chilies

Ancho: A relatively mild chili with a rich, smoky flavor. Sometimes poblanos are dried and sold as anchos.

California: Usually made from the mature red Anaheim chile.

Chipotle: The dried, smoked form of jalapeño. Most commonly available canned as "chipotle in adobo," in which the chili is combined with garlic and herbs.

New Mexico: A group of long, red chilies that are commonly dried to create a toasty, rich, medium-hot flavor (hotter than the California).

Pasilla: Sometimes a dried ancho, but usually a distinct variety. Very dark, smoky flavor with a hint of tobacco. Also known as chili negro.

Pequin: A family of small chilies, yellow to orange in color, that are very hot. They are related to cayenne.

To Peel Chilies

The easiest way to peel chilies is to char them over the open flame of either a grill or a gas stove. Once the outside blisters, place them in a plastic or paper bag to "sweat" for about an hour. Then, simply peel off the charred skin under running water. It is not always necessary to peel chilies, by any means, but the charring adds an interesting toasted flavor.

All hot chilies must be handled with care! Either wear rubber gloves, or be sure to wash hands thoroughly with soap and water after handling them. Do not touch eyes, nose, or other sensitive areas while working with hot chilies as they can cause severe irritation.

Fiddlehead Ferns

Although fiddlehead ferns are a difficult-to-find delicacy, they are worth the search as they offer a wonderful flavor and textural addition to many game dishes. With farm-raised game, the connection is probably more one of association than diet.

The coiled, emergent growth stage of a new fern is called a fiddlehead, and is known to be a prime ingredient in the diet of many wild game animals who forage for it regularly on the forest floor. The northeastern United States, principally Maine and Vermont, and Nova Scotia are known to be prime fiddlehead fern areas, but the shoots are plentiful in many states on the eastern seaboard. Fiddlehead season runs from April to June, depending on locale.

Fiddleheads must be picked in their infancy, while they are still coiled in a tight, firm ball. They are extremely perishable, so they must be cooked soon after purchase, or frozen for later use.

We recommend either boiling them for 1 to 2 minutes, or sautéing them with shallots and mushrooms to accompany any number of game dishes. Fiddleheads have a distinctive taste, somewhat akin to green beans or artichokes, and a pleasing crunchy texture. Be careful not to overcook them.

Disagreement exists about the level of carcinogens in some fern varieties. The widely available ostrich fern is considered to be noncarcinogenic; the bracken fern is still under serious scrutiny. Make sure when buying fiddlehead ferns that your supplier knows the difference.

Herbs

It's difficult to imagine cooking game without herbs playing a prominent role. But then again, it's difficult to imagine any type of cooking without the use of herbs. Herbs are one of nature's most basic flavoring agents, and they provide a diverse range of aromas, flavors, and decorative shapes that greatly enhances any game meat or bird.

Rosalind Creasy, the noted culinary garden writer, observed that "cooking without herbs is like cooking in mono instead of full stereo." We agree, except to add that it's more like multichannel surround sound! Herbs, when used judiciously, add dimension and complexity to game of all kinds. As American cuisine evolves, more and more top chefs are turning to herbs as a healthful, satisfying replacement for salt and fat in their dishes.

There are so many different herbs that anything more than a brief coverage of the topic suggests a whole book in itself. In fact, many volumes have been written on the subject of herbs, which releases us from the task.

Herbs existed long before the written word. The earliest records date back to transcriptions on Babylonian clay tablets around 3000 B.C. Much of what we know about herbs today, however, has come to us through legend and folklore. Herbs have historically been used in medicine to the extent that many are reported to have magical properties.

Yet, it's surprising how many Americans know very little about *fresh* herbs. Perhaps it's the success that the dried herb and spice manufacturers have had in teaching the public what they do know. Many people think of herbs primarily as something you find in a small tin rather than in the backyard garden.

The pleasures of fresh herbs notwithstanding, high-quality dried herbs that have been properly packaged and stored are suitable replacements for their fresh equivalents. In fact, certain dried herbs, such as oregano, often have more flavor and aroma than their fresh counterparts. It's important to store dried herbs in a cool, dry place, away from the damaging effects of sunlight and stove heat.

A brief discussion of the most popular herbs in game cooking is in order.

Basil: A native of either Thailand or India, basil has been used to cure nervous headaches and to induce sleep and fragrant dreams. In Jewish lore, it is held in the hand to provide strength when fasting; in Greek it's called *basilikón,* meaning "king." In Latin, it translates as "fire-breathing dragon." Basil was found growing around Christ's tomb after the Resurrection, and in the Greek Orthodox church it is sometimes used to prepare the holy water. Basil is also one of 130 herbs that form Chartreuse liqueur.

A regal member of the mint family, basil has some of the same aromatic characteristics as its kin. It has a warm, spicy, sweet fragrance with an overtone of licorice and cloves. There are some 150 types of basil, including anise, lemon, cinnamon, mammoth, and purple varieties.

Basil was guaranteed culinary immortality with the invention of pesto, that wondrous Italian concoction that combines the herb with olive oil, garlic, cheese, and pine nuts in the classic version. There are so many variations on pesto, however, that in Parma, Michigan every year there is a Pesto Challenge, something akin to a barbecue sauce cook-off. A well-made pesto is a fine companion to a grilled game bird when a simple, low-cholesterol meal is in order.

This versatile herb also works beautifully with game stews and ragouts; in corn, zucchini, and squash side dishes; and in herb-tinged olive oils and vinegars for salad dressings with game birds.

Chives: Long, thin members of the onion family with a unique taste, chives are always useful for garnishes and provide a backbone for delicate sauces. Waverley Root described them poetically: "Suppose, in the symphony of tastes, you described the onion as the cornet: the chive would be the oboe."

Cilantro: Also known as coriander or Chinese parsley, cilantro is an increasingly popular herb with a complex soapy, rubbery, citrus-peel, parsleylike aroma and an intriguing spicy flavor. It is essential in Latin and Oriental-influenced dishes and is probably the most multicultural herb available, with wide applications in many cuisines. The dried seeds of the cilantro plant are usually called coriander seeds, but, in the market, coriander and cilantro are often used interchangeably. Strangely, as lovingly as cilantro is embraced by many cooks, its unusual smell and flavor are extremely unpleasant to some.

Dill: Used less in game cooking than many other herbs, dill has an aroma that seems better applied to seafood and vegetable dishes. Dill is, however, well suited to flavoring cabbage or sauerkraut to accompany game birds or *confits*.

Mint: A distinctive, clean fragrance and pungent, cool, cleansing taste make mint a useful counterpoint to stronger flavors in many dishes. Mint can enliven sauces and natural reductions, and its pronounced character, derived from the oil menthol, perfumes many salad dressings as well (see Warm Quail Salad Yerba Buena, page 175). Mint is also thought to be an appetite enhancer. Pliny wrote, "The smell of mint stirs up the mind and appetite for food."

Oregano: Widely used in Italian cooking, oregano has fairly versatile applications in game cooking because of its pungent aroma and savory flavor. The different varieties of oregano grown throughout the world, such as Mexican, Greek, and Italian, are very different from one another in terms of strength and pungency. Thus, it helps to know the source of your oregano when cooking with it. Oregano shines particularly in tomato-based sauces.

Sage: A strongly aromatic herb with a mildly resinous flavor, sage has a particular affinity for game birds. It is often tucked under the skin of quail, squab, or pheasant to season the flesh and is used extensively in the flavoring of game sausages. Sage is often found in stuffings for game birds, commonly accompanied by onion; its aromatic character helps permeate the stuffing and the cavity of the bird.

Tarragon: Another strongly aromatic herb, tarragon has a hint of licorice and a subtle tang. Some people find a vanilla tone in tarragon, which often helps marry it to

Chardonnay, particularly when it's used in white wine–based butter sauces (*beurre blanc*), hollandaise, béarnaise, and béchamel.

Thyme: A wonderful perennial herb, full of legend and lore, thyme means "burn sacrifice" and has inspired praise from the likes of Virgil and Kipling, who wrote, "a wind-bit thyme that smells of dawn in Paradise." The Greeks denoted its graceful elegance; Roman soldiers bathed in thyme water to give themselves vigor before a battle; Scottish highlanders drank copious amounts of wild thyme tea for strength and courage. Thyme was planted by the colonists in Virginia in 1610, and was grown extensively in Thomas Jefferson's garden at Monticello.

Many of the recipes for braised and grilled dishes employ thyme in a pivotal role. It is also essential in the marinade for Greek lamb *souvlaki*, in the Cajun specialty red beans and rice, and is one of the herbs used in Benedictine liqueur. A traditional *bouquet garni* mixture blends thyme with sage, parsley, bay, and oregano.

Thyme is sometimes described as having aromas of peppermint, nutmeg, tangerine, pine, coconut, and varnish. In more general terms, it seems to have an intense, warm, distinctively sweet fragrance. There are estimated to be about 400 different varieties of thyme, but the most common ones include English thyme, lemon thyme, caraway thyme, and silver thyme. Thyme combines well with parsley, oregano, marjoram, sage, and dill. Finally, about thyme, we'll simply quote the old cook's rule: "When in doubt, use thyme."

Juniper Berries

Juniper berries and game, particularly venison and pheasant, are a marital pair with dependability and longevity. They've been used together for centuries, both in the grand cuisine of Europe and by the American Indians of the Northwest. Over the years, juniper berries have come to be considered the classic flavoring for game.

Particularly noteworthy is the continuing tradition of using gin and juniper (from which gin is made) to create the basis for sauces for pheasant (page 151). One traditional method is to pour 2 ounces of warmed gin over 8 to 10 crushed berries, ignite the berries, and then allow the flame to burn out to help concentrate the unique aroma of the berries. This mixture is used to infuse sauces and marinades with great effectiveness.

Another classic utilization of juniper berries is Alsatian *choucroute garni*, which combines sauerkraut, white wine, boiled potatoes, slab bacon, and preserved goose or smoked pork. Brillat-Savarin considered this to be one of the great dishes of French cuisine, and its reputation has not faded.

Juniper berries should be used fresh whenever possible and can be foraged for on the prickly bushes on which they grow, or on ground cover where they fall. Initially, juniper berries are green and then turn from dark blue to black as they get riper.

Dried juniper berries are widely available in whole berry form, about half the size of small blueberries. To use them, crush them to release the intense, piny, resinlike perfume that will infuse and add complexity to marinades and sauces. Juniper berries mix nicely with peppercorns, bay leaves, tarragon, allspice, and fennel. Most of the references in this book call for dried juniper berries; these are usually finely crushed when used in stocks and sauces. If crushing is not indicated, leave the berries whole.

MUSHROOMS

Mushrooms have a special place alongside (and inside) game. From the common hot-house white and brown varieties to the more exotic wild varieties, mushrooms add a unique, earthy flavor to game and are worthy of a special exploration of both cultivated and wild-harvested types.

COMMON NAME	OTHER NAMES
Cultivated	
Button	Common Domestic
Shiitake	Black Forest, Golden Oak, Chinese Black
Bearded Tooth	Pom Pom Blanc™, Bear's Claws
Oyster	Shimeji (Japan)
Clam Shell™	Hon Shimeji (Japan)
Hen of the Woods	Mitake (Japan)
Wood Ear	Cloud Ear, Black Fungus
Wild-Harvested	
Chanterelle	Pfifferling (German), Egg, Girolle
Hedgehog	Pied de Mouton (French), Chicken Fat
Black Trumpet	Black Chanterelle, Horn of Plenty, Trumpet de Mort
Cèpe	Porcini (Italian), Boletus
Morel	Fairy Mushroom, Morille (French)
Pine	Matsutake (Japan)

All of these are worth searching out. In almost all instances, cook fresh mushrooms quickly in a little butter or olive oil in a hot sauté pan. Slow cooking or braising tends to turn fresh mushrooms to mush and to destroy their subtle, ethereal texture.

Many of the mushrooms—morels, black trumpets, wood ears, and cèpes—are more readily available in their dried form, usually in gourmet stores and delicatessens. They need to be reconstituted in water until softened, usually 30 minutes to an hour, and then sautéed very quickly. The texture of the finished product doesn't really compare with the fresh, but the flavor is often more intense. Save the soaking liquid, strain it, and use it in stocks, soups, and sauces for added flavor.

Mustard

Mustard may seem initially like an odd ingredient in the game cook's repertoire, but it is quite useful. Mustard in all its various forms—seeds, powdered, and in various condiment preparations—has a place in game cooking.

Whether used in marinades or sauces, or as coating for a venison or a buffalo roast, mustard's slightly nutty, sharp flavor mellows and sweetens as it cooks, resulting in an excellent flavoring agent. The tartness of many vinegar-laced bottled mustards adds a restorative acid element to many dishes as well. Mustard seeds also release a natural oil that can help baste and flavor roasts quite effectively.

The use of mustard seeds in cuisine dates back to the ancient Egyptians, Romans, and Hindus, all of whom popped mustard seeds into their mouths while eating various meats to help flavor them. This was the humble beginning of what cooks have known for centuries: "A little bit of mustard in a dish is a magical ingredient which is truly unsurpassed and cannot be duplicated."

Peppercorns

Hailed as the "king of spices," the use of peppercorns with game meats is legendary. The intense gaminess of many wild game meats takes well to the subtle heat of pepper, which acts as both a flavor enhancer and a mellowing agent. Black peppercorns, particularly those from Madagascar and the Tellicherry peppercorn from the Malabar coast of India, are prized for their fruity aroma and intense perfume.

Green, white, and black peppercorns all come from the same plant (*Piper Nigrum*). Green peppercorns are the immature berries that are usually brined or pickled and have a relatively mild flavor. Black peppercorns are the mature berries that are dried and have the most potent flavors. White peppercorns are the black berries that have been soaked and the black husk removed.

Pink and red peppercorns are not true peppercorns at all, but the dried berries from a relative of the rose family.

Like salt, peppercorns were used in early cultures as a form of payment, and, in fact, were considered a more stable commodity than gold during many historical eras. When first introduced to the Mediterranean world, pepper was considered more a medicine than a food.

Green, black, and white peppercorns abound in the annals of game cuisine; much of the choice of which ones to use depends on personal taste and availability. Always grind pepper fresh, either with a spice grinder or in a mortar with a pestle, since this releases more aroma and flavor from the peppercorns. In fact, if you don't have a pepper grinder in your culinary arsenal, we're not coming to dinner!

Pomegranate

Although a prominent ingredient in Persian and Mediterranean cooking, a symbol of fertility in Chinese, Greek, Roman, and Hebrew cultures, and an expression of hope in Christian art, pomegranates are not widely eaten in the United States. The sweet-sour contrast of the fruit, like that of the sun-dried cherry, plays a vivid and flavorful role in many game preparations, particularly in such venison dishes as the one on page 246.

The pomegranate offers shiny, red seeds of striking intensity that must be scraped out from their encasing membranes (or cells) in order to be eaten. A spoon or the tip of a knife works best in pulling out the seeds without puncturing them.

In many gourmet markets and Arabic food stores, pomegranate juice can be purchased and used to flavor sauces. In the fall, when pomegranates are fresh, the glistening seeds make an attractive, tasty garnish for many of the quail, pheasant, and squab salads that are included in this book.

Ultimately, we might look to Mohammed for the best explanation of pomegranates: "Eat the pomegranate for it purges the systems of envy and hatred."

Salt

It may seem unnecessary to include salt in this list, but it is perhaps the *most essential* entry. Salt is taken for granted by many of us, yet the flavors of salts are very different.

The use of salt as a preservative for wild game is basic, particularly prior to the days of refrigeration. Because it inhibits bacterial growth, salt is also basic to both the wet and dry brines used on game meats that will be smoked.

Salt has been the basis for trade and barter in many cultures, from Roman and Greek to Egyptian, Norse, Flemish, and Venetian. References to salt in the Old Testament include one in which it is prescribed as an offering to God. Roman soldiers were paid their wages, a *salary*, in order to buy salt, and words such as *salutary* and *salute* are derived from the name of the Roman god of health, Salus. The French Revolution began with a popular revolt against a new "salt tax."

Superstitions abound with regard to salt. Among them is one that suggests that you must throw salt over your shoulder if you spill it in order to avoid bad luck—a direct reference to Leonardo da Vinci's *Last Supper,* which shows Judas upsetting the salt. Asian cultures view salt as a spiritual purifier. For example, Sumo wrestlers throw salt before each match to both appease the gods and purify their spirit.

In recent years, salt has gotten a bad name due to its excessive use in the American diet, particularly in canned, packaged, and fast-food cooking. It's estimated that the average American consumes about 10 times the amount of salt required in the diet, a fact that many medical authorities believe contributes greatly to this country's abnormally high cardiovascular problems. When used to excess, salt will destroy any dish; when used sparingly, its effect is sublime, as it augments taste and helps draw out the natural flavor of the meat.

The salts of choice (and the ones sometimes, although not always, called for in this book) are kosher salt and sea salt. They can be experimented with and used interchangeably as your taste dictates. Kosher salt has less sodium by volume than regular table salt, and, to our taste, a kind of sweetness that adds an interesting flavor note. Sea salt is derived either from the ocean or from salt marshes along the coasts of the world; many salt connoisseurs have noticed dramatic differences in these salts, depending upon their origin. A useful analogy here is the differences found in Cabernet Sauvignon, for example, in the Bordeaux region of France and in California's north coast wine country. The same grapes go into the wine, but the environment and soil in which they are grown produce a considerably different end product. And so with sea salt.

Sun-Dried Cherries and Cranberries

The use of sour cherries in game dishes is widespread in the cuisines of Eastern Europe and Russia. Their preserved counterpart, the sun-dried cherry, is a fairly recent gourmet discovery, however. Sun-dried cherries offer a sweet-tart flavor that is a wonderful embellishment for game sauces, chutneys, and relishes.

They are derived primarily from the Montmorency, a sour cherry variety grown principally in Michigan. American Spoon Foods in Petoskey, Michigan, is the principal commercial supplier, although many cherries are dried and sold locally throughout the country in season. Sun-dried cranberries are a related delicacy that offer many of the same advantages and uses.

Sun-dried cherries and cranberries should be reconstituted in liquid before using. They infuse a sauce with a wonderful flavor, and they can be strained out of the sauce before serving if desired. In our minds, part of the beauty of the fruit is its pleasing texture, so we suggest that you do not strain the sauce.

Although we've mentioned two of the most unusual dried fruits, we hasten to add that there is a wonderful affinity between many dried fruits, notably apples, apricots, pears, and prunes, and game dishes of all kinds.

TRUFFLES

We include truffles here more for their historical role in game cooking than for their prominence on the home table, since their scarcity and subsequent cost make them all but a revered novelty for most of us. While canned truffles can be found, they lack the pungency and allure of fresh ones.

Truffles date back to the Mesopotamian culture of 1800 B.C., but they became legendary in the Périgord region of France in the 19th century when Brillat-Savarin wrote that "the truffle is not at all a positive aphrodisiac; but it can, on certain occasions, make women more tender and men more amiable." Both Napoleon and Louis XIV reportedly ate copious amounts of truffles to enhance their potency, and many others have waned rhapsodically about both their pleasures and their potency.

Called "the black diamond of the kitchen," "black gold," "the jewels of poor soils," "the underground empress," and "a fragrant nugget" by writers and gastronomes throughout history, the luxurious truffle—in reality, a mere underground fungus—has played a prominent role at feasts and celebrations involving game for centuries. Often stuffed into turkeys, they were prized for their heady perfume, which echoes hints of the earth, nuts, and licorice.

Truffles are found most often around scrub oaks, buried deep in subterranean hideaways where they are discovered by pigs or dogs whose mouths are tied to prevent them from eating the treasures before they are unearthed by man. They are hunted mostly at night, when their aroma seems to be most pronounced. While the Périgord region of France and the area just south of Périgord around Cahors and Quercy remain the truffle capitals of France, the Umbria region of northern Italy is also very highly regarded for producing an evocative white truffle with an intriguing garlic aroma that is prized in many Italian restaurants in the United States as well as Italy.

Truffles remain a luxury in many game dishes since, depending on the season, they can exceed $1,000 per pound. They can either be shaved atop a sauce or studded in it to add complexity and fragrance. Some truffle aficionados like to tuck small shavings under the skin of wild turkeys, pheasants, or small game birds to intensify their aroma. Ultimately, we look to the French writer Colette on truffles: "If you love her, pay her ransom regally, or leave her alone. But, having bought her, eat her on her own, fragrant, coarse-grained, eat her like the vegetable that she is, warm, served in sumptuous portions. She will not give you much trouble; her supreme flavour scorns complexity and complicity."

GAME AND WINE: THE PERFECT MARRIAGE

Game and wine have existed together on the tables of so many cultures for so long that they seem inseparable. Like a perfect marriage, the two function well on their own, but beautifully in tandem. Accompanying one another, there is harmony, depth of expression, and a sensual interaction that is truly sublime.

It can also be argued that game and wine are the oldest food and wine pairing known to mankind. The history of wine dates back thousands of years and wild game has been on our tables since mankind searched for food. The enjoyment of the two together is therefore no surprise.

There are many reasons for this seductive partnership. These have to do with the compatibility of flavors, the balance of textures, and the harnessing of the basic components of taste found both in game and in wine. As these elements interact, the impression of both food and wine changes for the diner; the initial separateness comes together and creates an overall harmony.

Flavors: To understand the synergism in flavors between wine and food, we need to look closely at the elements that create the interplay. If you dined on a piece of simple roasted venison with a glass of good red wine, you would, no doubt, find plenty of satisfaction. However, the accompanying flavors of many venison dishes—berries, mushrooms, olives, root vegetables, herbs, stocks—greatly enhance the natural taste and complexity of the venison meat itself.

These additional flavor layers offer greater opportunities to marry the dish with the subtle nuances of a fine Cabernet Sauvignon or Merlot. For example, venison with a currant- or cherry-based sauce will reflect the currant-cherry flavors in Cabernet Sauvignon or Merlot, just as a mushroom-based sauce will point up the earthy flavors found in Pinot Noir.

Likewise, a quail or duck dish, marinated in white wine and citrus juices and grilled or sautéed to perfection, matches the flavors of many white wines, particularly

Chardonnay and Sauvignon Blanc, depending on the type of sauce and accompanying flavors.

An example of contrasting flavors to achieve a successful match might be the use of a fruity red wine and a spicy rabbit stew. The contrast of the fruity wine versus the spicy flavors of the dish enlivens the palate.

Using flavors that either contrast with or match one another is one of the easiest ways to accomplish a successful partnership on the table, but there are many others.

Texture: Another key element in the marriage of game and wine is texture. The leanness of most wild and domestic game is widely heralded. Therefore, the texture (or body) of the wine that accompanies a certain dish can mirror the texture of the dish, such as a refined, elegant Cabernet Sauvignon with a tender loin of venison, or a buttery Chardonnay with the slightly fatty texture of duck. Naturally, the matching of textures in a specific dish with a wine will depend greatly on the accompanying ingredients as well, not just the texture of the meat itself.

Conversely, a wine might also be chosen to contrast with the texture of the dish, such as a delicate Johannisberg Riesling with a robust quail stew. Such a match refreshes the palate. Both the food and the wine shine.

Taste: The most important element in the marrying of wine and food involves the interplay of the four basic components of taste—sweet, sour, salty, and bitter. If food and wine combinations are selected for their similar taste components, such as the pairing of a venison dish with walnuts (bitter taste) and a young Cabernet Sauvignon with slightly bitter, youthful tannins, you might discover that the bitterness in the walnuts helps offset the youthfulness of the tannins in the wine.

Another partnering of taste components might involve a sweet white wine, such as certain styles of Johannisberg Riesling or Gewürztraminer, paired with a game bird and a slightly sweet fruit sauce. The two taste components match—sweet wine with sweet sauce.

On the other hand, one might select taste components for their contrast. In this instance, a slightly sweet wine could be chosen to contrast with the slightly salty taste component of a smoked duck or game bird dish.

There are innumerable possibilities when it comes to enjoying game and wine. An understanding of flavors, taste components, and textures, and how they are either similar to or contrast with one another, provides the foundation for satisfying choices. We can only proclaim the absolute delight we feel when a dish we've created is raised to even greater heights by the selection of the perfect wine to accompany it. On the other hand, wine and food pairing is not, and should not be, looked upon as a science.

Our basic rule is: "If you place good food, fine wines, and great people together at the table, you will *always* have a great match."

The following general guidelines on wine assume a basic understanding of the beverage and attempt to identify certain commonly found characteristics in the major California varietal wines, which are the primary focus for the wine recommendations in this book. These should be considered broad guidelines only, since specific wines will vary enormously. Many other European varietals also have a place on the game table.

Red Wines

Cabernet Sauvignon

Flavors: Currants, berries, cherries, olives, chocolate, mint, eucalyptus, vanilla, cedar, tobacco
Texture: Medium-full body, sometimes slightly coarse in young wines
Taste: Slightly astringent and puckery, which, with a little age, matures into a velvety, sensuous quality

- Serve with roasted venison, boar, and buffalo, particularly when accompanied with reduction sauces. Best when aged 3 to 5 years from vintage date.

Gamay Beaujolais

Flavors: Light cherry, fresh floral, sassafras
Texture: Very light body, sometimes with a hint of spritz
Taste: Slightly tart and very lively

- Serve with game-bird salads and smoked dishes or with grilled game meats with relishes. Best when young and served chilled.

Merlot

Flavors: Cherries, currants, earthy-herbal, tealike
Texture: Soft, engaging mouthfeel with more roundness and suppleness than Cabernet Sauvignon
Taste: Typically shows a lot of ripe fruit character in its youth and develops complexity as its matures

- Serve with venison, boar, and buffalo dishes, braised or accompanied with reduction sauces. Also nice with darker meat game birds, such as squab and partridge. Best when aged 2 to 4 years from vintage date.

Petite Sirah (or Syrah)

Flavors: Ripe blackberry, peppery, licorice, cinnamon-clove spice, vanilla
Texture: Full body, round mouthfeel; can be quite coarse and astringent when young
Taste: Some bitterness from tannins when young

- Serve with venison, boar, and buffalo, particularly with intense sauces and spicy flavors. Needs 2 to 4 years of bottle age from vintage date for optimum enjoyment.

Pinot Noir

Flavors: Cherries, berries, earthy-herbal, tomatoes, cinnamon-clove spice, vanilla, mushrooms
Texture: Light-medium body with a softer mouthfeel
Taste: Occasionally slightly tart when young, becoming more graceful as it ages

- Serve with game meats with lighter sauces and with grilled squab, partridge, and rabbit. Also good with roasted pheasant and as contrast to many braised dishes. Very enjoyable when young, but increasingly complex with bottle age.

Zinfandel

Flavors: Blackberries, raspberries, cinnamon-clove spice
Texture: Traditional style emphasizes medium-full body with slightly higher alcohol than other red wine varieties; lighter style tends toward lower alcohol and weight
Taste: Some ripeness from fruit

- Serve with venison, boar, and buffalo with hearty sauces or when grilled with intense marinades and spicy accompaniments. Also excellent with many deeply flavored braised rabbit and duck dishes that use tomato.

White Wines

CHARDONNAY

Flavors: Apple, pineapple, lemon, orange, tropical fruits, butter-oil, vanilla, toasty
Texture: Medium-full body with viscous nature, often quite mouthfilling and buttery, although many styles emphasize medium weight
Taste: Hint of sweetness or lushness with ripeness of fruit

- Serve with braised pheasant, quail, rabbit, and duck dishes, with cream and butter sauces, and with moderately sweet fruit-based relishes or chutneys. Best when consumed 1 to 3 years from vintage date.

CHENIN BLANC

Flavors: Melons, apples, citrus fruits
Texture: Light to medium body
Taste: Crisp, often lively; some styles have a hint of residual sugar, others are completely dry

- Serve with lighter quail and pheasant salads and with appetizers and first courses. Best when young.

GEWÜRZTRAMINER

Flavors: Pineapple, apples, oriental spice, rose petal, tropical fruits, honeysuckle
Texture: Medium body with a certain delicate nature
Taste: Slight hint of bitterness balanced by some residual sugar in some styles; other styles are completely dry (note label for residual sugar content: above 2 percent indicates medium sweet; above 6 to 8 percent indicates very sweet)

- Serve with spicy game bird dishes, particularly those using curries or chili peppers, or with *foie gras* or duck *confit*. Best when young.

JOHANNISBERG RIESLING

Flavors: Sweet citrus fruits, apples, rubberbands (principally from the bouquet), metallic, earthy-chalky
Texture: Light to medium body

Taste: Ranging from dry and slightly tart to very sweet, depending on style; most have modest amounts of residual sugar (see note on Gewürztraminer)

- Serve with game bird salads that have a fruity or sweet character. Best when young, except for late-harvest, sweeter styles that require aging.

SAUVIGNON BLANC (FUMÉ BLANC)

Flavors: Melons, figs, new-mown grass, citrus fruits, chalky, herbs (thyme, dill, oregano)
Texture: Medium body in most styles
Taste: Often quite tart and lively

- Serve with more highly flavored game bird dishes, including salads with light dressings, pestos, and salsas. Best when young.

II
A COOK'S TOUR OF GAME BIRDS AND MEATS

Marinated Loin of Venison Roasted in Mustard, Served with Creamy Polenta
with Wild Mushrooms (page 250)

Grilled Rabbit with Peanut-Chili Sauce,
Served with Spaghetti Squash
(page 196)

opposite
Grilled Quail Salad with Grilled Plums
and Prosciutto with Black Muscat Vinaigrette
(page 173)

Sautéed Squab with Blood Orange–Cumin
Sauce, Served with Spiced Couscous
(page 221)

From left to right: **Buffalo Rib Roast with Five Seeds, Served with Carrot–Sweet Potato Purée (page 91); Squab Roasted on the Spit, Served with Grilled Eggplant and White Corn Salsa (page 213); Broiled Quail with Mustard Butter, Served on French Bread (page 169); and Fettucine with Braised Rabbit, Sun-Dried Tomatoes, and Herbs (page 190)**

Grilled Duck Breast with Raspberry–Sweet Onion Relish (page 105)

opposite
Stuffed Pheasant with Orange and Ginger Butter Sauce (page 160)

Big Dog Venison Chili Verde, Served with Avocado Salsa (page 253)

In this section, the heart of the book, we present an overview of game cooking by focusing in detail on each of the major game varieties available. While it is difficult to describe what are often subtle distinctions in taste—of game birds, meats, or any food for that matter—we think it's possible to make general statements that will help to distinguish between the many farm-raised products now on the market.

The following chart offers general taste characteristics of the game featured. You can use it to help make substitutions in the recipes when a given bird or meat is not available.

The Taste of Farm-Raised Game

GAME TYPE	FLESH COLOR	TEXTURE	TASTE	SIMILARITY	SUBSTITUTION
Wild Boar	Medium-dark	Firm	Nutty, sweet, rich	Pork	Buffalo
Buffalo	Dark	Coarse	Sweet	Lean beef	Venison
Duck	Light pink to dark red	Medium	Buttery, beefy, nutty	Beef or young lamb	Goose
Goose	Medium-dark	Firm	Buttery	Dark turkey	Duck
Partridge	Dark	Medium	Piny, woodsy, earthy	Squab	Squab
Pheasant	Light-medium	Delicate breast, firm legs	Sweet, creamy	Free-range chicken	Quail
Quail	Light-medium	Delicate	Sweet, nutty	Poussin	Pheasant
Rabbit	Light	Dense	Mild, delicate	Chicken	Wild boar
Hare	Dark	Dense, chewy	Earthy, gamy	Dark turkey	Rabbit
Squab	Dark	Delicate	Earthy, mildly gamy	Beef or liver	Partridge
Wild Turkey	Dark	Dense	Rich, smoky	Duck	Duck
Venison	Dark	Firm, dense, velvety	Sweet, herbal, nutty	Lean beef	Buffalo

WILD BOAR

Wild boar is distinguished from the domestic pig, although it is related and can taste somewhat similar. To those who know and love pork, the taste of wild boar, with its slightly nutty, sweet flavors, should be enlightening—a glimpse of the "real thing."

The origin of the ancestral wild boar is thought to be the Crimea. In parts of Europe, the Middle East, and Asia, it was considered sacred and was eaten only at ceremonial feasts. Wild boar was also prized by the Florentines, who hunted it in the forests between Rome and Pisa, and it is still hunted with fervor in parts of Italy, France, and many parts of America.

In the words of the great eighteenth-century epicure, Grimod de la Reynière, "Everything in pig is good. What ingratitude has permitted his name to become a term of opprobrium?" Grimod also described pig as "the encyclopedic animal, a veritable walking repast. One throws no part of it away, even to the feet, one eats it all."

Despite its keen intelligence, capacity for learning, and plentiful nature, the pig is not always held in such esteem. Monselet observed, "His ignoble gluttony is echoed in terrible fashion. . . . The pig is nothing but an immense dish which walks while waiting to be served. . . ." This sentiment is evidenced by the important role the pig has played in cultures ranging from the early Etruscans, who trained their pigs to march to the sounds of the trumpet, to the poor people of the American South, who have virtually lived on pig for decades.

Wild boar pose a menacing image to many, since they can be an extremely vicious and highly protective animal. They are hunted mostly from November to March, and forage on a diet of greens and nuts, primarily acorns, which contribute to their apparent nutty flavor. Boar also have a keen sense of smell, as evidenced by their employment as truffle hunters in Bordeaux and Périgord in France.

The native American wild pig or boar is often called the javelina (sometimes spelled jabalina) or peccary, and it primarily lives in the southwestern United States. The razorback is a domestic pig that has perpetuated itself in the wild in certain parts of the southern United States. Wild boar was reintroduced in England about ten years ago, and is growing in popularity.

Larger, older boar (those with a dressed carcass weight over 100 pounds) will exhibit distinctive gaminess and are a different flavor altogether from pigs raised on preserves in Texas, Tennessee, North Carolina, California, and New Hampshire.

Most of the wild boar sold in this country are actually from a domestic pig species that has become feral. There are, however, descendants from the Russian boar that have mated in the wild with the feral domestic species. This is considered the highest quality boar available in this country and is somewhat more costly than the feral pig.

Boar is still one of the most difficult game meats to find, although it can be ordered through many of the suppliers listed in the back of this book. We consider boar to be an extraordinary delicacy, rich in flavor, and well worth the search for a special meal.

Shopping for Boar

The most important thing to consider when shopping for boar is to deal with a reputable supplier. Only then will you be assured that you're getting meat from a young boar that has been handled properly, rather than tough meat from an older animal. The best quality boar meat comes from boar that have a dressed carcass weight of 60 to 100 pounds.

Probably the most common of all boar cuts are chops, which are cut from the saddle or loin. The saddle and tenderloin can also sometimes be found, and they provide very succulent meat. Less expensive hind leg cuts and stew meat are also often available; the latter is ideal for the various braised dishes that follow.

Six to eight ounces of boneless meat or twelve to sixteen ounces of bone-in meat per person is the proper serving size for boar.

Cooking Tips

Remove fat and any silver membrane from boar meat before cooking. The hind leg of boar is ideal for roasting or braising and should be cooked until a meat thermometer registers 160°F at the thickest part. Let the meat rest in a warm place for 10 to 15 minutes before carving into thin slices, parallel to the leg.

If cooking older boar, many people prefer to soak it in buttermilk or cold water with baking soda for a few days to lessen the gaminess. We recommend the former over the latter.

Boar chops are best suited to grilling or sautéing. Because of their delicate flavor they don't require marinating, but they do take well to marinades nevertheless. Boar is cooked very much in the same way as ordinary pork, so if you have a favorite pork recipe, it can be adapted to boar fairly easily. It is even leaner than domestic pork, however, so cooking times should be reduced to keep the meat from drying out. Many people are timid about eating pork cooked less than well-done. Our personal preference is to cook pork, particularly the loin cuts, so that it is slightly pink and remains moist. The key is to get the temperature to 155 to 160° F to kill any harmful microorganisms. Other people feel comfortable eating pork only if it has been cooked to 170° F.

One of our favorite ways to prepare boar chops is to cut the meat off the bone, scallopini style, and sauté it very quickly so that it is still slightly pink inside.

Classic Dishes

Charles Lamb wrote lavishly about pig: "He must be roasted. . . . There is no flavor comparable, I will contend to that of the crisp, tawny, well-watched, not over-roasted, crackling, as it is well called—the very teeth are invited to their share of the pleasure at this banquet in overcoming the coy, brittle resistance . . . the cream and the quintessence of the child-pig's yet pure food—the lean, no lean, but a kind of animal manna—or, rather, fat and lean (if it must be so) so blended and running into each other, that together make one ambrosian result or common substance."

Of less grandiose claims, we fondly recall the rich flavors of boar served with an intense wine-and-game-stock reduction at Maurice et Charles Bistro in San Rafael, California. The rich flavors of the boar were counterpointed by a sweet chestnut purée. This dish presented us with a whole new realm of gastronomy, an awakening of sorts to this particularly tasty, but foreboding creature of the wild.

Classic Recipe

SPIT-ROASTED WILD BOAR WITH APPLE-ONION STUFFING

MAKES ABOUT 8 CUPS

Recommended Wine: A full-bodied Chardonnay with good acidity or a lively Zinfandel matches this dish perfectly.

Spit-roasted wild boar is a great culinary delicacy. Almost primordial in its ritualistic portrayal, with a taste both sublime and heady, it has been known to everyone from the Indian to the game hunter.

This dish is fun to prepare, but, of course, takes a good motorized spit or frequent hand turning to accomplish. We prefer cooking the stuffing separately since cooking times can be regulated more easily. If you wish to stuff the boar itself, you'll need to skewer shut the cavity.

Depending on the size of the boar, it will take awhile to cook, so begin early in the day. Prepare a baste (page 19) and use it every 30 minutes or so while the boar is cooking and turning on the spit. Slow cooking is the key. Make sure the boar is at least 3 feet above a large bed of moderately hot coals, and keep replacing the charcoal as necessary to provide even heat.

You can also cook the boar in the oven, if it will fit. Place it on a rack in a large roasting pan. Roast at 325° F for 20 to 25 minutes per pound, or until a thermometer registers 160° F. Baste regularly.

Whether you are doing the boar on the spit or in the oven, be sure to cover the ears, tail, snout, and other small exposed parts with foil so that they don't overcook. The theatrical presentation is important and you want your pig to look as beautiful as possible.

1 dressed 20 to 25 pound young boar

STUFFING

2 cups chopped onion
4 tablespoons butter or vegetable oil
4 cups peeled, sliced tart apples
⅓ cup Cognac or brandy
⅔ cup golden raisins
2 teaspoons minced fresh sage
2 teaspoons minced fresh thyme
4 cups coarsely chopped dry French bread crumbs
Salt and freshly ground black pepper to taste

In a large skillet, melt butter and sauté onions until lightly colored. Add apples and sauté for 3 minutes.

While apples are cooking, combine brandy and raisins in another saucepan and bring to a boil. Remove from heat. Stir brandy-raisin mixture into apple mixture. Add sage and thyme and gently stir in bread crumbs. Season with salt and pepper. Let cool and stuff into boar before roasting.

WILD BOAR CHOPS WITH CITRUS ZEST, SHALLOTS, AND MUSTARD CREAM SAUCE

SERVES 4

Recommended Wine: A full-throttle Zinfandel or Petite Sirah with hints of pepper and spice would be an ideal accompaniment to this hearty, flavorful boar dish.

Adapted from a recipe by Mark Stech-Novak, a Northern California chef and an artist when it comes to game cooking, this simple method showcases the flavor of wild boar chops. Stech-Novak's original recipe calls for ¼ cup dried rose hip pieces instead of the citrus zest.

1 recipe Basic Dry Game Marinade (page 28)
4 thick-cut wild boar chops (5 to 6 ounces each)
1½ tablespoons butter or olive oil

SAUCE

2 tablespoons mixed chopped lemon zest and orange zest, or
1 tablespoon finely chopped dried rose hips
¼ cup finely chopped shallots
¼ cup red wine vinegar
¼ cup red wine
3 tablespoons honey
¼ cup cream
1 tablespoon Dijon-style mustard
2 tablespoons butter (optional)

Prepare marinade and sprinkle enough of it on the chops to coat lightly. Rub into meat on both sides. Refrigerate for 4 to 5 hours.

Preheat oven to 300°F. In a nonstick pan, sauté chops in butter until browned on both sides. Place in preheated oven and cook until cooked through but still juicy, 12 to 15 minutes.

While chops are cooking, make sauce. Place citrus zest, shallots, vinegar, wine, and honey in a small saucepan and reduce over medium-high heat until 1 tablespoon remains. Add cream and mustard and reduce by half. If desired, swirl in butter. Strain sauce, pour over chops, and serve immediately.

SMOKED SADDLE OF WILD BOAR WITH CURRANT SAUCE

SERVES 6

Recommended Wine: The intense, curranty flavors in the sauce make the dish an ideal match for a well-balanced, rich Cabernet Sauvignon.

This dish, an adaptation of one created by chef Amy Ferguson-Ota during a stint at Charley's 517 in Houston, was previously published in Ellen Brown's *Cooking with the New American Chefs.* Ferguson-Ota now heads the kitchen at the Hotel Hana-Maui in Hawaii.

The curranty flavors of the sauce are the perfect counterpoint to the smoked boar. If boar cannot be found, a saddle of pork or venison can be used. Chestnut Purée (page 48) and braised leeks are ideal accompaniments.

1 recipe Basic Wet Brine for Game Meats (page 35)
1 saddle of wild boar or pork (6 to 8 pounds)

SAUCE
½ cup dried currants
½ cup crème de cassis
½ cup red wine
¼ cup black currant jam
2 cups veal, beef, or Basic Game Meat Stock (page 40)
3 shallots, chopped
2 teaspoons fresh lemon juice
½ teaspoon Dijon-style mustard
2 tablespoons unsalted butter
Salt and freshly ground black pepper to taste

A couple of days in advance of cooking, prepare brine and place boar in it.

Prepare grill for smoking. Using indirect-heat method (page 33), smoke boar on grill with hickory, pecan, and applewood chips that have been soaked for about 30 minutes in water and drained. Keep cover on grill and smoke until meat is cooked, 1½ to 2 hours. Replenish coals and chips as necessary.

To make sauce, in a small saucepan, soak currants in crème de cassis and wine for 45 minutes. Add all remaining ingredients, except butter, salt, and pepper, and reduce over medium heat to a light sauce consistency. Swirl in butter. Season with salt and pepper. Keep warm.

Remove boar from grill and let rest a few minutes. Carve boar and serve with sauce.

ROASTED LOIN OF WILD BOAR WITH APPLE CHARLOTTE

SERVES 6

Recommended Wine: A full-bodied Chardonnay will marry nicely with the apple flavor in the charlotte. A Zinfandel will emphasize the meaty flavors of the boar. Either wine is a treat with this dish.

Boar is a greatly ignored meat in the chef's repertoire. While admittedly difficult to find, it can be special ordered, and it is a sublime gastronomic treat. This homespun preparation by Joe Mannke, chef at Rotisserie for Beef and Bird in Houston, marries the boar with a tasty apple charlotte that is the perfect companion.

1 loin of wild boar (4 to 5 pounds, with chine bone removed by butcher)
1 tablespoon kosher salt
½ tablespoon freshly ground black pepper
1½ teaspoons dried thyme
½ cup water

CHARLOTTE

3 cups peeled and diced green apples
Pinch minced lemon zest, ground ginger, ground cinnamon, and ground cloves
2 tablespoons brown sugar
1 cup white wine
4 ounces Calvados
1 cup high-quality tart applesauce
Salt to taste
3 egg yolks
¼ pound butter, melted
3 cups white or French bread cubes with crust (1 inch)
Fresh thyme sprigs for garnish

Preheat oven to 450°F. Rub boar on all sides with salt, pepper, and thyme. Place boar in a roasting pan and add water to pan. Roast in preheated oven for 40 minutes.

Remove roasting pan from oven. Prepare charlotte by adding apples, zest, ginger, cinnamon, cloves, brown sugar, wine, and Calvados around the roast. Return pan to oven and bake for 15 to 20 minutes, or until apples are cooked through. Mix together applesauce, salt, and egg yolks and pour over apples. Return to oven for 5 minutes longer. Mix the butter with the bread cubes. Sprinkle over the apple mixture and bake for 10 minutes longer, or until golden brown, or when meat thermometer registers 160°F.

Remove roasting pan from oven, remove boar, and let rest for a few minutes. Slice boar on the bias. Using a spatula, transfer charlotte to a large serving platter. Place sliced boar atop charlotte. Garnish with thyme sprigs and serve.

WILD BOAR WITH ANCHO CHILIES, PINEAPPLE, AND TAMARIND
Served with Fried Onion Rings in Beer Batter

SERVES 10 TO 12

Recommended Wine: A lively, young Zinfandel with good acidity will mirror the tart-sweet quality in this dish.

Stephan Pyles of Routh Street Cafe/Baby Routh in Dallas is known for redefining (or defining, as the case may be) contemporary Southwest cooking. With this exotic boar dish, he extends the boundaries by incorporating such decidedly non-southwestern tropical ingredients as pineapple and tamarind. The combination of sweet-tart-spicy flavors is very harmonious and extremely satisfying. Duck breast may be substituted with great success if boar is not available. We've added the onion rings as a suitable accompaniment.

5 ancho chili peppers, seeded and deveined
2 to 3 pounds boneless loin of wild boar, trimmed of fat and cut into small cubes
2 tablespoons olive oil
1 large onion, chopped
2 carrots, peeled and chopped
4 large cloves garlic, chopped
½ teaspoon ground cumin
½ teaspoon cayenne pepper
1 red bell pepper, seeded, deveined, and chopped
½ teaspoon salt, plus salt to taste
About 4½ cups Basic Game Meat Stock or water (see page 40)
2 cups chopped fresh pineapple
Dash ground cinnamon
1 tablespoon tamarind concentrate (See Note)
Fried Onion Rings in Beer Batter (recipe follows)

Preheat oven to 450°F. Arrange ancho chilies in a small pan and roast in preheated oven for 2 to 3 minutes. Transfer to a bowl and add warm water to cover. Let stand until needed.

In a large pot, sauté boar, onion, carrots, garlic, cumin, cayenne, bell pepper, and ½ teaspoon salt in oil until vegetables are slightly wilted and boar is lightly browned. Add stock just to cover and bring to a boil. Skim surface and reduce heat. Let simmer, covered, for 15 minutes. Strain and skim again, if necessary. You should have about 4 cups liquid.

Place ancho chilies and 1 cup of the cooking liquid in a blender or food processor and purée. Add purée to pot along with pineapple, cinnamon, and tamarind. Bring to a simmer and continue cooking, uncovered, for 15 minutes. Season with salt and serve with onion rings.

NOTE: Tamarind concentrate can be found in Asian markets.

FRIED ONION RINGS
IN BEER BATTER

SERVES 10 TO 12

2 bottles (12 ounce) beer (not dark)
2¾ cups all-purpose flour
2 teaspoons salt
1 tablespoon Hungarian paprika
4 large red onions
1 cup flour for dusting
Vegetable oil for deep-frying

In a bowl, whisk together beer, 1¾ cups of the flour, salt, and paprika. Let batter stand for 1 hour before using.

Slice onions ¼-inch thick and separate into rings. In a deep fryer or heavy-bottomed sauté pan, heat at least 1 inch of oil to 375°F, or until a small bit of bread turns lightly golden within seconds of being dropped in oil. Dust onions with remaining 1 cup flour and then dip into the batter to coat thoroughly. Fry onions in oil, in batches, until golden. Remove with a slotted utensil to paper towels to drain. Serve hot with boar.

WILD BOAR WITH ROASTED RED PEPPER SAUCE AND FETA-MINT YOGURT

SERVES 4 TO 6

Recommended Wine: This flavorful Mediterranean-influenced dish works beautifully with a vibrant, youthful Petite Sirah or Zinfandel.

Food writer Marlena Spieler inspired this sauce combination, which she created to go with lamb brochettes. We've adapted her basic concept to accompany a roasted loin of boar; the flavors of the two sauces seem to marry perfectly with the mildly gamy flavors of the boar. This dish works nicely with a simple baked potato on the side; the yogurt sauce is delicious on the baked potato as well.

1 loin of wild boar, trimmed of excess fat (5 to 6 pounds, with chine bone removed by butcher)
¾ teaspoon salt
2 teaspoons paprika
1 teaspoon ground cumin
¼ cup vegetable oil

PEPPER SAUCE

1 clove garlic, peeled
1 jar (7 ounce) roasted red peppers, drained
¼ teaspoon ground cumin
⅛ teaspoon cayenne pepper
2 tablespoons olive oil
1 teaspoon fresh lemon juice
½ teaspoon chopped fresh oregano
½ teaspoon chopped fresh basil
Salt and freshly ground black pepper to taste

YOGURT SAUCE

1 medium shallot
½ cup loosely packed fresh mint leaves
4 ounces feta cheese
⅓ cup plain yogurt
2 teaspoons olive oil

Preheat oven to 400°F. Rub boar on all sides with salt, paprika, and cumin. Place boar in a large roasting pan and add oil to pan. Roast for about 1 hour, or until thermometer registers 160°F. Remove from pan and let rest under aluminum foil for a few minutes before carving.

Meanwhile, make the accompanying sauces. To make pepper sauce, place garlic in a food processor or blender and mince. Add all remaining ingredients and process until smooth. (This sauce can be made in advance and refrigerated for 2 to 3 days.)

To make yogurt sauce, place shallot in a food processor or blender and mince. Add mint and feta cheese and process to form a paste. Add yogurt and oil and process until smooth. (This sauce can be made in advance and refrigerated for 2 to 3 days.)

To serve, slice boar into chops. Arrange on individual serving plates and crisscross the sauces over the top, or serve each sauce on the side of chop in a large dollop.

WILD BOAR BORSCHT

SERVES 8 TO 10

Recommended Wine: A lightly chilled Gamay Beaujolais or lighter-style Zinfandel contrasts with the heartiness of the soup and provides an interesting textural counterpoint.

Hearty soups and stews are perfectly suited to cold day suppers and this one serves the need well. This recipe also works well with stew meat from buffalo, venison, elk, and similar animals.

1½ pounds boar stew meat, fat and sinew removed and cut into 1-inch cubes
2 tablespoons light olive oil
1 cup diced carrot
1½ cups sliced yellow onion
2 tablespoons slivered garlic
½ cup thinly sliced celery
3 cups diced beets
1 cup seeded, diced tomatoes
2 quarts beef stock or Basic Game Meat Stock (page 40)
2 cups hearty red wine
1 teaspoon fennel seed
2 teaspoons minced fresh thyme, or 1 teaspoon dried thyme leaves
1½ cups diced red potatoes
1½ cups finely shredded red cabbage
Salt and freshly ground black pepper to taste
2 tablespoons balsamic vinegar
¼ cup chopped fresh parsley
Sour cream or crumbled feta cheese for garnish

In a heavy-bottomed stockpot, lightly brown meat in 1 tablespoon of oil. Remove meat with slotted spoon and set aside. Add another tablespoon of oil along with carrots, onion, garlic, and celery to stockpot and sauté until vegetables just begin to color. Return meat to pot and add beets, tomatoes, stock, red wine, fennel, and thyme. Bring to a boil, reduce heat, and simmer 1½ to 2 hours, carefully skimming any scum that forms on surface.

Add potatoes and cabbage and cook for 10 minutes longer, or until potatoes are just done. Season with salt and pepper. Stir in vinegar and parsley just before serving. Garnish with a dollop of sour cream.

WILD BOAR SAUSAGE WITH CUCUMBER CHUTNEY

SERVES 6

Recommended Wine: A fruity Zinfandel supplies the liveliness and texture to support this tasty sausage.

Many sausage mixtures are heavy and usually contain a fair amount of fat. This version is quite light and epitomizes today's concern about eating healthful foods. The flavors are intriguing and reminiscent of the eastern Mediterranean. The sausages are also excellent grilled over hot coals. Cucumber chutney is a refreshing accompaniment.

CHUTNEY

1½ cups thinly sliced, seeded, unwaxed cucumber (see Note)
3 tablespoons thinly slivered shallots
1 teaspoon thinly sliced, seeded serrano chili pepper
2 tablespoons sugar
1 teaspoon sea salt
3 tablespoons white wine vinegar
1 teaspoon finely chopped fresh mint

1 cup chicken stock
¾ cup bulgur (cracked wheat)
2 tablespoons minced garlic
½ cup finely chopped green onion
5 tablespoons olive oil
2 pounds boneless lean wild boar shoulder, coarsely ground
2 teaspoons salt
½ teaspoon freshly ground white pepper
1 teaspoon ground cumin, lightly toasted
¼ cup chopped fresh mint
¾ cup walnuts, toasted and roughly chopped
¾ cup plain yogurt
¼ cup minced fresh parsley
⅓ cup golden raisins (optional)
Sausage casings or caul fat
Plain yogurt seasoned with minced red onion and minced fresh mint for garnish

To make chutney, combine all ingredients in a nonreactive bowl, cover, and refrigerate for at least 1 hour before serving.

In a small saucepan, heat chicken stock to boiling. Pour stock over bulgur and let stand a few minutes until all liquid is absorbed and mixture is cool.

In a small skillet, sauté garlic and green onion briefly in 3 tablespoons of oil until soft but not browned. Let cool and mix with bulgur. Add all remaining ingredients, except sausage casings, to bulgur mixture and blend well.

Form into twelve patties or stuff into casings or wrap in caul fat. Sauté in remaining oil until browned on the outside and cooked through, about 4 minutes per side over moderate heat.

Serve with fresh cucumber chutney and garnish with a dollop of yogurt seasoned with red onion and mint.

NOTE: Most cucumbers in supermarkets have been waxed. Peel these before using. If you're lucky enough to get cucumbers from the yard, leave the peel on.

BRAISED LOIN OF WILD BOAR IN MILK

SERVES 4

Recommended Wine: A full, rich Chardonnay supports the subtle richness of the dish.

This is our version of the classic Italian *arrosto di maiale al latte*. It may not sound all that appealing, but the end result is so succulent and delicate that you'll want to try it often with boar or domestic pork. The milk magically transforms the sauce into a nutty, brown concoction of indescribable flavor.

3 tablespoons butter
2 pounds boneless loin of wild boar, with a thin layer of fat left on and tied
2 teaspoons finely slivered garlic
2 teaspoons finely minced fresh rosemary
3 cups milk, or as needed
½ pound fresh mushrooms, finely diced
Salt and freshly ground black pepper to taste
¼ cup minced fresh flat-leaf parsley

In a heavy-bottomed pot, melt 2 tablespoons of the butter and brown the loin thoroughly. Add garlic, rosemary, and 3 cups milk. Cover and simmer slowly until boar is very tender, 1½ to 2 hours. As boar cooks, milk will thicken and brown. Check occasionally to make sure milk is not cooking too fast. Add additional milk if necessary.

While boar is cooking, sauté mushrooms in remaining 1 tablespoon of butter until lightly golden brown; set aside. When boar is finished cooking, remove strings and set on platter. Cover with aluminum foil to keep warm. Add mushrooms to pot and whisk juices over medium heat until a smooth sauce forms. Add a bit more milk if sauce is too thick. Season with salt and pepper and whisk in parsley.

Slice boar in ¼-inch-thick medallions and pour sauce over.

BUFFALO

Although its sweet, coarsely textured meat is utterly delectable, the overwhelming image of the buffalo has been created not by its culinary merit, but by its physical image and place in history. Despite the somewhat exotic notion of buffalo, the meat is quite similar tasting to beef, and is not at all gamy. In fact, in blind taste tests, many people have a difficult time differentiating the two.

Nowhere is the legacy of game cookery in America more visible than with the magnificent buffalo. When Christopher Columbus arrived in America in 1492, it is estimated that there were more than 30 million buffalo on the Great Plains; later estimates record the buffalo population reaching as high as 125 million. Coronado, one of the first explorers to see an American buffalo, described them as "hunchback cows," and a report of his expedition described their presence in America with awesome magnitude: "So many animals fell in [the canyon] that they filled it up and the rest passed over with their bodies."

Indigenous to and almost symbolic of America, the buffalo was the sustenance for the Plains Indians who roamed the land. *Tatonka,* as the buffalo was called, also provided the Indians with shelter, tools, clothing, weapons, fuel, grease, and thread, and was the symbol of "The Great Spirit." One of the Indians' first culinary triumphs was to preserve buffalo meat, turning it into dried "jerky" that they could carry with them as they roamed the plains. Buffalo tongue was considered sacred and was taken like a sacrament.

The prevalence of buffalo in our country is best evidenced by a notation from Tom McHugh's *The Time of the Buffalo,* in which he quotes zoologist Joel Allen observing the herds in Kansas in 1871: ". . . such a quantity of them that I do not know what to compare them with, except the fish in the sea . . . numerous as the locusts of Egypt . . . we could not see the limit either north or west. . . . The Plains were black and appeared as if in motion . . . the country was one robe."

In the late 1800s the buffalo became the bounty for throngs of hunters who prized its hide and, only occasionally, its meat, which they called humpback beef. Once a magnificent wild creature that foraged on our grasslands, the legendary buffalo all but disappeared from our country and our table as the predatory killing increased. One of the most notable enemies of the buffalo was Buffalo Bill Cody, who is reported to have shot over four thousand of them in a year and a half. At the turn of the century only a few hundred buffalo remained in North America, mostly on preserves in Yellowstone Park and in zoos.

In Europe, the bison (as the buffalo was called there) provided sustenance for prehistoric Europeans, and the beautiful animal was often depicted in cave paintings from the Stone Age. It was forced into extinction by the twentieth century primarily because of the eradication of its food supply from the forests of Switzerland, Germany, and France, where it lived primarily on the foliage and nuts from the forest rather than grass.

Clearly, it has taken a dedicated breeding program by ranchers in Texas, California, Colorado, Idaho, Wyoming, Kansas, Montana, and the Dakotas to rejuvenate the very existence of the buffalo. Today there are between eighty thousand and one hundred thousand buffalo in the United States and Canada, and they are raised very much like natural, prime range beef. Even the United States government maintains a herd of about twelve thousand wild bison.

As a source of meat, buffalo has significant advantages over beef. It is high in protein, extremely low in cholesterol (approximately 30 percent less than beef), and low in fat (approximately 50 percent of the calories and 10 percent of the fat of beef). For many people with cardio-vascular problems, buffalo is a satisfying replacement for beef, and it is even recommended on some medically approved diets in this country.

Buffalo is one of the most efficient grass-eating animals in the world, thus it is more economical to raise than cattle. The grass diet of buffalo is supplemented with natural grains and sun-cured hay. Over the years, buffalo has proven relatively free from disease, therefore antibiotics are rarely required. Another interesting discovery is that buffalo almost never get cancer, a fact that has animal scientists still looking for answers. And, if we don't have enough praise for buffalo, its meat is also nonallergenic.

Buffalo mature at six to seven years, but often live until they are thirty. Those selected for slaughter are done so at about thirty months, however, when their meat is at its prime. Buffalo measure six feet tall at the hump, and they weigh close to two thousand pounds. Despite its size, the buffalo is a very fast animal and can run up to thirty-five miles per hour.

Less available, but offering many of the same benefits as the farm-raised American bison, is the Asian water buffalo. Currently there are only about thirty-five hundred Asian buffalo in the United States. They are sturdy, low-maintenance animals that feed on leaves, weeds, and grass and produce a rich milk from which a highly prized mozzarella cheese is made.

Shopping for Buffalo

Buffalo comes in cuts similar to those for beef. Because of a low supply-to-demand ratio, it currently costs considerably more, however, so it is not yet as attractive to a large segment of the population as it might be. The premium price is readily absorbed by those favoring buffalo for its nutritional (lean) value. It is also important to note that smaller amounts of buffalo tend to go further than beef because of its dense, "all-meat" nature.

Commonly found cuts are the less expensive chuck roast and top round, as well as the more expensive cuts—rib eye, tenderloin, New York strip loin, and rib roast. Since buffalo is not carried by most supermarket meat departments, it normally requires special ordering at a game purveyor. We recommend letting your regular butcher know of your interest in buffalo; it's likely that he or she will be able to special order it for you, and perhaps carry it on a regular basis if the demand is great enough.

In the past few years there has been a notable escalation in the availability of high-quality, range-fed beef raised without the use of hormones and antibiotics. On the West Coast, the Niman-Schell and Harris Ranch products are exceptional. In this respect, beef is beginning to draw closer to the natural quality of buffalo.

Six to eight ounces of boneless or twelve to sixteen ounces of bone-in meat per person is the proper serving size for buffalo.

Cooking Tips

Trim any visible fat before cooking buffalo. Since buffalo meat is not marbled with fat like beef, it doesn't need to be cooked at as high a temperature for as long. Fat acts as an insulator to heat, so it takes less time for heat to penetrate the meat of buffalo than of beef. Regardless of cooking method, buffalo meat needs to be cooked rare to medium-rare; well-done meat will render a dry, chewy, tasteless mass of little merit.

A buffalo rib roast should be cooked slowly at low heat (approximately 325°F) with oil and seasonings rubbed into the surface of the meat to help with internal basting.

If grilling buffalo steaks or chops, cook them quickly at least 6 inches from the heat source and baste to keep the meat moist. Ground buffalo patties may need to be combined with a little ground pork to add a slight amount of fat to the meat.

Classic Dishes

Traditional preparations of buffalo focus on simple roasts, steaks, ground patties, loafs, and wine and tomato-based stews. In fact, many of today's buffalo dishes are directly related to the campfire cuisine of our ancestors. Like other game meats, however, the preparation of buffalo is undergoing change and is infinitely flexible in terms of seasoning and flavor accompaniments. Virtually any beef recipe can be adapted to buffalo with adjustments in cooking times as noted above.

Classic Recipe

BUFFALO JERKY

Recommended Wine: As a snack food, it's unlikely that jerky will be served with wine. Should the occasion arise, a fruity Gamay Beaujolais or lighter-style Zinfandel contrasts the salty components in the jerky.

Jerky has become a curious snack for us today, but not too long ago it was basic survival food for the American Indian and early pioneers. Jerky is dried, not cooked, meat and can be easily made at home with any of the red meat game. Like potato chips, once you start eating jerky, it's difficult to stop. We've given this version a little twist with some Asian flavoring.

2 pounds lean buffalo roast, from round or leg
⅓ cup dry sherry
½ cup soy sauce
⅓ cup chicken stock or Basic Game Meat Stock (page 40)
3 tablespoons rice wine vinegar
1 tablespoon brown sugar
2 teaspoons chopped fresh ginger
2 cloves garlic, slivered
1 teaspoon freshly ground black pepper

Remove all fat from meat. Wrap meat in plastic wrap and place in freezer until almost frozen solid, about 2 hours. This step will make the meat easier to slice. Remove and cut with the grain into neat ⅛-inch-thick slices. Arrange meat in a shallow dish.

Mix all remaining ingredients together in a saucepan and bring to a boil. Let cool and pour over sliced meat. Marinate overnight in the refrigerator, stirring once or twice.

Preheat oven to 250°F. Pat meat dry with paper towels. Arrange meat in a single layer on a roasting rack and place in preheated oven. Immediately reduce heat to 140° F and allow meat to dry slowly for 8 hours or so. Meat should be stiff but still "bendable." Store in an airtight container in the refrigerator.

SAUTÉED BUFFALO SIRLOIN STEAKS WITH FRESH HERBS AND MUSHROOMS
Served with Parsnip Fries

SERVES 2

Recommended Wine: The straightforward flavors of this dish lend themselves to showcasing an elegant, refined Cabernet Sauvignon where the complexity of the wine can really embellish the dish.

The lean meat of buffalo is presented here without a lot of embellishments. French-fried potatoes or parsnips are a terrific accompaniment to maintain the simple pleasure. An assortment of shiitakes, cèpes, or porcini mushrooms would be excellent with this dish.

MARINADE

2 tablespoons soy sauce
2 tablespoons olive oil
1 teaspoon minced fresh oregano, or ½ teaspoon dried oregano leaves
1 teaspoon minced fresh tarragon, or ½ teaspoon dried tarragon leaves
Few drops Tabasco sauce
Few drops Worcestershire sauce

2 buffalo sirloin steaks (8 to 10 ounces each)
½ pound mixed fresh mushrooms, sliced
3 tablespoons butter or olive oil
Salt and freshly ground black pepper to taste
Parsnip Fries (recipe follows)
Fresh oregano or thyme sprigs for garnish

Combine all ingredients for marinade and marinate steaks for 2 to 3 hours at room temperature. Remove steaks from marinade and pat dry with paper towels.

In a large skillet, sauté mushrooms in 1 tablespoon of the butter for 2 to 3 minutes. Remove from pan and keep warm. Add remaining 2 tablespoons butter to skillet and sauté buffalo steaks until rare, 1½ to 2 minutes per side. Season with salt and pepper.

Serve steaks topped with sautéed mushrooms and Parsnip Fries. Garnish with oregano sprigs.

PARSNIP FRIES

SERVES 2

½ pound fresh parsnips
2 cups vegetable oil for deep-frying

Peel parsnips, removing a ⅛-inch-thick layer. With a mandolin or vegetable slicer, slice parsnips very thinly lengthwise. Pat dry. Heat oil to 350° F, or until just shimmering. Working in batches so as not to crowd pan, slip parsnips into oil and carefully fry until crisp and golden. Remove with a slotted utensil to paper towels to drain. Fries can be done ahead and reheated in a low oven. Strain oil and save for other uses.

GRILLED MEDALLIONS OF BUFFALO TENDERLOIN WITH ROAST CORN SAUCE
Served with Wild Rice Fritters

SERVES 4

Recommended Wine: This hearty dish will stand up to the intense fruit of a fine Cabernet Sauvignon, which helps tie all the flavors together.

Tim Anderson, the chef at Goodfellow's in Minneapolis, excels at cooking game. The combination of buffalo tenderloin with corn and wild rice is a distinctively Heartland touch and an excellent juxtaposition of flavors. If the tenderloin is not available, this dish can be prepared with buffalo steaks.

CORN SAUCE
2 ears of corn, husks intact
¼ cup chopped carrot
½ yellow or red bell pepper, seeded, deveined, and chopped
1 clove garlic, crushed
¼ cup chopped yellow onion
1½ cups chicken stock
½ cup heavy cream
Salt and freshly ground black pepper to taste

1½ pounds buffalo tenderloin
¼ cup vegetable oil
Salt and freshly ground black pepper to taste

To make corn sauce, preheat oven to 400°F. Place corn with husks intact on a baking sheet, and roast them in preheated oven until husks are brown and somewhat dry, about 30 minutes. Remove from oven, let cool slightly, and peel off husks and silk.

Cut corn kernels from cobs and place in saucepan with carrot, bell pepper, garlic, onion, and stock. Cook over medium heat until carrots are soft, about 15 minutes. Add cream and cook for 5 minutes. Remove from heat and purée in blender or food processor until smooth. Strain sauce, season with salt and pepper, and keep warm. (Sauce can be thinned with chicken stock, if necessary, to consistency that coats the back of a wooden spoon.)

To prepare buffalo, prepare a fire in a charcoal grill. Cut meat into 8 even medallions. Coat with oil, then season with salt and pepper. Cook over hot coals until medium-rare, 2 to 3 minutes per side.

To serve, place 2 buffalo medallions on each serving plate. Pour corn sauce around edge of medallions. Garnish with fritters.

WILD RICE FRITTERS

SERVES 4

1½ cups all-purpose flour
1½ teaspoons baking powder
3 eggs
1 cup half-and-half
3 shallots, chopped
3 cloves garlic, chopped
1½ cups cooked wild rice
½ cup chopped carrot
2 tablespoons molasses
Salt and freshly ground black pepper to taste
About 1½ cups vegetable oil for frying

In a mixing bowl, sift together flour and baking powder. Add eggs and half-and-half and blend together well with a whisk; reserve. Combine all remaining ingredients, except oil, in a food processor and chop until rice is broken up. Add this to flour-egg batter and mix well. Season with salt and pepper.

To fry fritters, coat bottom of a skillet with about ⅛ inch oil and heat until lightly sizzling. To form each fritter, spoon 1 tablespoon of batter into pan. Don't try to cook too many at once or they will turn greasy. Turn fritters constantly and cook for approximately 5 minutes. Test one to see if center is cooked through. Remove from pan with a slotted utensil and drain on paper towels; keep warm. Add oil to pan as needed after each batch is cooked.

BUFFALO CHILI

SERVES 6 TO 8

Recommended Wine: The flavors of this deeply flavored chili are amplified by a rich Petite Sirah or Zinfandel.

This buffalo preparation by Joe Mannke of Houston's Rotisserie for Beef and Bird emphasizes straightforward flavors and is equally great on a cold winter night or a hot summer day. Any leftover cooked buffalo meat from roasts can be added just long enough to warm it thoroughly.

Mannke likes to serve his chili with beans and brown rice, which helps mop up the zesty flavors. Leftovers can be refrigerated and served within a couple of days or frozen.

½ pound bacon, chopped
2 large yellow onions, chopped
6 cloves garlic, minced
3 pounds buffalo stew meat, coarsely ground or cut into ½-inch pieces, depending on preference and quality of the meat
About ¼ teaspoon freshly ground black pepper or hot-pepper flakes
About ¼ teaspoon dried thyme
About ¼ teaspoon dried rosemary
Salt to taste
¼ cup ground red chili or chili powder (see Note)
2 teaspoons ground cumin
1 tablespoon flour
1½ cups dark beer
1 can (35 ounces) Italian plum tomatoes, drained and chopped
½ cup plus 2 tablespoons tomato paste

In a large heavy cast-iron skillet or pot, combine bacon, onion, and garlic and cook over low heat until onions are soft and translucent. Drain off any fat.

Season the buffalo meat with pepper, thyme, rosemary, salt, ground chili, and cumin. Dust with flour. Add meat to skillet and cook over high heat, stirring with a large spoon, until lightly browned. Add beer, tomatoes, and tomato paste and bring to a boil. Reduce heat, cover, and cook for 2½ hours, stirring occasionally. Taste and adjust seasonings. Skim any fat from surface.

NOTE: Ground red chili, made exclusively from dried chilies, can be found in Latin American markets. Chili powder varies with the manufacturer, but it is always a blend of chili with other spices, such as cumin, coriander, and cloves.

BUFFALO RIB ROAST WITH FIVE SEEDS
Served with Carrot–Sweet Potato Purée

SERVES 8 TO 10

Recommended Wine: This elegant, flavorful roast is nicely complemented by a fine Cabernet Sauvignon or Merlot to highlight the succulent meat.

Mark Stech-Novak, a gifted San Francisco chef, shares his recipe for roasting buffalo. It brings out the flavor of the meat itself, and is highlighted by an interesting combination of seeds, which acts as both a coating and a flavoring agent for the meat. One of the real delights of this dish is the intriguing aroma that permeates the kitchen during the slow roasting of the buffalo.

This elegant presentation would be ideally suited to a holiday dinner with the appropriate accompaniments—sweet potato purée, braised leeks, or potato gratin.

1 buffalo rib or top sirloin roast (7 to 9 pounds)
1 tablespoon anise seed
1 tablespoon coriander seed
1 tablespoon fennel seed
1 tablespoon yellow mustard seed
1 teaspoon celery seed
1 teaspoon kosher salt
1 tablespoon Tellicherry black peppercorns
1 tablespoon safflower oil
1½ cups dry red wine
1 cup beef stock, veal stock, or Basic Game Meat Stock (page 40)
1 teaspoon Dijon mustard
Carrot–Sweet Potato Purée (recipe follows)

One day prior to cooking, carefully trim roast to remove all but a thin layer of fat. Tie securely.

In a mortar with a pestle or with a spice grinder, crush all seeds with salt and peppercorns. Do not pulverize them. Rub meat with oil. Rub seed mixture thoroughly over meat. Refrigerate meat for 12 hours or overnight.

Preheat oven to 450°F. Place meat on a rack in a large roasting pan and roast for 15 minutes. Reduce heat to 325° F and continue to cook about 16 minutes per pound for medium-rare, or until a thermometer registers 130°F. Do not overcook meat or it will be chewy.

Remove roast from pan and cover with aluminum foil to keep warm. Remove any fat from the pan. Add wine, stock, and mustard to pan and bring to a boil, scraping brown bits into liquid. Reduce slightly and then strain sauce, pressing down hard on solids to extract more flavor. Slice roast into chops and serve with pan juices.

Serve with Carrot–Sweet Potato Purée. Any leftover roast may be refrigerated or frozen for use in Buffalo Chili (page 89).

CARROT–SWEET POTATO PURÉE

SERVES 8 TO 10

3 large sweet potatoes or yams (about 2 pounds)
1 pound carrots, peeled and quartered lengthwise
2 cups water
Salt to taste
1 tablespoon honey
1 tablespoon chopped fresh ginger
3 tablespoons unsalted butter, at room temperature
½ cup crème fraîche or sour cream
⅛ teaspoon freshly grated nutmeg
½ teaspoon finely minced orange zest
Cayenne pepper to taste

Preheat oven to 375°F. Cut a shallow cross in top of each potato. Place potatoes in middle of preheated oven and bake until tender when pierced with a fork, about 1 hour. Reduce oven temperature to 350°F.

Cut carrots into 1-inch lengths. Place in a saucepan with water, salt, honey, ginger, and butter. Bring to a boil over medium heat and cook, uncovered, until tender, about 30 minutes. Add additional water, if necessary. Drain.

Remove and discard peel from potatoes and place pulp in a food processor. Add carrots, remaining 6 tablespoons butter, and crème fraîche and process until smooth. Add nutmeg and orange zest and blend well. Season with salt and cayenne.

Transfer mixture to an ovenproof casserole dish, cover, and bake in preheated oven until thoroughly heated, 20 to 25 minutes.

GRILLED BUFFALO STEAKS WITH CHILI-CORN SAUCE

SERVES 4 TO 6

This colorful, flavorful sauce is adapted from a recipe by Larry Forgione, whose An American Place in New York City continues to help define the state of cooking in this country. The sauce can be spiced up by a more assertive use of cayenne and chili powder, if desired, but it is nicely balanced and quite complex in its present form. It also works very well with venison medallions or boar chops.

Recommended Wine: An asser-tive, young Zinfandel or Petite Sirah helps balance the tasty corn-chili sauce effectively and brings out its smoky, spicy character.

SAUCE

2 ears of corn, husked, or ¾ cup frozen corn kernels
1 tablespoon vegetable oil
½ medium yellow onion, chopped
½ red bell pepper, seeded, deveined, and finely diced
½ green bell pepper, finely diced
½ jalapeño pepper, seeded and minced
½ clove garlic, minced
1½ tablespoons chili powder
½ teaspoon cumin seed, toasted and crushed
Cayenne and freshly ground black pepper to taste
⅓ cup dry white wine
2 cups beef stock or Basic Game Meat Stock (page 40)
¾ cup heavy cream, or less, if desired
Salt to taste

6 buffalo steaks (10 to 12 ounces each)
1 tablespoon olive oil
Salt and freshly ground black pepper to taste

Using a serrated knife, remove kernels of corn from cobs; reserve both kernels and cobs for sauce. Set aside.

In a heavy, 2-quart saucepan, heat oil over low heat, add onion, peppers, and garlic, and cook, covered, for 2 to 3 minutes. Add chili powder, cumin, and cayenne and black peppers, and stir over low heat for 3 minutes. Add wine and stir until smooth. Add stock and reserved corn cobs and bring to a boil. Reduce heat, and cook, uncovered, stirring occasionally, until volume is reduced by half, approximately 20 minutes. The sauce should have a syrupy consistency.

Add cream and simmer over low heat for 7 to 10 minutes. Remove and discard cobs. Add corn kernels and simmer for 3 minutes. Taste and adjust seasoning with salt; keep warm.

Prepare a fire in a charcoal grill. Coat buffalo steaks with oil and season to taste with salt and pepper. Grill over hot coals until rare to medium-rare, 2 to 3 minutes per side. Do not overcook meat or it will be chewy.

To serve, spoon sauces onto individual serving plates and top with steaks.

BUFFALO STEAKS WITH JACK DANIELS SAUCE

SERVES 6

Recommended Wine: The power and intensity of the sauce demand a hearty Petite Sirah or Zinfandel.

Jack Daniels, the South's time-honored sour mash whiskey, is more than a good drink. It's a useful flavoring agent for the sauce for this unusual buffalo preparation. The same sauce can be used with venison with equal success.

6 boneless buffalo rib steaks (10 ounces each)
Salt and freshly ground white pepper to taste

SAUCE
¼ cup minced shallots or green onion
½ cup sliced fresh mushrooms
4 tablespoons unsalted butter, at room temperature
2 cups beef stock or Basic Game Meat Stock (page 40)
¾ cup dry white wine
2 tablespoons green peppercorns, lightly crushed
½ cup plus 5 tablespoons Jack Daniels or other high-quality bourbon
½ cup heavy cream (optional)
Salt and freshly ground white pepper
Drops of fresh lemon juice

2 tablespoons butter or olive oil

Season buffalo steaks with salt and pepper to taste and let them rest for 1 hour at room temperature.

To make sauce, in a saucepan, sauté shallots and mushrooms in 2 tablespoons butter until golden brown. Add stock, wine, ½ cup bourbon, 1 tablespoon of the peppercorns; reduce over medium heat by half. Add cream and reduce to a light sauce consistency. Whisk in remaining 2 tablespoons butter little by little. Add remaining 1 tablespoon peppercorns, 5 tablespoons bourbon, and lemon juice to taste; keep warm.

Sauté buffalo steaks in butter until medium-rare, 2 to 3 minutes per side. Do not overcook steaks or they will be chewy.

Arrange one steak on each plate and top with sauce.

DUCK

Nothing is quite as savorous, as utterly satisfying, as perfectly cooked duck, oozing with flavorful juices and complemented by a finely honed sauce or condiment that doesn't overwhelm the duck's natural flavors.

In America, most of the domestic ducks eaten at the table can trace their origins to China, where duck has always been an important food. By the second century B.C., duck, along with pig, goat, and hen, was China's primary food animal. Duck remains an essential part of the Chinese diet. In Beijing the famous Pien Yi Fang restaurant offers more than one hundred duck dishes on its menu, including one with thirty duck tongues in each serving.

Duck also played a prominent role with the ancient Egyptians and the Romans, who kept wild birds in net enclosures until they were ready to feast on them. It is reputed that the Romans ate only the breast meat and the brains of these wild ducks.

Nowhere was duck more prominent, however, than in early America. In 1608 famed explorer Captain John Smith reported that great numbers of wild ducks abounded. Wild ducks played a prominent role in the "swamp floor cuisine" of the Acadian settlers in Louisiana in the eighteenth century. Their principal settlement, St. Jacques de Caboncey on the Mississippi River, in fact was named after the Indian word *caboncey*, meaning "clearing where mallard ducks roost." The local Indians—the Houmas, Choctaw, and Chetimaches—instructed these first Acadian settlers in new ways of preparing duck and other game birds, although the Acadians had a long history of cooking duck in their northern outpost in Canada.

Likewise, the Creoles in New Orleans concocted a vast array of wild game dishes from the bounty brought to them by Cajun fur trappers and hunters and the local Indians. Mallard and canvasback ducks were turned into a Cajun stew called salmi, in which the duck was braised slowly in wine for hours. Duck and andouille sausage gumbo was another dish that evolved out of the early Creole and Cajun kitchens of Louisiana.

French gastronome Brillat-Savarin chastised the preparation of certain sauces for duck as "monstrous, degrading and dishonorable," but he also expressed some fondness for the bird, writing that it was "slightly exciting" and that it provoked dreaming.

In the wild, the gamy mallard and the lesser-known but highly regarded teal, pintail, gadwall (cherished in England), canvasback (a particularly delectable variety), nantais (a 2- to 3-pound duck fancied by the French that is a cross between a domestic duck and a wild drake), shoveler, coot, scoter (which lives principally on fish and thus offers a very different taste), widgeon (a grass eater known as whistler in America), ringneck, and black duck are all prized by hunters and offer sublime tastes to the knowing gourmet. The preceding list is an abbreviated notation, as there are known to be close to one hundred varieties of duck. The meat of these wild birds is dark and rich compared to that of domestic ducks.

Most commercial ducks now come from farms in Northern California or the Midwest states, especially Indiana. As with most other birds, the farm-raised duck has considerably more fat than its wild counterpart, which is virtually devoid of fat. This is due not only to the age and physical activity of the wild bird, but to its diet, which often consists of fish rather than the corn and grain diet of most farm-raised ducks.

The old adage "You are what you eat" is valid not only for ducks but basically for all farm-raised game discussed in this book. To wild game purists this might be a simple drawback, but we think that the subtler flavors, the predictability of tenderness and cooking times, and certainly the availability which comes from farm-raised game are the key reasons for its growth in popularity.

Farm-raised ducks are thought to have their genesis in America in 1873, when a clipper ship from China transported three dozen Pekin ducks into the San Francisco Bay on its way to New York. A dozen of the ducks were sidetracked to Northern California, where they became the basis for contemporary duck farms. The other two dozen became the foundation for the well-known, but often poorly-cooked Long Island duck. Urbanization has supplanted the duck farming industry on Long Island, so this term is relatively meaningless on menus today.

Shopping for Duck

Frozen duck is perfectly acceptable, but—as with most products—fresh is preferred. In the case of duck, availability of birds is happening with much greater frequency, particularly in large metropolitan areas and in areas where there is a large indigenous Chinese population. Many of these same areas also offer a Chinese roasted duck which is sold ready to serve. Check for a crisp, mahogany-colored skin that will ensure a relatively fat-free duck. In Chinese homes, a whole roast duck is considered a delicacy, and is often presented with traditional plum or hoisin sauce and slivered scallions.

On the farm today, the overwhelming choice is the Chinese white Pekin, distantly followed by the less fatty, but more flavorful musky Muscovy (a South American jungle bird by origin), and the moulard or mullard, the sterile offspring of Muscovy and Pekin that is particularly prized in the south of France. Muscovy ducks are also raised in the south of France where they are bred with Rouen or Nantes ducks, and are known by the name barbary (sometimes spelled barbarie). Paula Wolfert observes in her cookbook on the southwest of France that "ducks are to the South-West what steaks are to Texas."

The relatively lean barbary variety is also being farmed in the United States, particularly at Maple Leaf Farms in Indiana. The plump breasts of these birds are very flavorful, and are often smoked for additional flavor. Some mallard and other wild varieties are also being raised, but this is usually for later release in the wild.

Moulards are selectively bred for their supple breasts, reddish flesh, and the production of *foie gras,* the enlarged liver that results from forced feeding of corn. In California's Sonoma County, both the moulard and the Muscovy are being bred for the production of *foie gras* by a company called Sonoma County Foie Gras.

Domestic *foie gras* production was started in upstate New York, where the industry is still flourishing. *Foie gras* itself has been considered a delicacy throughout the ages; its recorded history can actually be traced to pictographs on the walls of Egyptian tombs, and it was plentifully consumed during Roman feasts.

Foie gras is graded by the size, color, and firmness of the liver. Grade A is the largest, best-colored, and firmest liver and is the most desirable. Grades B and C are still entirely wholesome and acceptable for cooking.

Breeding programs are producing ducks with larger breasts and less fat. If you are buying fresh duck, look at the fat around the breast and buy those that appear leanest. Plump, meaty breasts are highly desirable; the cavity should look and smell fresh. Yield is best from ducks that weigh at least 4 pounds, although many mallards weigh only 2 to 3 pounds. The moulard and the Muscovy are among the larger varieties of duck, weighing approximately 6 to 8 pounds. Unlike chicken, a 4- to 5-pound Pekin duck serves only 2 people, because there is a relatively high proportion of fat.

As ducks get older, they increase in toughness. Therefore, younger ducks—particularly if they are wild ducks—are desirable. Since most farm-raised ducks are killed at 45 to 52 days old, pick the largest you can find. If you're buying from a butcher, be sure you're getting birds that are not more than 8 weeks old. These will invariably be fully plucked and cleaned. If frozen, the duck will need to be defrosted in the refrigerator before cooking. Older ducks, which are usually used for breeding and egg production, may range in age up to 1½ years. They are very tough and good only for stewing or for use in pâtés and terrines.

A word about price: Duck is still considered an exotic meat in many parts of the country and is often sold at exotic prices. In one Northern California market, fresh ducks sold for $1.40 per pound at wholesale, but at retail some markets were charging as much as $6.00. Needless to say, this causes duck producers much concern and limits the potential enjoyment of this marvelous bird.

Cooking Tips

The differences between the cooking procedures required for wild and farm-raised ducks couldn't be more dramatic. If roasting whole Muscovy or mallard ducks, barding of the breast may be necessary to prevent them from drying out, since they have very little fat. Some cooks of wild duck rub the skin with ginger or lemon, then fill the cavity with sliced onion, chopped celery, and fruit (sliced apple, orange, or lemon), and slow roast in a moderately hot oven, basting frequently with a cooking liquid. Some other duck fanciers, however, prefer to cook at a high temperature (approximately 500°F) for a shorter time. The danger in cooking duck at a high temperature is in overcooking it.

Either method can be effective as long as the meat is not overcooked. To test for doneness, cut a tiny slit in the breast meat. The juices should run clear yellow for farm-raised birds; wild ducks will release a reddish pink juice and should never be overcooked, or they will be profoundly dry.

An average rule of thumb for a 4½-pound domestic duck is 1 hour and 15 to 20 minutes in a 350°F oven for medium-rare, and an additional 25 to 30 minutes for well-done. Domestic ducks can be roasted, grilled, or sautéed with equal success and with little concern for basting.

Many knowledgable chefs prefer to cook duck pieces separately because the cooking times for the breast and leg-thigh pieces differ significantly due to their varying muscle tissue. The leg-thigh pieces take well to slow braising in liquid to reduce their inherent toughness; the prized breast is best suited to faster cooking methods, such as sautéing and grilling, and it should be cooked rare to medium-rare. In France the *magret*, or "breast," is peppered, cooked, and sliced on the bias to preserve tenderness. It is served simply, with a pile of freshly cooked fries. Despite the fatty layer, breast meat is very lean and cooks quickly.

When removing the legs from the duck, make sure to leave enough skin around them to cover the meat. Bend the leg away from the carcass enough so that you can make a complete cut through the ball and socket (see technique on page 19). The neck, wings, gizzard, and carcass should always be saved and reserved for making stock. In France the extremely tiny duck heart is usually reserved for the cook.

Always reserve the duck fat. It can be used in the cooking of many foods (particularly *confit*), if desired, and is especially favored by the French. Slowly roasted duck renders a great deal of fat, which Brillat-Savarin described as "sublime in roasting potatoes." Dietary considerations aside (half the fat of duck is in the skin itself), duck fat is a very flavorful alternative to other fats for cooking.

Classic Dishes

Chinese students of cuisine are required to take a one-year course devoted entirely to the art of preparing Peking roast duck. Most Chinese cooks, however, purchase their ducks from a roasting house rather than going through the process themselves. In the classic training, the first three months are concerned only with the fattening, slaughter, and cleaning of the bird. The ducks are killed but left intact. They are plucked, singed, and drawn. Then, the entire bird is inflated by forcing air into it. This process used to be done by the cook himself blowing into a small hole in the neck, but now a more hygienic method incorporates a mechanical pump.

The duck is then dipped in boiling water, and the skin is brushed with a syrup of malt sugar. It is hung by the neck for a few hours in a cool, dry place until the skin is dry and hard. In olden days in China, one could see ducks hanging on breezy porches. Finally, the duck is suspended in an open-mouth wood-burning oven and roasted until it is crisp and mahogany colored. Temperature is all important: If too low, the skin will not be crisp and succulent. If too high the skin will stretch and be too thin. A setting of 400°F for an hour is generally perfect for a 3- to 4-pound duck.

The skin is highly prized. It is carved into small squares and rolled up inside a thin wheat pancake with hoisin sauce and spring onions. Traditionally, this mixture was sweet soy and rice. In China, the flesh of the duck is carved and served as a less appealing side dish or saved for leftovers; in America the meat itself is often used inside the pancake. A simplified Peking duck recipe appears on page 101.

European pressed duck is another classic of the genre. The most famous source for this complicated and time-consuming dish is the Tour d'Argent restaurant in Paris, but numerous variations have evolved over the years. The common themes are to salt and pepper the cavity and skin of the duck, usually a prized Rouen, and cook it in a moderate oven for 10 to 12 minutes. The skin is then removed from the breasts, and the breast meat is sliced and reserved. The remains of the carcass are placed in a press where the juices are extracted. The intensity of the juices is largely due to the fact that Rouen ducks are strangled at death, allowing the blood to remain in the body.

A sauce is then made of currant jelly, Worcestershire and hot sauces, and the duck essence from the press. A separate sauce is made by sautéing the duck liver with shallots, carrots, herbs, and dry sherry. The two sauces are blended at the end and served on top of the breasts—a classic, formal presentation that may not quite have the appeal that it once did.

The 1973 edition of the venerable *Joy of Cooking* relates the difficult process of making a classic salmi as follows: "Obviously, a classic salmi, fully accoutered, is only for the skilled cook whose husband is a Nimrod and has presented her with more than a single bird. If she is less well endowed, she will have to base her sauce on the backs, wings and necks of the bird that is being presented. . . . Needless to say, the dish is rarely presented in its original form. And the salmis that appear on menus are usually made from reheated meat, with sauces which have been previously confected."

Duck à l'orange is probably the world's most famous and most abused duck dish. There have been more variations on this traditional European warhorse than one cares to even think about, most prepared in America with Long Island ducks and sickly sweet, goopy sauces that do little justice to the meat. Although thought of as a traditional French dish, the true heritage of duck à l'orange seems to be Florentine.

Why this elegant dish has evolved into such a gloppy mess in the United States is difficult to understand, except that it was one of the first attempts at translating a classic European game dish and was probably not well understood by many of the cooks who've attempted it. Achieving the right consistency and balance of sweetness and natural acidity is clearly the key, as is evidenced by the recipe that follows.

Classic Recipe

DUCK WITH ORANGE

SERVES 4

This is a version of the classic duck à l'orange. It really is quite a simple dish to make and is an old standby on traditional French menus. Although often abused, when made correctly and freshly, it's a stunning dish that is well worth adding to your repertoire.

1 large duck (4 to 5 pounds)
Salt and freshly ground black pepper to taste
2 medium oranges
2 medium lemons
Boiling water, as needed
¼ cup sugar
⅓ cup white wine vinegar
3 cups chicken stock or Basic Game Bird Stock (page 40)

Recommended Wine: A well-balanced Chardonnay or Johannisberg Riesling with good acidity will underscore the citric flavors in the sauce.

⅓ cup Grand Marnier or other orange-flavored brandy
2 teaspoons cornstarch
1 tablespoon red currant jelly or apricot jelly (optional)
½ cup dry white wine
Freshly ground white pepper to taste

Preheat oven to 350°F. Season duck inside cavity with salt and black pepper to taste. Place breast side up on a rack in a roasting pan and prick thighs and breast with a fork to allow fat to escape. Roast in preheated oven until juices run clear when the thigh is pricked, about 1½ hours or until thermometer registers 155° to 160°F.

While duck is cooking, remove zest from the oranges and lemons and cut into fine julienne. Squeeze juice from the oranges and lemons and set aside. Blanch zest in boiling water to cover for 3 minutes; drain and set aside.

In a heavy-bottomed saucepan over moderate heat, melt sugar and cook until it begins to brown lightly. Add vinegar, orange and lemon juices, and stock and reduce over medium heat to a light sauce consistency.

In a small bowl, mix together Grand Marnier and cornstarch and stir into stock mixture. Simmer briefly until slightly thickened. Stir in jelly, if used, and keep sauce warm.

When duck is cooked, remove from pan and cover with aluminum foil to keep warm. Scoop off fat from pan juices. Quickly deglaze roasting pan with wine, scraping up the brown bits. Strain into sauce. Add reserved zest and simmer until slightly thickened. Carve duck, place on a warm serving platter, and pour sauce over pieces.

A SIMPLIFIED PEKING DUCK WITH CHINESE PANCAKES

SERVES 2 TO 4

Nothing, of course, can beat the authentic recipe for Peking duck, in which the bird is inflated to pull the skin away from the meat, resulting in a heavenly crisp skin. We can still remember the bemused faces at our local gas station when we took our ducks there to inflate them with the pressurized air hose. Somehow we could never quite convince the gas station attendants of the need to do that step! This recipe is a good approximation and a whole lot easier to accomplish. It also works well with other birds; adjust cooking time accordingly.

These pancakes are adapted from Ken Hom's wonderful book *Fragrant Harbor Taste*. If in a big rush, it wouldn't be a cardinal

Recommended Wine: Although it may seem a little odd, we like a dry sparkling wine with this dish, especially those from California. A slightly sweet Gewürztraminer also works well.

sin to use flour tortillas, ready-made pancakes, or crêpes instead, but the results are not quite the same. Any exotic ingredients required to cook the duck can be found in Asian markets.

1 large duck (4 to 5 pounds)
1 teaspoon freshly ground white pepper
1½ tablespoons ground cinnamon
1½ tablespoons ground ginger
¾ cup firmly packed brown sugar
¾ cup red wine vinegar
1 teaspoon sesame oil
2 teaspoons peanut oil
½ teaspoon ground star anise
Hoisin and slivered green onions for serving

PANCAKES

2 cups all-purpose flour
1 cup boiling water
2 tablespoons minced green onion
2 tablespoons sesame oil

Fill a pot, large enough to hold duck, with water and bring to a boil. Remove from heat, plunge duck in water, and let stand for 5 minutes. Remove duck and pat dry.

Combine pepper, cinnamon, ginger, sugar, vinegar, sesame oil, peanut oil, and star anise in a small saucepan and bring just to a boil. Remove from heat and let mixture cool to room temperature. Liberally coat the duck with the mixture and let stand at room temperature until coating dries completely, about 3 hours.

To make pancakes, in a large mixing bowl, combine flour and water, stirring constantly until all water is absorbed. Add more water if mixture seems dry; dough should just hold together in large lumps.

Add green onion. Gather up dough and knead on a lightly floured board until smooth, about 5 minutes. Wrap in plastic and allow to rest at room temperature for 30 minutes.

Unwrap and knead again on a lightly floured board for 5 minutes. Form into a log about 18 inches long and 1 inch in diameter. Cut roll into 20 equal pieces and roll each piece into a ball. Dip one side of the ball in the sesame oil and place oiled side on top of oiled side of another ball. On a lightly floured board, roll out each pair of balls into a circle about 6 inches in diameter (rolling the balls together helps keep them moist inside).

Heat a dry sauté pan over low heat. Put rolled-out circle into pan and cook until dry on one side, about 1 to 2 minutes. Flip and cook until dry on second side, about 1 to 2 minutes. Remove pancakes, peel them apart, and set aside. Cover with plastic wrap until ready to use.

Preheat oven to 350°F. Place duck breast side up on a rack in a roasting pan. Roast until skin is crisp and brown, about 1½ hours. Check occasionally and adjust temperature so that the coating does not burn.

To serve, let duck cool to room temperature. Steam pancakes briefly to reheat or wrap in plastic wrap and heat in microwave. Carefully carve flesh from the bone, being sure to include the crisp skin. Roll up in pancakes with a dab of hoisin sauce and slivered green onions.

SMOKED DUCK BREASTS WITH PERSIMMON, KIWIFRUIT, AND TROPICAL FRUIT SAUCE

SERVES 2

Recommended Wine: The spicy, floral characteristics of Gewürztraminer go beautifully with the fruit flavors in this dish. A hint of sweetness in the wine will harmonize particularly well with this sauce.

The combination of smoked meats and fruits is a time-honored tradition in many cuisines, particularly tropical ones. While not precisely tropical, the tart-sweet quality of the different fruits used in this dish balances the smoky duck breasts and makes for a tantalizing contrast of flavors.

2 smoked half duck breasts (4 to 5 ounces each), prepared with Basic Wet Brine for Game Birds (page 34) or Basic Dry Brine for Game (page 35)

SAUCE

1 tablespoon chopped shallots
⅓ cup Gewürztraminer or other fruity white wine
1 cup unsweetened pineapple juice
1 fresh serrano chili pepper, seeded and diced
1 tablespoon passion fruit syrup or thawed, frozen pineapple or orange juice concentrate
1 persimmon, peeled, seeded, and chopped
2 kiwifruits, peeled and chopped
2 tablespoons heavy cream or half-and-half (optional)

Preheat oven to 300°F. Wrap smoked duck breasts in foil and warm slowly in preheated oven for 15 to 20 minutes. Be careful not to dry them out.

Meanwhile, make sauce. Combine shallots and wine in a small saucepan and place over medium heat until reduced by three-fourths to a near-syrup consistency. Add pineapple juice and chilies and reduce by half. Add passion fruit syrup or concentrate, persimmon, and kiwifruits and simmer to reduce to a light sauce consistency, about 3 to 5 minutes. Stir in cream, if used.

Place warmed breasts on plate and top with sauce.

ROAST LACQUERED DUCK WITH MUSCAT-TAMARIND SAUCE

SERVES 2

Recommended Wine: The slightly sweet-tart flavors of this dish will contrast nicely with a spicy Gewürztraminer or fruity Johannisberg Riesling with a hint of sweetness, or they can be further amplified by a ripe Zinfandel.

This Far East–influenced dish combines the intense flavors of tart tamarind with ginger, licorice-flavored star anise, and Black Muscat wine for the decidedly nontraditional sauce. The duck should have a crispy skin, which is accomplished through air drying. In France, this is called lacquering. Thanks must be given to Ken Hom, the noted Chinese scholar and cooking teacher, for the inspiration for the lacquering process and the salt-and-pepper combination.

BASTING LIQUID

4 cups water
2 tablespoons honey
3 tablespoons soy sauce

1 large duck (4 to 5 pounds), with neck

DRY MARINADE

2 tablespoons Sichuan peppercorns (see Note)
1 tablespoon kosher salt
2 star anise, crushed (see Note)
2 tablespoons chopped green onion

SAUCE

¾ tablespoon chopped shallots
½ cup Black Muscat wine or port
½ teaspoon crushed star anise
1 teaspoon chopped fresh ginger, or ¼ teaspoon ground ginger
1 cup chicken stock or Basic Game Bird Stock (page 40)
½ teaspoon tamarind concentrate (see Note)
1½ tablespoons butter (optional)
Salt and freshly ground white pepper to taste

Fresh cilantro sprigs and thinly sliced green onion spears for garnish

In a large pot, combine all ingredients for basting liquid and bring to a boil. Place duck in boiling mixture for 1 minute. Remove duck and pat dry with paper towels. Reserve basting liquid.

Hang duck by neck in a cool, dry, drafty place for 6 to 8 hours or overnight, or near an electric fan for 2 to 3 hours. This will dry the skin of the duck and make it slightly brittle.

To make marinade, combine peppercorns and salt in a dry skillet over low heat and heat until lightly toasted, 3 to 5 minutes. Crush peppercorns, then combine with star anise and green on-ions. Rub mixture in cavity of duck.

Preheat oven to 400°F. Place duck on rack in roasting pan and pour reserved basting liquid into pan. Roast in preheated oven, basting frequently to glaze the skin, until skin is crispy and brown, 1 to 1¼ hours.

To make sauce, combine shallots, wine, star anise, and ginger in a small saucepan and reduce over high heat by half. Add stock and tamarind concentrate and reduce by half again. Swirl in butter, if desired. Season with salt and pepper.

Separate leg-thigh pieces and breasts from duck. Slice meat thinly off the breast, including some skin with each slice, and arrange on a serving platter. Top with sauce. The leg-thigh pieces can be served next to sliced breast meat. Garnish dish with cilantro and green onions.

NOTE: These ingredients can be found in Asian markets.

GRILLED DUCK BREAST WITH RASPBERRY–SWEET ONION RELISH

SERVES 4

The inspiration for this dish comes from Patrick O'Connell, whose Inn at Little Washington in Virginia is famous for its regional specialties. The relish is a perfect counterpoint to the smoky grilled duck and is a fresh, healthful preparation devoid of cream and butter.

RELISH

2 cups chopped raspberries
¾ cup chopped Vidalia or other sweet onion
4 teaspoons raspberry vinegar
2 teaspoons fresh lemon juice
1 tablespoon chopped fresh sage, or ½ tablespoon dried sage
½ teaspoon crushed red-pepper flakes
3 tablespoons crème de cassis, or more to taste

Recommended Wine: A fruity, raspberry-tinged Zinfandel makes the perfect partner to this dish with its strong emphasis on raspberry flavors from start to finish.

MARINADE

¼ cup olive oil
½ teaspoon freshly ground black pepper
½ teaspoon salt
1 clove garlic, minced
1 teaspoon chopped fresh sage, or ½ teaspoon ground sage

4 half duck breasts (4 to 5 ounces each), boned and skinned
8 raspberries and fresh mint sprigs for garnish

In a nonreactive bowl, combine all ingredients for relish and mix thoroughly. In a separate nonreactive bowl, mix all ingredients for marinade together; add ⅓ cup of the relish and stir well. Place duck in marinade for 2 to 4 hours, refrigerated, turning occasionally. Refrigerate remaining relish.

Prepare a fire in a charcoal grill, preferably with mesquite. Grill duck breasts, skin side down, over hot coals for 5 to 7 minutes. Turn and continue grilling until done, 3 to 4 minutes. Duck should be medium-rare. To serve, slice duck breasts on bias and arrange on individual serving plates. Garnish each serving with 2 raspberries and a mint sprig. Dollop relish over the duck.

DUCK SAUSAGE

MAKES 20 6-INCH LINKS

Recommended Wine: We like a dry to medium-sweet Gewürztraminer or Johannisberg Riesling if the sausage is served on its own. When incorporated into pastas or pizza, a hearty, forwardly fruity Zinfandel works beautifully.

Duck sausage is an absolutely wonderful addition to many dishes. It can be used in salads, soups, pastas, and pizzas, but it's also quite delicious on its own. We like this Cajun-inspired recipe of John Folse's sliced into pieces and served as an appetizer with spicy Creole mustard. Folse, owner of Lafitte's Landing in Louisiana, makes his version with mallard duck, but virtually any kind of farm-raised duck can be used as long as the amount of fat used is decreased slightly. The recipe can also be adapted to other meats, such as rabbit, venison, buffalo, or even alligator.

1 wild mallard duck (about 2½ pounds), boned
2½ pounds boneless pork shoulder or butt
½ pound pork fat
½ pound bacon
¼ pound butter
2 cups diced yellow onion
1 cup diced celery
½ cup chopped green onion
2 tablespoons chopped garlic
½ cup port

¼ cup Cognac
1 tablespoon dried thyme leaves
1 tablespoon cracked black pepper
½ cup chopped fresh parsley
Salt and cayenne pepper to taste
6 feet sausage casing
Vegetable oil for sautéing

Using the fine cutting blade of a meat grinder or food processor, grind duck, pork, pork fat, and bacon. Once ground, place in a mixing bowl and remove any visible sinew or bone that may have passed through the blade. Set aside.

In a heavy-bottomed sauté pan, melt butter over medium-high heat. Add onion, celery, green onion, and garlic and sauté until wilted, 3 to 4 minutes. Remove from flame and add port and Cognac. Return to stove top and carefully ignite with a long match. Let burn for about 2 minutes, then continue to cook until liquid is reduced by half. Add thyme and pepper and blend well. Remove from heat and cool to room temperature.

Add sautéed vegetables to ground meat and mix thoroughly. Add parsley and season with salt and cayenne. (To check for proper seasoning, form a small patty and sauté in hot oil for a few minutes. Taste and adjust if necessary.) Stuff mixture into casings, using the sausage attachment on your grinder.

In a sauté pan, add water to a depth of ¼ inch. Heat until water simmers, add sausages, and cook until water evaporates, 5 to 7 minutes, on all sides. Add a few drops of oil and sauté over moderate heat until golden brown on all sides.

HONEY- AND CHILI-GLAZED GRILLED DUCK BREASTS WITH SPANISH SHERRY WINE–CHILI SAUCE
Served with Fried Plantains

SERVES 4

Recommended Wine: The smoky, tart, slightly hot flavors in the sauce call out for a hearty, ripe Zinfandel or Petite Sirah for balance.

This intriguing dish takes some time to prepare, but is well worth the effort. It has a sun-drenched, Mediterranean, south-of-the-border spirit and is the creation of Norman Van Aken, the enormously talented south Florida chef whose a Mano in Miami Beach epitomizes his vibrant approach.

GLAZE

2 tablespoons olive oil
6 cloves garlic, slivered
1 poblano chili pepper, seeded, deveined, and julienned
1 ancho chili pepper, toasted in a dry skillet, soaked in water to cover, drained, and roughly chopped
3 tablespoons Spanish sherry wine vinegar
½ cup honey
Salt and freshly ground black pepper to taste

SAUCE

6 ounces bacon, diced
3 tablespoons olive oil
3 tablespoons butter
1½ cups carrot, peeled and diced (about 4 carrots)
1½ cups yellow onion, diced (about 1 medium onion)
1 cup diced leeks, white part only
½ cup diced celery
1 head garlic, cut in half crosswise with skin intact
1 cup Spanish sherry wine vinegar
1 cup Spanish sherry wine
2 quarts chicken stock or Basic Game Bird Stock (page 40)
12 black peppercorns
¼ cup cumin seed, toasted
2 dried ancho chili peppers, toasted in a dry skillet and seeded
2 dried chipotle chili peppers, toasted in a dry skillet and seeded, or 1 tablespoon canned chipotle chili peppers in adobo, drained
1 bay leaf, crushed

4 half duck breasts (preferably moulard or Muscovy)
Pinch salt, freshly ground black pepper, and freshly ground cumin seed
Fried Plantains (recipe follows)
Fresh cilantro leaves for garnish

To make glaze, heat oil in a small saucepan. Add garlic and poblano and ancho chilies and sauté for 2 to 3 minutes. Add vinegar and reduce over medium heat by half. Add honey and remove from heat. Let steep for 20 minutes and then strain. Season with salt and pepper. (It may be necessary to reheat the mixture slightly in order for it to pass through the strainer effectively.)

To make sauce, place a heavy-bottomed saucepan over medium-high heat and cook bacon in oil and 2 tablespoons of the butter until browned. Add carrot, onion, leeks, celery, and garlic and continue to sauté until lightly browned. Add vinegar and wine and reduce over medium heat by half. Add stock, peppercorns, cumin seed, chilies, and bay leaf and reduce to a light sauce consistency, about 45 minutes. Strain sauce, pressing down hard on the vegetables to extract all juices.

To finish sauce, reheat in a saucepan and whisk in remaining 1 tablespoon butter. Keep warm.

Prepare a fire in a charcoal grill. Score duck breast skin with 3 or 4 incisions. Season duck with salt, pepper, and cumin. Place breasts on grill, skin side down, and cook for 5 to 7 minutes. Brush with glaze, turn, and cook until done, 2 to 3 minutes.

Slice duck breasts on the bias. Spoon some sauce onto individual serving plates. Arrange duck slices on top of sauce. Place plantains opposite the duck. Garnish with cilantro.

FRIED PLANTAINS

SERVES 4

½ cup all-purpose flour
¼ teaspoon salt
¼ teaspoon freshly ground black pepper
¼ teaspoon ground cinnamon
1 very ripe plantain, red banana, or regular banana, peeled and sliced crosswise on a sharp bias
1 tablespoon butter
2 tablespoons peanut oil

In a shallow bowl, combine flour, salt, pepper, and cinnamon. Dredge plantain slices in seasoned flour and shake off excess. In a skillet, heat butter and oil. Fry plantain slices for 1 to 2 minutes. Remove to paper towels to drain. Keep warm until serving.

BRAISED DUCK IN RED CHILE SAUCE

SERVES 4

Recommended Wine: Spicy, chili-based sauces often play havoc with wine. We find this dish works quite nicely with a chilled Gamay Beaujolais or lighter-style Zinfandel. The fruitiness and liveliness of these wines offer a refreshing quality much in the same way that beer does with spicy food.

Chef Robert Del Grande of Houston's Cafe Annie created this dish for chicken, and we've adapted it for duck. While it works beautifully for breasts and leg-thigh pieces, it's also a great way to utilize only the leg-thigh pieces when you've collected enough of them. This dish captures the essence and complexity of Southwest cooking. It should be served over rice.

1 tablespoon olive oil
1½ teaspoons kosher salt
½ teaspoon freshly ground black pepper
1 large duck (4 to 5 pounds), cut into breast and leg-thigh pieces, or 8 leg-thigh pieces
6 cups water
4 plum tomatoes, quartered
½ yellow onion, roughly chopped
4 cloves garlic, minced
6 dried pasilla chili peppers, seeded
4 dried ancho chili peppers, seeded
½ teaspoon cumin seeds, lightly toasted in dry skillet and crushed

GARNISHES
¼ cup crème fraîche or sour cream
1 ripe avocado, peeled, pitted, and cubed
½ yellow onion, finely chopped
4 red radishes, thinly sliced
Fresh cilantro sprigs
Lime wedges

In a large saucepan, heat oil until very hot. Salt and pepper duck pieces and sauté, skin side down, until the fat has rendered and duck is browned. Turn and brown on second side. Pour off excess fat. Add water and bring to a boil. Reduce heat and simmer, covered, for 15 to 20 minutes. Remove duck from liquid and reserve.

Add tomatoes, onion, garlic, chilies, and cumin seeds to the liquid. Bring to a boil, then simmer, covered, for 30 minutes. Transfer to a blender or food processor and purée until smooth. Return duck and purée to pan and simmer, covered, for 30 minutes. If sauce is too thick, add additional water. Taste and adjust seasoning with salt and pepper.

Arrange duck pieces on individual serving plates and spoon sauce over top. Drizzle crème fraîche over duck. Garnish with avocado, onion, radishes, cilantro, and lime wedges.

SAUTÉED DUCK BREASTS WITH RHUBARB SAUCE AND CRACKLINGS

SERVES 6

Recommended Wine: The tart-sweet quality of the rhubarb sauce is nicely balanced by a lively Zinfandel.

Anne Rosenzweig of Arcadia in New York City does wonderful things with all kinds of game. This is a perfect spring dish featuring two of the pure pleasures of the season, rhubarb and asparagus, along with duck fillets. The cracklings are an added bonus provided by the rendering of duck fat.

6 boneless duck breast halves
½ cup water
Kosher salt
4 stalks young rhubarb, cut into ½-inch pieces
1 cup port
½ cup raspberry vinegar
¾ cup chicken stock or Basic Game Bird Stock (page 40)
6 cups loosely packed arugula or spinach leaves
1 pound medium asparagus, trimmed, steamed, and cooled

VINAIGRETTE

Juice and finely grated zest of 1 orange
2 tablespoons chopped fresh parsley
2 tablespoons chopped fresh chervil or oregano
Salt and freshly ground black pepper to taste
½ cup light olive oil or soy oil

Remove skin and fat from duck breasts and cut skin and fat into ¼-inch dice. Reserve 2 tablespoons of fat. To make cracklings, combine skin and remaining fat in a saucepan with water and place over medium heat to render fat. When cracklings are light brown and crispy, remove with a slotted utensil, drain on paper towels, and toss with kosher salt. Let cool, then reheat just before serving. Discard fat from saucepan and set pan aside.

Place breasts between sheets of plastic wrap and pound with a mallet or cleaver until they are half their original thickness. Set aside.

Marinate rhubarb in a mixture of port and raspberry vinegar for at least 30 minutes. Add rhubarb, marinade, and stock to saucepan used for cracklings. Cook until reduced to a medium sauce consistency. Keep warm.

Heat a large sauté pan over high heat and add reserved 2 tablespoons fat. Salt duck breasts on both sides and then sear on both sides. Reduce heat to medium and continue to cook until medium rare, about 4 minutes, depending on thickness. They should feel springy to the touch. Remove breasts to paper towels to absorb any fat and keep warm.

To make vinaigrette, mix together orange juice and zest, parsley, chervil, salt, and pepper. Slowly whisk in oil, blending thoroughly. Toss arugula and asparagus with vinaigrette and arrange on 6 individual serving plates. Slice duck breasts on the bias and arrange on top of greens. Spoon rhubarb sauce over breasts. Top with warm cracklings that have been warmed in paper towels in the oven.

BRAISED DUCK IN THAI RED CURRY

SERVES 6

Recommended Wine: A chilled Gamay Beaujolais or lighter-style Zinfandel are the ideal wine choices for this exotic dish.

Susan Feniger and Mary Sue Milliken of the City Restaurant in Los Angeles are two of our favorite people and favorite cooks. Their travels to the Orient and Europe have provided them with abundant inspiration for their personalized, eclectic cuisine. This bold stew takes its cues from authentic Thai curry dishes, and it absolutely resonates with intriguing tart, sweet, and spicy flavors. A bed of basmati rice is the perfect accompaniment.

2 large ducks (4 to 5 pounds each)
Salt and freshly ground black pepper to taste
¼ cup vegetable oil or rendered duck fat
16 medium shallots, thinly sliced
8 cloves garlic, minced
2 tablespoons grated fresh ginger
¼ cup Thai red curry paste (see Note)
5 cups chicken stock or Basic Game Bird Stock (page 40)
¼ cup Thai fish sauce (see Note)
1 can (14 ounce) unsweetened coconut milk (see Note)
3 tablespoons brown sugar or palm sugar
¼ cup fresh lime juice (about 3 limes)
2 bunches fresh cilantro, trimmed and chopped
2 limes, peeled and diced
1 bunch green onions, all white and half green stalks, trimmed and sliced on diagonal

Bone ducks and remove skin. Reserve carcass for stock and skin for rendering. Cut breasts in half lengthwise, then cut each half breast crosswise into 3 equal pieces. Chop leg-thigh pieces into 3 or 4 pieces each. Sprinkle with salt and pepper to taste.

Heat oil in a heavy-bottomed dutch oven over high heat. Brown duck on all sides, then transfer meat to a platter. Reduce heat to medium-low, add shallots, and cook until brown. Add garlic and ginger, cook about 1 minute, then add curry paste.

Cook, stirring constantly, about 3 minutes. Return duck meat to pot along with stock and simmer, uncovered, until meat is tender, approximately 40 minutes.

With slotted utensil, transfer meat to a platter and keep warm. Purée sauce in a blender or food processor and strain back into pot. Cook over high heat until liquid is reduced by one third. Stir in fish sauce, coconut milk, sugar, and lime juice and bring to a simmer. Remove from heat. Stir duck back into warm sauce. Serve garnished with cilantro, diced lime, and green onions.

NOTE: These ingredients can be found in Asian markets and well-stocked supermarkets.

BRAISED DUCK WITH DRIED APRICOTS AND APPLES

SERVES 4

Recommended Wine: A rich Chardonnay offers the textural balance for this flavorful braised dish.

This delicious braised duck dish is nicely balanced by the slight sweetness and tartness of the fruit. We particularly enjoy it when the bounty of fall apples is upon us, and we have a wide variety from which to choose.

4 large duck leg-thigh pieces (about ¾ pound each)
4 tablespoons vegetable oil
1 cup sliced yellow onion
¼ cup slivered garlic
½ cup chopped carrot
½ cup chopped celery
1 teaspoon black peppercorns
2 large bay leaves, crumbled
8 juniper berries, crushed
2 cups hearty red wine
2 cups chicken stock or Basic Game Bird Stock (page 40)
⅔ cup dried apricots, sliced lengthwise
½ cup walnut halves
Salt and freshly ground black pepper to taste
1 cup peeled, sliced green apples
2 tablespoons butter

Trim all visible fat and excess skin from duck pieces. In a saucepan, heat 2 tablespoons of the oil. Add onion, garlic, carrot, and celery and sauté until lightly browned. Add peppercorns, bay leaf, juniper berries, and wine, cover partially, and simmer for 10 minutes. Cool completely and then add duck pieces; refrigerate for 8 hours or overnight.

Remove duck from marinade, reserving marinade with vegetables, and pat dry with paper towels. In a large, heavy-bottomed pot, sauté duck in remaining 2 tablespoons oil until golden brown. Add marinade with vegetables and stock and simmer slowly, covered, until duck is tender, about 1 hour. Remove duck and keep warm.

Strain cooking liquid and then remove fat. Place liquid in a saucepan and reduce over high heat to a light sauce consistency. Add apricots and walnuts and heat through. Season with salt and pepper.

In a sauté pan, sauté apple slices in butter until lightly browned. Divide apples among warm serving plates. Top with duck and surround with sauce.

ROAST DUCK WITH ACHIOTE AND PEPPERS
Served with Sweet Potato Polenta

SERVES 4

Recommended Wine: A lively Sauvignon Blanc with good acidity and slightly herbal character will balance this pepper-oriented dish.

Jimmy Schmidt, the creative chef at Detroit's Rattlesnake Club, features American cuisine in his repertoire. Here, he takes duck in a Southwest direction through the use of achiote paste, chili peppers, and cilantro. This successful merging of flavors is nicely offset by the accompaniment of Sweet Potato Polenta.

2 large ducks (4 to 5 pounds each)
¼ cup achiote paste (see Note)
2 tablespoons corn oil

SAUCE

1 red bell pepper, roasted, peeled, seeded, and deveined
1 red onion, roasted in 375°F oven for 30 minutes and peeled
¼ cup balsamic vinegar
3 cups chicken stock or Basic Game Bird Stock (page 40)
Salt
1 tablespoon chipotle pepper in adobo or to taste (see Note)
4 tablespoons unsalted butter, or less to taste
¼ cup roasted, peeled, and diced red bell pepper
¼ cup chopped fresh chives
¼ cup roasted, peeled, and diced fresh poblano chili pepper
¼ cup chopped fresh cilantro

Sweet Potato Polenta (recipe follows)
Fresh herb sprigs (thyme or basil) for garnish

Preheat oven to 450°F. Place ducks on a rack in a large roasting pan. In a small bowl, stir together achiote paste and oil until smooth light paste is formed. Rub paste all over surface of ducks, especially legs and thighs. Reserve some paste.

Place ducks in lower third of preheated oven and cook for about 15 minutes. Reduce heat to 350°F, baste again with remaining paste, and cook until well browned, about 1 to 1½ hours or until thermometer registers 160°F. Remove and let rest for 30 minutes before carving.

Remove breasts and leg-thigh pieces from birds. Remove thigh bones. Strip excess fat from all pieces. Place pieces, meat side down, on baking sheet and reserve.

To make sauce, combine 1 bell pepper, onion, and vinegar in a blender or food processor and purée until very smooth. In a large saucepan, bring stock to a boil over high heat. Reduce for about 20 minutes. Add puréed pepper-onion mixture and reduce until sauce coats the back of a spoon, about 15 minutes. Adjust seasoning with salt and chipotle purée. Strain.

Return sauce to pan and bring to a simmer. Whisk in butter, 1 tablespoon at a time. Add diced bell and poblano peppers, chives, and cilantro. Remove from heat and keep warm.

Slip ducks in preheated broiler to reheat and crisp skins. Spoon sauce onto individual serving plates, and arrange duck pieces attractively on top. Serve with Sweet Potato Polenta and garnish with herb sprigs.

NOTE: Achiote paste is an intensely colored red paste made from annatto seeds. Its earthy flavors are quite prized in Southwest and Mexican cooking. It can be found in Mexican markets, as can chipotle pepper in adobo.

SWEET POTATO POLENTA

SERVES 6 TO 8

2 large sweet potatoes (about 1½ pounds)
1½ cups milk
1½ cups chicken stock or Basic Game Bird Stock (page 40)
Salt and freshly ground black pepper to taste
½ teaspoon freshly grated nutmeg
1 cup coarse yellow cornmeal
4 tablespoons unsalted butter, plus unsalted butter for sautéing

Preheat oven to 400°F. Place sweet potatoes in roasting pan on lower rack of oven. Bake until well done and very tender, about 1 hour. Remove and allow to cool slightly. Scoop flesh from potatoes into a food processor. Add ⅛ cup of the milk and purée until smooth. Keep warm.

In a large saucepan, combine remaining 1⅜ cups milk, stock, salt, pepper, and nutmeg. Bring to a simmer over medium-high heat. Gradually whisk in cornmeal. Stir with a spatula or wooden spoon until polenta is thick enough for spoon to stand upright in it, about 10 minutes. Add potato purée and 4 tablespoons butter. Adjust seasoning with salt and pepper.

Oil a 9-by-12-inch cake pan and pour polenta into it. Smooth and level surface. Cover and refrigerate until firm, about 4 hours.

Remove cover and run a thin-bladed knife around edge of pan to loosen polenta. Invert pan on a cutting surface to unmold. With a knife or cookie cutter, cut polenta into desired shapes (triangles, rectangles, diamonds, moons, etc.). Refrigerate until ready to cook. Extra polenta can be frozen for another use.

In a nonstick skillet over high heat, melt butter as needed to cover bottom of pan. Carefully add polenta and cook until browned on both sides, about 2 minutes on each side. Remove to paper towels to drain briefly, then serve at once.

PERUVIAN DUCK CEVICHE

SERVES 2 TO 4

Recommended Wine: This unusual presentation of duck will work with a number of wines. The bottom line is to choose a wine with good acidity, either Chardonnay, Johannisberg Riesling, or Gewürztraminer, so that the acid structure will contrast with the small amount of fat in the duck and cracklings and will echo the citrus tones from the marinade.

Chef Felipe Rojas-Lombardi of New York City's The Ballroom created this dish based on a traditional recipe from the ancient Peruvian city of Huacho. The concept of an acid base marinade to "cook" the duck is similar to the way seafood ceviche is presented; in this case, the duck is then braised in the citrus marinade. The dish can be served as a first course or as a light dinner entrée with brown rice. Chef Rojas-Lombardi likes to serve it at room temperature, but we prefer it hot. It can be made a couple of days in advance and then reheated in a saucepan just before serving.

1 large duck (4 to 5 pounds)
½ cup water
Salt to taste, plus 1 teaspoon salt
2 small dried hot chili peppers, seeded and crumbled
½ cup fresh lime juice (6 to 8 limes)
1 teaspoon salt
2 large cloves garlic
1½ cups fresh orange juice
1 medium red onion, thinly sliced
1 teaspoon ground cumin
¼ teaspoon freshly ground white pepper
2 sprigs fresh cilantro
2 sprigs fresh flat-leaf parsley

Cut duck into 6 pieces. Remove skin from breasts and thighs and reserve. Reserve wings for another use.

Slice reserved duck skin into 1-inch-wide sections. Combine skin and water in a small saucepan and bring to a boil. Simmer, stirring occasionally, until water evaporates, skin is golden brown, and all the fat is rendered, about 15 minutes. Remove skin with a slotted utensil, drain on paper towels, and chop for cracklings. Sprinkle cracklings with salt to taste. (Cracklings can be stored in an airtight container for up to 3 days.) Reserve ¼ cup rendered fat and set aside; discard the remaining fat or save for another use.

Combine chilies, lime juice, and 1 teaspoon salt in a food processor or blender. Crush 1 of the garlic cloves, add to processor, and purée mixture until smooth. Place duck pieces in a bowl. Add puréed chili mixture, orange juice, and onion; mix to coat duck. Let stand at room temperature for 2 hours, or refrigerate overnight.

Remove duck from marinade. Strain marinade through a fine sieve, reserving onions and marinating juices separately. Pat duck dry with paper towels.

To cook duck, heat the ¼ cup reserved fat in a dutch oven or deep skillet. Add duck pieces, in batches if necessary, and sear on both sides, about 5 minutes. Remove duck pieces with a slotted utensil and set aside.

Mince remaining garlic clove. Add to pan in which duck was seared, along with half of reserved onions from marinade, cumin, and white pepper. Cook until onions soften, 3 to 4 minutes. Add reserved marinating juices, cilantro, and parsley; bring to a boil. Reduce heat, return duck to pot and simmer, until tender, about 15 minutes. Remove breasts. Continue cooking legs for another 10 to 15 minutes. Add remaining reserved onions and simmer to heat through, about 2 minutes.

Transfer to a large serving dish, and sprinkle liberally with lightly salted cracklings.

DUCK BREAST WITH MINT-HAZELNUT PESTO

SERVES 8

Recommended Wine: The berry-spice flavors of Zinfandel bolster the richness of the duck and echo the aromatic presence of mint in the pesto.

Ralph Tingle is a talented, young chef and caterer in California's wine country. We like this preparation of his because of the use of the light, flavorful pesto as opposed to a sauce. This dish is particularly tasty at the height of summer when fresh mint abounds. The same dish can be prepared as a summer salad, served atop greens that have been drizzled in a light vinaigrette. You can also cook the duck breasts over hot coals in a covered grill.

PESTO

2 cups loosely packed fresh mint leaves
½ cup ground hazelnuts
2 tablespoons chopped garlic
½ cup extra-virgin olive oil
Sea salt and freshly ground black pepper to taste

8 half duck breasts
Salt and freshly ground black pepper to taste
¼ pound Parmesan cheese for garnish

To make pesto, combine mint, hazelnuts, and garlic in a food processor or blender. Process until smooth. With machine running, slowly add oil to form a smooth paste. Season with salt and pepper to taste. Set aside at room temperature.

Season duck breasts on both sides with salt and pepper. Place in a sauté pan, skin side down. Sauté for 5 to 6 minutes, depending on the size of the breasts. Turn, and continue to cook for 2 to 3 minutes. To test doneness, push finger into breast; if meat springs back, breasts are medium-rare.

Slice breasts on the bias and arrange on individual serving plates. Drizzle with pesto. With a cheese slicer or sharp knife, shave thin strips of cheese over pesto. Serve immediately.

BRAZILIAN DUCK TART IN A SWEET CORNMEAL CRUST

SERVES 6 TO 8

The Brazilian reference comes from trying to describe the hot-sweet flavors. At John Ash & Company we originally called it a Sonoma summer tart, but that lacked pizzazz. When we called it a Brazilian tart, it sold like crazy!

CORNMEAL CRUST

½ cup unsalted butter, at room temperature
¼ cup sugar
1 cup yellow cornmeal
2 eggs, at room temperature
1 teaspoon kosher salt
1½ cups all-purpose flour

Recommended Wine: The hot-sweet flavors marry nicely with an off-dry Johannisberg Riesling or Gewürztraminer, or a Merlot is a good contrast.

FILLING

4 cups thinly sliced yellow onion (about 3 onions)
3 tablespoons slivered garlic
1 teaspoon minced, seeded fresh serrano chili pepper
2 cups finely julienned, seeded red and/or yellow bell pepper
¼ cup olive oil
¾ cup chicken stock or Basic Game Bird Stock (page 40)
½ cup dry white wine
⅔ cup dried currants or golden raisins
½ teaspoon ground cinnamon
½ teaspoon ground cumin
½ teaspoon red-pepper flakes
1½ cups finely diced, seeded ripe tomatoes

5 ounces boneless smoked duck meat, shredded (page 34)
½ cup walnuts, lightly toasted and chopped
5 ounces jack cheese (preferably Sonoma jack), cut in tiny cubes
Baby greens dressed with walnut oil vinaigrette for garnish

To make crust, in a mixer or food processor blend butter and sugar until smooth. Add cornmeal, eggs, and salt and blend until well combined. Add flour and mix until dough forms a ball. Mixture should be soft and moist. Gather into a ball and wrap in plastic wrap. Chill for 1 hour.

Preheat oven to 350°F. On a lightly floured board, roll out dough into a 12-inch round. Oil a 9-inch tart pan with 2-inch sides and transfer dough round to pan. Gently press dough against bottom and sides of pan. Trim off excess dough and attractively crimp edges along pan rim. Wrap and save any leftover dough in the freezer. Prick tart shell with a fork in several places. Bake until shell is just set, 4 to 5 minutes. Let cool.

To make filling, leave oven set at 350°F. In a large sauté pan, sauté onion, garlic, and chili and bell peppers in oil until soft but not browned. Add stock, wine, currants or raisins, cinnamon, cumin, and pepper flakes and cook until most of liquid has evaporated. Remove from heat and strain off any liquid.

Stir in tomatoes. Spread half of onion mixture in prepared tart shell. Scatter duck, walnuts, and cheese evenly over the onion mixture. Top with remaining onion mixture. Gently press down to form an even, flat surface. Cover with aluminum foil and bake in preheated oven for 25 minutes. Remove cover and cook until filling is lightly brown, 5 to 10 minutes longer.

Let cool and serve warm or at room temperature. Garnish with vinaigrette-dressed baby greens.

BRAISED DUCK WITH POBLANO CHILIES AND TOMATILLOS

SERVES 4

Recommended Wine: A crisp Sauvignon Blanc supplies the necessary acidity to contrast this hearty duck stew.

Poblano chilies look something like ordinary green bell peppers, but they have a unique, almost smoky flavor that makes them unlike any other chili. When dried, they are known as ancho chilies. They are not hot, but do have an intense flavor. This is a delicious Latin-tinged dish that is actually a type of *mole*. The approach works equally well with other game birds. Adjust cooking times as required by size.

8 meaty duck thigh-leg pieces
4 tablespoons light olive oil or vegetable oil
¾ cup unsalted pepitas (see Note)
½ cup walnuts
½ cup almonds
2 cups sliced yellow onion
2 tablespoons minced garlic
3 cups fresh tomatillos, husks discarded and quartered
6 fresh poblano chili peppers, seeded, deveined, and coarsely chopped
2 to 3 cups chicken stock or Basic Game Bird Stock (page 40)
⅓ cup loosely packed fresh cilantro leaves, chopped
Salt and freshly ground black pepper to taste

Trim all fat from duck pieces. In a deep, heavy-bottomed sauté pan over medium-high heat, add 2 tablespoons of the oil. Brown duck legs in oil on all sides. Remove and set aside. Pour off fat.

In a dry skillet over low heat, lightly toast the pepitas. Let cool and then place in blender with almonds and walnuts. Pulverize mixture and set aside.

Add remaining 2 tablespoons oil to pan and sauté onion and garlic until lightly browned. Add tomatillos and poblanos and cook over moderate heat until chilies are soft, about 10 minutes. If mixture is too dry, add a little stock to keep it moist.

Add pepita mixture to pan along with enough stock and reduce to a light sauce consistency. Add duck pieces, cover, and simmer until meat is tender, about 45 minutes. Remove legs to a serving platter and keep warm. Skim off any visible fat. Add cilantro and additional stock, if desired. Correct seasoning. If sauce looks "curdled," whisk briefly. Reheat, pour over duck legs, and serve immediately.

NOTE: Pepitas, or pumpkin seeds, can be found in Mexican markets.

FRESH SPINACH PASTA WITH SMOKED DUCK, OLIVES, AND PORCINI MUSHROOMS

SERVES 4

Recommended Wine: This is a classic dish for a good, hearty Zinfandel to echo the hearty notes of the pasta.

This recipe is extremely simple, just as most good pasta dishes are. Any smoked game breasts or legs could be used, not just duck.

With a food processor and a pasta machine, pasta dough is a snap to make on your own. If you don't have the equipment, the time, or the inspiration, there's plenty of good fresh pasta available in local markets.

SPINACH PASTA

1¾ cups all-purpose flour
2 large eggs, lightly beaten
½ teaspoon salt
½ pound spinach, cooked, well-drained, and puréed
1 tablespoon olive oil
About 1 tablespoon warm water, or as needed

1 ounce dried porcini mushrooms
1 cup warm water
⅓ cup slivered shallots
6 tablespoons olive oil
2 cups chopped, seeded ripe tomatoes
½ cup slivered, pitted oil-cured olives
½ cup loosely packed fresh basil leaves, chopped
½ pound boneless smoked duck meat, julienned (page 34)
Salt and freshly ground black pepper to taste
Toasted pine nuts and fresh basil sprigs for garnish

To make pasta, combine flour, eggs, salt, spinach, and oil in a food processor and blend with a steel blade just until dough begins to come together, about 15 seconds. Add drops of water if dough is too dry. It should be firm but not sticky. Turn machine on for 15 to 20 seconds longer to knead dough. Remove, wrap in plastic wrap, and let rest at room temperature for 1 hour.

After dough has rested, roll it out and cut it into fettuccine noodles on a pasta machine according to manufacturer's instructions. Drape noodles over a rack or place in a single layer on a flour-dusted towel until ready to cook.

Combine porcini and warm water and soak for at least 30 minutes. Remove mushrooms and carefully strain soaking liquid to remove any grit or sand. Coarsely chop mushrooms. In a sauté pan over moderate heat, sauté mushrooms and shallots in oil until shallots just begin to color.

Add tomatoes, mushroom soaking liquid, and olives and simmer, uncovered, until liquid is a light sauce consistency, about

10 minutes. Stir in basil and duck and warm through. Season with salt and pepper. Keep warm.

Fill a large pot with water and bring to a rapid boil. Add salt to taste and then add fettuccine. Cook until just tender, drain, and toss with duck sauce. Garnish with pine nuts and basil sprigs.

DUCK RILLETTE
Served with Apple-Ginger Chutney

MAKES 1 PATÉ, ABOUT 16 SLICES

Recommended Wine: A fresh, fruity Johannisberg Riesling or Gewürztraminer works nicely with the rillette as well as with the sweet chutney.

This is adapted from an old French recipe that traditionally used pork or goose. We like it a lot both as a cold "pâté" and served warm in small crocks with crusty French bread or tossed with freshly cooked pasta.

2 large ducks (4 to 5 pounds each), with giblets
3 tablespoons sea salt
3 teaspoons whole fresh thyme leaves
1½ teaspoons freshly ground black pepper
½ teaspoon red-pepper flakes
1 teaspoon fennel seed
½ teaspoon dried lavender blossoms (optional)
2 cups dry white wine
¾ cup minced shallots or green onions
3 tablespoons minced garlic
½ teaspoon dried sage
½ teaspoon dried oregano leaves
⅓ cup brandy
2 tablespoons green peppercorns, lightly crushed
3 tablespoons minced fresh parsley
1 tablespoon unsalted butter
4 ounces smoked ham, julienned
Melon or papaya slices, whole-grain mustard, cornichons, and walnut croûtes for garnish
Apple-Ginger Chutney (recipe follows)

Preheat oven to 350°F. Remove giblets from ducks and reserve livers. Mix together 2 tablespoons of the salt, 2 teaspoons of the thyme, 1 teaspoon of the black pepper, pepper flakes, fennel seed, and lavender and sprinkle over ducks and in cavities. Prick the ducks all over with a cooking fork and place in a deep roasting pan. Add wine to pan and cover with foil. Roast in preheated oven until the meat falls off the bone easily, 2½ to 3 hours. Remove ducks. Cool and reserve 2 cups of the cooking juice and fat, including scrapings from the bottom of the pan.

Place reserved juices and fat in a deep sauté pan. Add the

shallots, garlic, remaining 1 tablespoon salt and 1 teaspoon thyme, sage, oregano, and remaining ½ teaspoon black pepper and sauté until soft but not brown. Add brandy and cook for 5 minutes. Remove from heat and add peppercorns and parsley.

Pull meat off ducks and remove any skin, cartilage, or bone. Shred meat by hand or in short bursts in food processor. Stir in the shallot mixture. Taste the duck mixture and adjust seasoning with salt and pepper. Separately sauté the livers in butter until just pink and set aside.

To assemble the rillette, line a 6-cup pâté mold with parchment paper or plastic wrap. Fill the prepared mold halfway with duck meat mixture. Roughly chop the livers and scatter over the duck meat along with the ham. Fill the mold with remaining duck mixture to overflowing. Press mixture down hard and wrap in plastic wrap. Place in a larger pan and weight the top with heavy canned goods or a brick so that excess fat is squeezed out. Refrigerate overnight.

Unwrap the rillette and wipe off any excess fat. Unmold by running a thin-bladed knife around edges and inverting onto a cutting surface. Remove parchment or plastic wrap. Slice carefully and place slices on a chilled plate. Garnish with melon or papaya slices, whole-grain mustard, cornichons, walnut croûtes, and a small dab of chutney.

APPLE-GINGER CHUTNEY

MAKES 2 QUARTS

4 cups sliced yellow onion (about 3 onions)
6 tablespoons minced garlic
¼ cup light olive oil
6 pounds tart apples, peeled, cored, and thickly sliced (about 8 cups)
1 cup dried currants or golden raisins
6 tablespoons minced fresh ginger
1½ cups white wine vinegar
1½ cups firmly packed dark brown sugar
½ teaspoon red-pepper flakes
½ teaspoon ground mace
1 teaspoon ground cinnamon
½ teaspoon ground cloves
2 teaspoons sweet paprika
1 tablespoon kosher salt

In a nonreactive stockpot or saucepan, sauté the onion and garlic in oil until just beginning to color. Add all remaining ingredients and simmer until apples are just cooked through, about 40 minutes. Chutney should have a nice texture; be careful not to overcook.

Let cool and pack in jars with tight-fitting lids. Refrigerate for up to 3 months.

WARM DUCK *FOIE GRAS* SALAD WITH BLACKBERRY VINAIGRETTE

SERVES 4

Recommended Wine: Although vinegar is often a problem when matching with wine, a young Cabernet Sauvignon amplifies the hearty flavors of the duck liver and the vinaigrette.

In France especially, duck and goose livers are prized and expensive delicacies. Ducks (usually Muscovy) and geese are overfed on a diet of corn, which causes their livers to enlarge considerably. The liver of a 7-pound duck can reach almost 2 pounds. In America, these special duck livers are being produced by a few growers, primarily in California and New York. Although these nurtured livers are quite expensive, they are worth an occasional splurge for "lovers of the liver." We like to serve this recipe as a first course.

½ cup blackberry vinegar or black currant vinegar
½ cup light olive oil
2 teaspoons wild honey
1 teaspoon minced shallots or green onions
¼ teaspoon minced garlic
⅓ cup fresh blackberries or whole thawed, frozen blackberries, halved
Salt and freshly ground black pepper to taste
3 cups mixed baby salad greens, such as spinach, arugula, mâche, endive, and mustard greens
1 pound *foie gras,* cut into ¼-inch-thick slices

In a mixing bowl, whisk together vinegar, ¼ cup of the oil, honey, shallots, garlic, and blackberries. Season with salt and pepper. Set aside.

Arrange the greens attractively on chilled individual serving plates.

In a nonstick sauté pan, heat remaining ¼ cup oil over moderately high heat. Add the *foie gras,* season lightly with salt and pepper, and very quickly brown on both sides, about 2 minutes' total cooking time. Place the sautéed *foie gras* immediately on greens and drizzle the blackberry vinaigrette over. Serve immediately.

WARM DUCK BREAST SALAD WITH ASIAN SPICES AND HAZELNUT VINAIGRETTE

SERVES 4

Recommended Wine: The spiciness and complexity of flavors work well with a Gewürztraminer; the same qualities are a good contrast to a Pinot Noir.

We particularly enjoy this dish as a first course, as it seems to wake up the taste buds. Try to include some spicy greens—mizuna, red mustard, nasturtium leaves—in the mix. The challenging part of this dish is to serve it quickly so that the greens stay chilled and the duck is still warm.

MARINADE

1 teaspoon minced garlic
2 tablespoons minced green onions
2 teaspoons oyster sauce (see Note)
1 teaspoon light soy sauce
1 teaspoon rice wine or dry sherry
1 teaspoon sugar
½ teaspoon 5-spice powder (see Note)

VINAIGRETTE

1 tablespoon minced garlic
⅓ cup hazelnut oil
⅓ cup walnut oil or light olive oil
1 tablespoon minced chives
2 tablespoons balsamic vinegar
1 teaspoon light soy sauce
¼ teaspoon sugar
⅓ cup toasted, coarsely chopped hazelnuts

2 whole duck breasts (1 to 1¼ pounds each)
4 to 6 ounces mixed baby salad greens
Edible flowers (nasturtium, borage) for garnish (optional)

Bone duck breasts and trim off excess fat. Cut each breast in half and place in a shallow dish. Combine ingredients for marinade and coat breasts thoroughly. Allow to marinate for 2 hours at room temperature.

In a small bowl, combine all ingredients for vinaigrette at least 2 hours before serving, to allow the flavors to develop.

To assemble salad, preheat broiler or prepare a fire in a charcoal grill. Artfully arrange baby greens on individual serving plates. Wipe excess marinade off duck breasts and grill or broil until medium-rare, about 2½ minutes per side. Do not overcook.

Quickly slice breast on the bias and arrange on plates with greens. Drizzle vinaigrette over greens. Garnish with flower petals, if available. Serve immediately.

NOTE: These ingredients can be found in Asian markets.

PIZZA WITH DUCK SAUSAGE AND BASIL-MINT PESTO

MAKES ONE 12-INCH PIZZA

Recommended Wine: This multi-flavored pizza is perfectly suited to a chilled Gamay Beaujolais or lighter-style Zinfandel.

This favorite pizza of ours can be made with any type of game sausage, but we particularly like it with duck sausage. You can either use the sausage recipe in this book or purchase duck sausage.

PIZZA DOUGH

½ cup warm water (110° to 114°F)
2 teaspoons active dry yeast
2 teaspoons sugar
2 tablespoons chopped mixed fresh herbs such as basil, thyme, and oregano
¼ cup plus 1 tablespoon olive oil
2 teaspoons salt
3 cups all-purpose flour
Sprinkling of cornmeal

PESTO

½ cup loosely packed fresh mint leaves
½ cup tightly packed fresh basil leaves
2 tablespoons pine nuts or walnuts, lightly toasted
2 teaspoons roasted garlic purée (page 31)
½ cup olive oil
Salt and freshly ground black pepper to taste

1 cup coarsely shredded mozzarella cheese
½ pound sliced spicy duck (or other game) sausage, lightly sautéed and patted dry
¼ cup slivered, pitted Kalamata, niçoise, or other black olives
¼ cup crumbled feta cheese
½ cup chopped fresh basil or mint and toasted pine nuts for garnish

To make pizza dough, pour water into a bowl, sprinkle yeast into the water, and then sprinkle in the sugar. Let mixture sit until foamy, about 5 minutes.

Pour the yeast mixture into a food processor with a plastic blade. Add herbs, ¼ cup olive oil, salt, and flour and process until the mixture gathers together into a ball. Add more warm water if mixture is dry.

On a lightly floured board, knead the dough for a couple of minutes. If the dough is very sticky, use a little extra flour.

Oil a large plastic or ceramic bowl with remaining 1 table-spoon oil. Place the dough in bowl and turn to coat all surfaces. Cover bowl with plastic wrap and let dough rise in a warm place until it has doubled in bulk.

Preheat oven to 450°F. To make pesto, combine mint, basil, pine nuts, and garlic in a food processor or blender and purée. With motor running, slowly add oil to form a smooth paste. Season with salt and pepper.

On a lightly floured board, roll out dough into a 12-inch circle. Sprinkle cornmeal on a 12-inch pizza pan and place dough on it. Tuck dough neatly into corners and over top of pan, forming a ridge. (Alternatively, place dough on a baking sheet.)

Spread mozzarella evenly over dough. Arrange sausage and olives on cheese. Bake in preheated oven until cheese has melted and crust is lightly browned, 12 to 14 minutes. Remove from oven and sprinkle feta cheese and herb and pine nut garnishes over top. Dollop pesto evenly over pizza and serve.

GOOSE

*T*he full-flavored flesh of goose provides ample enjoyment unto itself. It also seems to benefit immensely from either slow roasting or braising with other ingredients that further enliven its rich meat.

With legends of goose abounding, it's sometimes difficult to separate myth from reality. The ancient Romans were the first to prize the humble goose; in fact, the goose, which they considered sacred, was attached to the Temple of Juno. The Greeks, too, domesticated geese and fattened them on grain. Geese remained popular in France and Germany throughout the Middle Ages, and were so revered that when a city was conquered in battle, the geese of the town were given to the Grand Master of the Crossbowmen as a symbol of distinction.

In Germany in the sixteenth and seventeenth centuries, goose was extremely popular, and in England it was the symbol of celebration for St. Michael's Day, September 29.

Goose has found its way into the eighteenth-century prose of Grimod de la Reynière, who called it "a snappy brunette, with whom we get along very well, especially in the absence of our dear blonde," which, no doubt, refers to the chicken. Balzac referred to the goose as "the pheasant of coopers," more than likely a reference to the fact that goose is food for the nobleman and the poor man alike.

Goose even found its way into the writings of Charles Dickens: ". . . Bob said he didn't believe there was ever such a goose cooked. Its tenderness and flavor, size and cheapness were the themes of universal admiration. Eked out by apple-sauce and mashed potatoes, it was sufficient dinner for the whole family; indeed, as Mrs. Cratchit said with great delight (surveying one small atom of a bone upon the dish) they hadn't ate it all at last! Yet every one had had enough, and the youngest Cratchits in particular were steeped in sage and onion to the eyebrows." The sage and onion reference here was the prominent combination for stuffing the goose in England for many years.

Odd that the plucky, nervous goose has generated so much humor and lyricism over the years. Expressions like "You sent me on a wild goose chase," "That's a sure way to cook your goose," "You silly old goose," "You honk like a goose," and "What is sauce for the goose may be sauce for the gander" are age-old testaments to the temperament, longevity, and elusiveness of the legendary waterfowl.

In contemporary times, nowhere is the difference between wild and farm-raised waterfowl more dramatically apparent than with goose. While hunters have savored for centuries the rich flavors of a recently bagged young Canadian, snow, German Embden, or blue goose after arduously plucking its pinfeathers, these wild waterfowl are truly a bird apart from their domestic kin. The critical difference between the two is the absence of fat in the bird of the wild due to its active flight patterns.

Shopping for Goose

Plumped up through their scavenging on fish, fallen apples, or emerging young onions from the garden, domestic geese can offer gastronomic triumph and provide immense satisfaction when they are cooked properly. The Toulouse goose, the most common of the farm-raised species, is of two distinct types. One is raised primarily for the purpose of *foie gras,* the succulent swollen liver of the goose. Additionally, it provides the rich fat that is used to preserve the goose in *confits.* The other Toulouse goose, the agricultural variety, is the one that is available commercially for eating purposes.

These geese are butchered before they are 9 months old (often as young as 6 months) at 8 to 12 pounds, when they tend to be tender with plump, supple breasts and more meat to bone than wild geese. Beyond this age, they lose much of their appeal. Youth should therefore be paramount in your search for goose.

Fresh goose is difficult to find except for during the holiday season, but frozen goose can be purchased the year around. It is best to defrost frozen goose slowly in the refrigerator for 1 to 2 days.

Although the ratio of meat to fat and bone is not as good with smaller geese as it is with larger ones, smaller geese offer more tenderness and flavor. An 8- to 10-pound goose will serve 4 to 6 people.

Cooking Tips

Whether wild or domestic, the traditional way to cook your goose is to roast it, although wild goose requires barding before cooking and steady basting to prevent the meat from drying out. Refer to page 36 in the Techniques section for further information on rendering goose fat effectively before roasting it. With older wild goose, braising is the preferred method of cooking.

A domestic goose is cooked when the juices from the breast run pale yellow when pricked. Unlike the breast meat of duck and squab, which is best served medium-rare to rare, goose breast meat needs to be fully cooked. Overcooking, however, will result in the dryness and fibrous texture that occur with any bird subjected to too much heat. The best cooking range for an unstuffed domestic goose is usually 13 to 15 minutes per pound. A stuffed goose will require 5 to 7 minutes more per pound than an unstuffed one. If the substantial layer of fat on the goose has not been rendered before roasting, basting with boiling water or stock every 20 minutes will help dissolve it. Beware of recipes with cooking times for wild geese which are smaller (4 to 5 pounds) and are considerably leaner.

Ultimately, the most accurate way to gauge the cooking time for roasted goose is to aim for 165° to 170°F on an instant-read thermometer. Remember that the temperature continues to rise after the bird is removed from the oven.

Save rendered goose fat for *cassoulets, confits,* or to brown breasts of other game birds, poultry, or meat. As with duck fat, goose fat is wonderful for sautéing potatoes. Goose livers are excellent for use in stuffings.

Classic Dishes

In Europe and the United States, goose is traditionally roasted with a stuffing of wild rice, roasted chestnuts, apples, onions, sage, and celery. Other classic variations incorporate bread crumbs, herbs, and dried fruits; another stuffing incorporates sauerkraut (or red cabbage) with paprika. Prunes are also a suitable accompaniment for goose; they are often simmered in port or white wine prior to using them in stuffings.

In *The Cooking of South-West France,* Paula Wolfert offers an interesting recipe for goose stew with radishes, based on an old Gascon recipe. The breasts of the goose are larded with strips of fat soaked in Armagnac and mixed with chopped garlic and herbs prior to a long, gentle simmering. The addition of the peppery radishes is a new twist on the classic idea of using baby turnips.

Goose also provides the knowing gastronome with supplemental treats. The richness of goose livers is highly prized, as is the rendered fat from the goose, which is often preserved in the refrigerator and used to make *cassoulet,* the savory mélange of white beans and sausage that is a signature dish of French country cooking. *Cassoulet* is served in so many variations throughout France that it inspires considerable controversy on its regional authenticity.

Goose *confit* is thought by many gastronomes to be the quintessential *confit*, since it offers a richer, more complex taste and smoother texture than that made from duck.

The saying in the southwest of France is "A spoonful of goose fat can raise soup to sainthood." Goose fat can also provide delicious morsels called cracklings, tiny pieces of skin and fat cooked until crisp and used as garnish in salads. Smoked goose is considered quite a delicacy, too, and is worth the effort of smoking it at home if it can't be purchased.

Classic Recipe

CHRISTMAS ROAST GOOSE WITH WINTER FRUITS

SERVES 6

Recommended Wine: A delicate Pinot Noir or chilled Gamay Beaujolais offers a contrast of texture to this rich dish.

Farm-raised geese are quite fatty. The key to a successful goose dish is the rendering of that fat. A description of how to do this can be found in the Techniques section.

1 goose (6 to 8 pounds)
1 pound yellow or red onions, unpeeled
2 tablespoons minced garlic
Olive oil for sautéing (optional)
4 cups dry French bread crumbs
¾ cup milk, heated to lukewarm
4 cups mixed dried fruits such as apples, pears, figs, and/or apricots
2 tablespoons minced fresh sage, or 1 tablespoon dried sage
¼ cup minced fresh parsley
¾ cup chopped walnuts or hazelnuts (optional)
½ cup diced celery (optional)
1 pound sweet Italian sausage, diced, sautéed, and drained (optional)
½ pint (8 ounces) fresh shucked oysters, chopped, with their liquor (optional)
¼ cup Calvados (optional)
Salt and freshly ground black pepper to taste
Freshly grated nutmeg to taste

Steam goose, if desired, to render some of the fat (page 36). Reserve the fat. Preheat oven to 375°F. Place unpeeled onions in a shallow pan and roast until tender, about 30 minutes. Cool, peel, and chop; set aside. Reset oven to 350°F.

In a small skillet, sauté garlic in a small amount of the rendered goose fat or olive oil until soft but not browned; set aside. Soak bread crumbs in milk until soft, then squeeze dry; set aside.

In a large mixing bowl, combine bread, onions, reserved garlic, dried fruits, sage, and parsley. If desired, add nuts, celery, sausage, and/or oysters with liquor. Season with salt, pepper, and nutmeg. Stuff the goose with the mixture, and truss cavity closed (page 37). Place on a rack in a roasting pan.

Roast goose in preheated oven until juices run clear when thigh is pricked with a fork, about 2½ hours or until a thermometer registers 165° to 175°F. Remove goose from pan and skim off fat from pan juices. Deglaze pan with a little Calvados, if desired, and pour over the goose.

BRAISED GOOSE WITH OLIVES AND WINTER VEGETABLES

SERVES 6 TO 8

Recommended Wine: The rich flavors of goose and the hearty texture of this braised dish are matched by a young Zinfandel or Pinot Noir.

This straightforward dish is rich with Italian flavors. Like many stews and braised dishes, a great part of the enjoyment of cooking the dish is reveling in the wonderful aromas that fill the kitchen during the process, an aromatic bliss that continues at the table. Duck may be used in place of goose.

1 goose (8 to 10 pounds)
Salt and freshly ground black pepper to taste
½ cup olive oil
6 cups sliced yellow onion
⅓ cup slivered garlic
4 cups chopped, seeded ripe tomatoes
3 cups dry white wine
2 pounds turnips, peeled and cut into ½-inch dice
1 pound fennel bulb, thinly sliced
1 pound parsnips, peeled and cut into ½-inch dice
¾ cup slivered, pitted green olives
2 large bay leaves
1 tablespoon minced fresh thyme, or 2 teaspoons dried thyme
About 4 cups Basic Game Bird Stock (page 40)
Fresh watercress sprigs and small wedge of Parmesan or Asiago cheese for garnish

Cut goose into 12 serving pieces, reserving the back, wing tips, and neck for stock. Season goose pieces with salt and pepper. In a heavy-bottomed pot over medium-high heat, add oil and sauté the goose, in batches if necessary, until brown on all sides.

Remove goose and discard all but ¼ cup of the oil from the pot. Add onion and garlic and sauté until very lightly browned. Return goose pieces to pot and add tomatoes, wine, turnips, fennel, parsnips, olives, bay leaves, and thyme. Add stock just to cover and bring to a boil. Reduce heat, cover, and simmer until goose is very tender, about 1½ hours.

Remove from heat and skim off excess fat. Strain cooking juices into saucepan and reduce over high heat to a light sauce consistency. Arrange goose and vegetables on a warm serving platter and pour reduced cooking juices over. Garnish with watercress sprigs. With a cheese slicer or sharp knife, shave thin strips of cheese over top.

BRAISED GOOSE WITH FRESH CHESTNUTS

SERVES 6

Recommended Wine: A rich, oak-aged Chardonnay will echo the nutty tones as well as the succulence of the goose.

We look forward to the late fall with its fresh chestnuts so that we can prepare this simple but lovely dish. The chestnuts must be peeled first, which is a little time consuming but worth the effort. Although canned peeled chestnuts are available, they are not recommended for this dish. Occasionally, frozen peeled chestnuts are stocked in specialty markets; these are a good substitute for fresh, but only if they haven't been frozen for too long.

1 goose (6 to 8 pounds)
2 tablespoons olive oil
2 tablespoons slivered garlic
3 cups sliced yellow onion
1 cup diced carrot
½ cup thinly sliced celery
2 cups dry white wine
4 tablespoons minced sun-dried tomatoes in oil
1 teaspoon juniper berries, crushed
3 bay leaves
2 teaspoons minced fresh thyme, or 1 teaspoon dried thyme
Salt and freshly ground black pepper to taste
Water or Basic Game Bird Stock to cover (page 40)
1½ pounds fresh chestnuts, peeled (page 47)
½ cup minced fresh parsley

Cut goose into serving pieces. Remove all visible fat. In a large, heavy-bottomed pot over medium-high heat, brown goose in oil on all sides until golden. Remove goose and pour off all but 2 tablespoons of oil.

Using the same pot, sauté garlic, onion, carrot, and celery in remaining oil until lightly colored. Return goose to pot, add wine, tomatoes, juniper berries, bay leaves, and thyme. Season lightly with salt and pepper.

Add water to cover goose and bring to a boil. Reduce heat, cover, and simmer for 2½ hours. Add chestnuts and simmer for 30 minutes longer. When goose and chestnuts are tender, remove from pot with vegetables and keep warm. Skim fat from cooking broth and reduce broth over high heat for 5 to 7 minutes to concentrate flavors and thicken slightly. Adjust seasoning and stir in parsley.

Arrange goose on a deep serving platter and surround with chestnuts and vegetables. Pour some of the cooking broth over and pass the rest in a bowl.

PASTA SALAD WITH CORNED GOOSE AND SWEET CORN

SERVES 6

Recommended Wine: A fruity Jo-hannisberg Riesling contrasts the slight salty component in this dish.

Corning is a very old technique for preserving meats, predating commercial refrigeration. *Corned* refers to the use of salt, which looked a bit like corn kernels and has nothing to do with real corn. Today we usually think of corned only in the context of beef, but it also adds an interesting flavor to game birds or chicken. A fair amount of salt remains in the meat even with the soaking, so be sure to match it with more neutral ingredients. Allow 5 days to prepare this recipe.

1 goose (6 to 8 pounds)
1 cup kosher salt or sea salt
½ cup firmly packed brown sugar
3 quarts water
6 garlic cloves, lightly crushed
12 whole cloves
1 teaspoon freshly grated nutmeg
1½ tablespoons juniper berries, crushed

PASTA

Salt to taste
1 pound fresh corkscrew (rotini) pasta, or ½ pound dried corkscrew pasta
1½ cups fresh corn kernels
½ cup loosely packed fresh basil leaves, julienned
⅓ cup extra-virgin olive oil
3 tablespoons fresh lemon juice, or more to taste
Freshly cracked black pepper to taste

Fresh basil sprigs and seeded, slivered ripe tomatoes for garnish

Combine salt, sugar, and water in a stockpot. Bring to a simmer and stir until salt and sugar dissolve. Remove from heat and stir in garlic, cloves, nutmeg, and juniper berries. Let cool to room temperature.

Put goose in cooled mixture, adding additional water if necessary to cover goose barely. Cover and refrigerate, turning the goose twice each day for 4 days.

Drain goose and rinse well. Place in a large vessel and cover with cold water. Weight the bird, if necessary, to keep it submerged and let it stand in the refrigerator for 8 hours. During this time, change the water at least 4 times.

Drain goose and pat dry. Steam goose to render some of the fat (page 36).

Preheat oven to 350°F. Pat goose dry, and truss cavity closed (page 37). Place goose on a rack in a roasting pan and roast in preheated oven until juices run clear when thigh is pricked with a fork, about 2½ hours or until a thermometer registers 165° to 175°F. Remove from oven and let cool.

Remove any skin or fat from the goose and julienne meat. You will need 1 pound of meat for the salad; reserve remaining meat for another use.

Fill a large pot with water and bring to a boil. Lightly salt water and add pasta. Cook pasta until just done, then drain and rinse with cold water. Drain well.

In a large bowl, combine cooked pasta, corn, basil, oil, lemon juice, and pepper. Toss gently and adjust seasoning. Divide pasta among 6 chilled plates. Top with reserved julienned goose and garnish with basil sprigs and tomato.

PARTRIDGE AND GROUSE

*P*artridge are so succulent, with their pronounced piny, gamy flavor, that it's a mystery why they aren't more widely available. We suspect that if offered more regularly, much in the way that domestic squab has been, partridge would quickly become a popular choice on the American table.

Partridge, grouse, ptarmigan, and a host of other wild birds are so closely related that they will be discussed as one here. We find them first referred to in history by the Romans in the first century A.D., when they were cooked by Apicius in their feathers and stuffed with dates from Jericho. These birds are often grouped together because they weigh between one and one and a half pounds, with some older birds weighing as much as three pounds.

Nowadays the most commonly domesticated bird in this group is the chukar partridge, a relative of the wild Scotish red-legged partridge. It offers particulary lean, tender meat that is somewhat like squab, plus it is slightly larger than some of the other partridge and grouse varieties.

Grouse and partridge abound in the wild in Europe, North Africa, and parts of Asia, where they are known (or confused as the case may be) by their variety: gray partridge, red partridge, Hungarian partridge (which was imported to the United States in the eighteenth century for sporting purposes), Greek partridge, ruffed grouse, sage grouse, black grouse, red grouse, Scotch grouse, and pintailed grouse. Of these, the red and gray partridge are generally thought to be the most flavorful; gourmets, however, have debated their respective merits for centuries.

All of these varieties are members of the same family, which are distinguished by their relatively short wings, legs, necks, and tails, and variegated but not particularly showy plumage. The flavor of these birds tends to vary, owing mostly to differences in locale and diet rather than kinship.

Grouse, which are considered to be an extraordinary delicacy by many gourmets, tend toward a darker flesh than partridge and feed on the tender shoots of heather, which might explain their earthy taste.

In America, due to variations in geographic nomenclature, there is considerable lack of distinction between grouse and partridge. In the north, the ruffed grouse is often called partridge; in the south, quail and partridge are virtually interchangeable.

Shopping for Partridge and Grouse

Connoisseurs of wild partridge swear that the only time to eat them is in the early months of fall—September, October, and November—although they are still quite edible in December. Charles Monselet, a nineteenth-century writer, offered that "after the first snowfall, partridge no longer exists except in a stringy state." This aphorism led us and the late food historian Waverley Root to wonder why the partridge would be found and cherished by true lovers on the first day of Christmas in a non-fruit-bearing pear tree?

For domestic partridge, invariably the chukar partridge, plan on a one-pound bird per person. Cost, unfortunately, is quite high, but they are a special treat.

Cooking Tips

Like other small game birds, farm-raised partridge differ significantly from the birds of the wild, although they can be cooked by the same methods. The wild birds are extraordinarily lean, so it's good insurance to bard them with bacon or pork fat and baste them often while cooking to prevent them from drying out.

Wild partridge and grouse take well to a variety of cooking methods, but roasting and braising are the most successful. One of the best methods for roasting involves placing small onions or shallots along with aromatic herbs inside the cavity of the bird, tenting it in aluminum foil or brown paper, and placing it inside a lidded casserole.

Farm-raised partridge take well to grilling and sautéing, as they are not nearly as prone to drying out as their wild cousins. Before cooking, they should be split by cutting along the backbone and pressing down firmly on the bird with a jolt from the hand. This presents a more uniform shape, and helps ensure even cooking. An oil-based marinade helps (see Basic Liquid Game Marinade, page 27) to keep the flesh moist. In any case, constantly monitoring the birds for doneness will ensure a good result.

Traditional presentations of these small, succulent birds include roast grouse with raspberries, grouse on toast (often creamed), grouse fricassee, partridge in a pear sauce (as opposed to a pear tree), partridge or grouse with oysters (a popular American colonial dish), and partridge braised in red cabbage. Partridge and grouse were particularly prized in the courts of Europe, where they are still considered an epicurean delicacy of the highest order.

Classic Recipe

PARTRIDGE "ON A STRING"

SERVES 4

Recommended Wine: A soft, supple Pinot Noir or Merlot would be the ideal accompaniment to this decadent dish.

Jean-Louis Palladin, of Jean-Louis at Watergate in Washington, D.C., shares with us a recipe that was prepared by his Spanish mother in the Gascony region of France. The authentic version is cooked with the partridge (or wood pigeon, grouse, woodcock, or other small game bird) hung from a string attached to an iron rod above a wood fire.

While certainly posing some logistical challenges for the home cook, the dish can be accomplished by hanging the string from the flue, as Jean-Louis does in his home in Virginia. He serves this rustic dish with a mousseline of potatoes, celery root, fresh chestnuts, or quince, or with a seasonal salad, but it can be adapted to any of the appealing side dishes in this book.

4 partridge or other small birds (about ¼ pound each), with giblets
12 slices pancetta or lean bacon strips
Fine sea salt and freshly ground black pepper to taste
½ cup rendered duck fat or peanut oil for basting
¼ pound fresh duck *foie gras*, diced
Peanut oil for sautéing
2 tablespoons Armagnac or Cognac
4 slices brioche, toasted just before serving

To prepare birds for roasting, clean them thoroughly and remove giblets. Reserve gizzard for another use. Chop remaining giblets into small dice; set aside.

Truss the birds tightly (page 37) and tie legs of birds with string, leaving about 2 feet extra to extend from the fireplace. Wrap each bird with 3 pieces pancetta and secure pancetta with toothpicks or more string. Lightly salt and pepper each bird and brush with some of the duck fat. Set aside.

Heat a small nonstick skillet over medium heat for 2 minutes.

Season *foie gras* with salt and pepper and add to skillet with a few drops of oil. Sauté for 2 minutes, add reserved giblets, and continue to sauté for 3 minutes. Deglaze pan with Armagnac and continue cooking for 30 seconds. Remove from heat and set aside until ready to serve.

To roast birds, hang them from chimney by attaching them to a flue or a horizontal rod. Cook for 25 minutes over hot wood coals, about 18 inches from coals. Baste birds with duck fat every 10 minutes and turn them to ensure even cooking.

To serve, spread briefly warmed giblet *foie gras* on toasted brioche. Remove birds from fire and untie all strings. Cut into quarters and arrange around brioche slices. Serve with lots of napkins.

GRILLED CHUKAR PARTRIDGE WITH SPICY GOLDEN PEAR SAUCE

SERVES 2

Recommended Wine: This subtly spicy dish is complemented by the luscious fruit and complex character of a Pinot Noir or by a slightly oaky Chardonnay.

This dish is adapted from a recipe created by the talented Dean Fearing at the Mansion on Turtle Creek in Dallas. Fearing's original recipe calls for venison, white port, and veal *demi-glace* in the sauce. He serves the venison with a wild rice compote that contains sun-dried pears, a hard-to-find ingredient. We've chosen to present the partridge with a slightly different sauce, we think with pleasing results. The same dish can easily be adapted to quail or squab with slight adjustments in cooking times for the birds. This dish is complemented by wild rice or spiced couscous (page 222).

MARINADE

¾ cup sweet vermouth
1 shallot, finely chopped
¼ cup olive oil
½ teaspoon finely minced orange zest
¼ teaspoon crushed black peppercorns
¼ teaspoon kosher salt

2 chukar partridge, backbone removed and bird flattened

SAUCE

¼ cup thinly sliced fresh mushrooms
1 tablespoon peanut oil
2 tablespoons finely chopped shallots
3 golden pears (Bartlett or Anjou), peeled, cored, and thinly sliced

1 teaspoon minced fresh thyme, or ½ teaspoon dried thyme
¾ teaspoon ground white pepper
1 teaspoon minced, seeded fresh serrano chili peppers
½ cup sweet vermouth
1 cup chicken stock or Basic Game Bird Stock (page 40)
1½ tablespoons butter (optional)
Salt to taste
Juice of ½ lemon, or more to taste

Mix together all ingredients for marinade. Place partridge in marinade and refrigerate for 4 to 6 hours or overnight.

To make sauce, in a large saucepan over medium-high heat, sauté mushrooms in oil until they begin to release their juices, 1 to 2 minutes. Add shallots and sauté for 1 minute. Add pears, thyme, pepper, chilies, and vermouth. Bring to a boil and reduce until there is 1 tablespoon of liquid remaining, about 10 minutes. Add stock and bring to a boil. Reduce over high heat to a light sauce consistency. Swirl in butter, if desired. Season with salt and add lemon juice. Keep sauce warm while grilling birds.

Prepare a fire in a charcoal grill. Remove partridge from marinade and pat dry with paper towels. Place birds, skin side down, over hot coals for 5 minutes. Turn and grill until juices run clear at the thigh when pricked with a fork, 3 to 5 minutes.

Spoon sauce evenly on individual serving plates. Arrange partridge on top of sauce.

ROAST PARTRIDGE WITH SHERRY VINEGAR
Served with Parsnip Purée with Saffron

SERVES 4

Vinegar is often used as a flavoring agent with full-flavored game. Since vinegars vary in strength, we usually add a bit less than the recipe calls for to begin with. Taste and decide if you want to add more. This recipe works very well with other birds such as grouse, pheasant, and guinea fowl.

4 partridge, or 2 large grouse
Salt and freshly ground black pepper to taste
1 medium lemon, quartered
4 cloves garlic, lightly crushed
4 tablespoons butter
⅓ cup Cognac or brandy
½ cup sherry vinegar
1 cup chicken stock or Basic Game Bird Stock (page 40)
6 ounces Smithfield ham or other dry cured ham, diced
¼ cup minced shallots

Recommended Wine: A lively
Zinfandel highlights the flavor of
the bird and the complex, smoky-
tart sauce.

½ tablespoon minced fresh tarragon, or 1 teaspoon dried
tarragon
¼ cup minced fresh flat-leaf parsley
½ cup fresh shiitake mushrooms, stemmed, slivered, and sautéed
briefly in butter
Parsnip Purée with Saffron (recipe follows)

Preheat oven to 400° F. Season bird cavities with salt and
pepper. Divide lemon quarters and garlic cloves equally among
cavities. In a heavy-bottomed sauté pan or oven-proof casserole
large enough to hold birds, heat 2 tablespoons of the butter over
moderate heat. Add birds and brown lightly on all sides. Pour
off fat and add Cognac. Carefully ignite with long match. When
flame dies down, add vinegar, stock, ham, shallots, and tarragon.
Cover pan and cook in preheated oven until juices run clear
when thigh is pierced with a fork, 30 to 35 minutes.

Remove birds from pan and cut in half. Discard lemon and
garlic from cavities. Place birds on a warm serving platter. Strain
sauce and return it to pan. Bring to a boil and reduce slightly. Remove from heat and quickly whisk in parsley and remaining butter.

Correct seasoning, add shiitakes, and pour over birds. Serve
immediately with Parsnip Purée with Saffon.

PARSNIP PURÉE
WITH SAFFRON

MAKES 3 CUPS

2 pounds parsnips or turnips, peeled and roughly chopped
Salt to taste
½ cup sliced yellow onion
⅛ teaspoon saffron threads
2 tablespoons butter or olive oil
¼ cup heavy cream
Drops of fresh lemon juice
Freshly ground white pepper to taste

In a saucepan, combine parsnips and lightly salted water to
cover. Bring to a boil and simmer until tender, 8 to 10 minutes.
Drain well.

While parsnips are cooking, in a small skillet, sauté onion
and saffron in butter until soft but not browned.

In a food mill or using short pulses in a food processor, purée
parsnips and onion mixture. Be careful not to purée too smoothly;
mixture should have some texture. Return mixture to pan, stir
in cream, and heat through. Season with lemon juice, salt, and
pepper.

ANDALUSIAN PARTRIDGE
Served with Beet-Horseradish Purée

SERVES 2 TO 4

Recommended Wine: A glass of good dry sherry is the obvious choice here. A crisp Sauvignon Blanc would also go very nicely.

This very simple dish is based on one we encountered in a small tapas bar in Spain. It was served cold, and we ate it with our fingers on a hot afternoon. Great memories are entwined with this recipe. The dish can also be made with squab or quail.

2 partridge
1 medium-sized red onion, thinly sliced
2 bay leaves
¼ cup high-quality sherry vinegar
Salt and freshly ground black pepper to taste
¾ cup high-quality sherry
½ cup chicken stock or Basic Game Bird Stock (page 40)
3 large cloves garlic
½ cup olive oil
6 whole cloves
2 tablespoons golden raisins
12 black peppercorns
Beet-Horseradish Purée (recipe follows)

Preheat oven to 350° F. Loosely fill cavity of birds with onion slices and bay leaves, reserving a few onion slices. Rub vinegar over birds. Season generously with salt and pepper.

Place birds, reserved onions, sherry, stock, garlic, oil, cloves, raisins, and peppercorns in an earthenware dish. Cover and bake in preheated oven until birds are very tender, about 45 minutes. Allow birds to cool in the cooking liquid.

Remove birds and serve at room temperature. Drizzle the cooking liquid over the partridge and save the remainder to flavor soup stocks. Serve Beet-Horseradish Purée on the side.

BEET-HORSERADISH PURÉE

MAKES ABOUT 1½ CUPS

1¼ pounds beets, trimmed
2 tablespoons butter
Salt and freshly ground black pepper to taste
½ cup sliced red onion
1 teaspoon freshly grated horseradish, or 1½ teaspoons prepared horseradish
1½ teaspoon raspberry vinegar

Preheat oven to 375° F. Lightly oil surface of beets with 1 tablespoon of the butter. Place beets in a small roasting pan, season lightly with salt and pepper, and cover. Place in preheated oven until skin is wrinkled and flesh is soft, 45 to 50 minutes. Remove from oven, cool slightly, and slip off and discard beet skins.

While beets are cooking, in a small skillet, sauté onion in remaining 1 tablespoon butter until soft but not browned. Purée beets and onions in a food processor or blender. Be careful not to purée too smoothly; mixture should have some texture. Stir in horseradish and vinegar and adjust seasoning to taste.

COLD PICKLED PARTRIDGE
Served with Preserved Lemons and Couscous Salad

SERVES 6

Recommended Wine: A youthful Zinfandel or Petite Sirah will off-set the tartness of the pickled partridge quite nicely.

Throughout history great feasts and banquets have often included a course of "little birds." This recipe works well with any of the small birds—quail, squab, grouse. It also translates nicely to poussin and Cornish hens. We've had some wonderful Spanish tapa assortments that have included little pickled birds as one of the dishes.

This unusual dish is ideal for picnics or lunches on a warm summer day. Pickling is a very old technique that was used to preserve game birds before refrigeration was widely available. It produces very interesting flavors and textures. This recipe and technique can be used for other small game birds as well. We strain and reuse the cooking liquid; it imparts more intense flavors the second time around.

6 whole partridge
2 teaspoons kosher salt
3 cups extra-virgin olive oil
1½ cups high-quality red wine vinegar
2 tablespoons black peppercorns
6 bay leaves
2 small heads garlic, separated into cloves and peeled
1 cup chopped green onions
2 tablespoons minced fresh thyme (lemon thyme preferred)
2 cups pearl onions
⅔ cup dried currants or golden raisins
Couscous Salad (recipe follows)
Preserved Lemons (recipe follows)
Watercress sprigs for garnish

Sprinkle partridge inside and out with some of the salt. Combine remaining salt, oil, vinegar, peppercorns, bay leaves, garlic, green onion, and thyme in a nonreactive pot. Add partridge and bring to a boil. Reduce heat, cover, and simmer for 15 minutes. Add pearl onions and currants and simmer until partridge is very tender, about 30 minutes longer.

Let cool, then refrigerate partridge in cooking liquid for 24 hours before serving. To serve, remove meat from partridge and slice breasts. Moisten with some of the cooking liquid. Arrange couscous attractively on plates and surround with watercress. Place sliced partridge breasts and leg-thigh pieces on top. Mince or julienne as much preserved lemon as desired and strew over partridge along with pine nuts from salad recipe. Finally, garnish with watercress sprigs.

PRESERVED LEMONS

MAKES 12 LEMONS

Preserved lemons are a staple of Moroccan cooking that we think deserve wider use. They are a terrific addition to the cook's palette of seasonings. Finely mince the lemon and add it to sauces or marinades. For best results, use Meyer or other thin-skinned lemon varieties; do not use ordinary thick-skinned types. If Meyers are unavailable, substitute limes.

12 ripe thin-skinned lemons
4½ tablespoons coarse sea salt or kosher salt
2 tablespoons fresh lemon juice

Scrub lemons well and place in a nonreactive container. Cover with cold water and refrigerate for 3 days, changing the water each day.

Drain lemons. With the point of a sharp knife, cut 4 incisions lengthwise all the way through each lemon to within ¼ inch of each end. The lemon should be held together at both ends.

Gently squeeze lemons open and place ½ teaspoon salt in center of each. Place lemons in a sterilized jar and sprinkle with remaining 2½ tablespoons salt. Add lemon juice and enough boiling water to cover completely. Top with lid and allow lemons to steep for 2 weeks at room temperature before using. Will keep indefinitely.

COUSCOUS SALAD

SERVES 6

1 cup chicken stock or Basic Game Bird Stock (page 40)
¾ cup couscous
3 tablespoons olive oil or pickled partridge cooking liquid
3 tablespoons finely chopped green onion
½ cup finely diced red bell pepper

½ cup diced yellow bell pepper
1 large tomato, seeded and finely chopped
¼ cup slivered, pitted niçoise or Kalamata olives
Fresh lemon juice, salt, and freshly ground white pepper to
taste
2 cups mixed salad greens, such as arugula, mâche, and
spinach
2 tablespoons pine nuts, lightly toasted, for garnish

In a small saucepan, bring stock to a boil. Remove from heat, pour over couscous in a mixing bowl, and let stand until cool. Fluff gently with a fork, add oil or cooking liquid, onion, bell peppers, tomato, and olives. Season with lemon juice, salt, and pepper. Keep warm, if necessary, before serving. Use greens and pine nuts when assembling with partridge.

PHEASANT

Of all the game birds, pheasant is perhaps the most delicious when cooked properly. It can be quite rich and gamy in the wild, but it is relatively mild and delicate when farm raised, with a hint of apples in the taste.

Long the prize of hunters because of its showy plumage, wild pheasant was traditionally hung in a cool, dry place to relax the muscles of the bird and to concentrate and intensify the gamy flavor so prized by some hunters and so disdained by others. In fact, this aged quality was so desirable to some that the hanging process was sometimes allowed to continue until the body of the pheasant severed from the neck.

The practice of hanging pheasant to the point of near decomposition is certainly European in origin. In the eighteenth century, Grimod de la Reynière wrote that "pheasant should be waited for like a governmental pension by a writer who has never flattered anybody." Some years later, Brillat-Savarin offered further insight into the practice of hanging pheasant to the proper degree of "ripeness," a state that he referred to as the pheasant's "apogee of excellence." Others refer to this state simply as "high" or "rotten."

Brillat-Savarin explained in some detail: "The peak is reached when the pheasant begins to decompose; then its aroma develops and mixes with an oil which must undergo a certain amount of fermentation, just as the oil in coffee can only be drawn out by roasting it. When the pheasant reaches this point, then, it is plucked, and not before, and it is larded carefully with the freshest and firmest of material. . . . Very careful experiments have taught us that pheasants which are left in their feathers are much more savory than those which have been naked for a long time. This may be because contact with the air neutralizes certain qualities in the aroma, or because part of the natural fluid which serves to nourish the feathers is reabsorbed and adds flavor to the meat."

It should be added that despite the European custom of hanging pheasant for long periods of time, the practice has never caught on in America to any significant degree, nor is it practiced nearly as widely in Europe as it once was.

146

The late noted food historian Waverley Root offered evidence that pheasant had been on the tables of noblemen and royalty for years. He reported that at one of the most lavish feasts ever known, the Banquet of the Vow of the Pheasant in 1453 in Lille, Philip the Good, Duke of Burgundy, made history by making his knights swear before a line of live, tethered pheasants that they would abstain from sleeping in beds and changing their clothes until Constantinople was taken back from the Saracens who had recently conquered it.

Apparently, after the revelry of pheasant and wine was over, these vows were later retracted so as not to annoy Charles VII, the king of France. "Swearing by a pheasant," however, was considered a valid ritual throughout much of the Middle Ages due to the bird's noble character. Pheasant were served with their beaks and legs gilded, a practice that apparently evolved from the Romans, who were known for their lavish table displays of the bird's plumage. Pheasant was also revered during King Henry VIII's reign, when one of his loyal servants was employed solely to take care of his pheasant flock.

Not all is praise for this handsome bird, however. Noting the tendency of the pheasant to flee danger by running rather than using its erratic flight patterns to confound hunters, the French writer Emile-Louis Blanchet observed: "God neglected to screw its brains down tight." To which, we can only say: "We don't love the pheasant for its brains."

After many years of domestication in Britain, pheasant have returned to the wild there only in the past two centuries. Thomas Jefferson, America's first real gastronome, wrote from France to James Madison that he intended to colonize the French pheasant in America, but it's not clear whether or not he ever fulfilled his desire.

Nowadays in America, pheasant are raised on farms in significant quantity, therefore they are far easier to find than they were ten years ago. This is a bit peculiar, because as recently as during the 1940s and 1950s, wild pheasant were in greater supply than chicken, and were very much a part of the American diet. It's estimated that in South Dakota alone, there were as many as 50 million pheasant inhabiting the marshlands and high-grass terrain.

Shopping for Pheasant

Ring-necked pheasant is currently the domesticated bird of choice, although there are 48 species and 128 subspecies of pheasant. Ring-necks are raised on farms all over the country, particularly in California and Pennsylvania. The Milan pheasant, a larger-breasted pheasant, is raised on the Grayledge Avian Farms in Glastonbury, Connecticut.

Regardless of locale there is considerable debate over the best diet, habitat, and slaughtering age of pheasant, since all of these factors play a prominent role in the flavor of the bird.

At Krout's Pheasant Farm in Sonoma County, California, pheasant are raised in 50-by-150-foot nylon-netted flight pens filled with lamb's-quarter, a tall cover crop with leafy, green foliage. At 7 weeks of age, the birds are fitted with "specs" that obscure their lateral sight and help cut down on the pecking and cannibalism that is common with domesticated birds. Growth hormones or steroids are not used in the raising of these pheasant.

The pheasant are fed on a high-protein soybean and corn diet. They develop supple, plump breasts with a very thin layer of fat by the time they are slaughtered at 20 to 22 weeks old. The cooking technique suitable for pheasants raised in this manner is considerably different than that of wild birds, since the wild pheasant does not necessarily get a full ration of food and has virtually no fat whatsoever.

A farm-raised pheasant, regardless of its handling, is a bird apart from the wild fowl, and exhibits much less gamy flavor than a bird that has been shot in the wild, hung for a few days to a week, and then plucked. To connoisseurs of the reddish purple meat of wild pheasant, the farm-raised version will seem insipid and tasteless. To the new pheasant devotee, however, the mild, pinkish white flesh, similar to that of a free-range chicken in some ways, can be greatly appreciated over the acquired taste of the wild bird.

If choosing a bird from the wild, select a young pheasant with a flexible breast bone and beak, gray legs, and pointed tip wing feathers. Older birds are often very tough and have an unpleasant aroma; they should be avoided whenever possible.

Many chefs prefer to use birds that have been dry plucked rather than those that have been dressed by the more common wet-plucking method. In the latter method, the feathers are removed after a hot-water bath. Dry plucking, these chefs contend, retains more of the natural flavor of the pheasant.

Commercially raised female birds with plump, lean breasts, weighing between two and three pounds, are highly desirable when they can be found. Their appeal is even greater if they've been allowed to forage outdoors for nuts and insects as they do on some farms, rather than being raised on a straight corn diet.

Pheasant raised in pens tend to be slightly fattier and milder than free-range pheasant. The latter come closer to exhibiting the flavors of a wild bird, but are still quite different. The age of the bird is another determining factor in its taste, since older pheasants will be considerably tougher. They must be cooked using a wet-cooking method or with substantial barding.

A pheasant typically weighs between 2 and 3 pounds and will serve 2 people.

Cost is somewhat high, but these delicious birds are worth it. Baby pheasant, weighing about 1 pound, are quite a delicacy as well, but they are even more expensive and more difficult to find. For the most part, guinea fowl should be considered interchangeable with pheasant in the recipes in this section.

Cooking Tips

Pheasant, one of the most widely consumed of all feathered game, poses some problems for the home cook who approaches it like chicken. Yet it is very simple to prepare and offers immense satisfaction for those who follow some simple guidelines. The mild, pinkish white meat invites a bevy of wonderful accompaniments, and is quite delicious when cooked moist and tender, with its juices intact. In fact, many gourmets consider pheasant and grouse to be the most delectable of all game birds.

As with squab and quail, careful attention must be paid to not overcooking the delicate pheasant meat, particularly the plump, white breast meat. Because of the large variation between the tender flesh of the breast and the muscular, tougher legs, particulary with wild pheasant, many chefs prefer to debone the birds and cook the breasts separately. If an older wild bird is being prepared, a moist cooking method with barding of the breasts will almost surely be required to deal with the natural leanness of the fowl. Many cooks prefer to roast wild pheasant breast side down on a rack so that the juices flow into the breasts.

Although not necessary with farm-raised birds, the cook will be similarly rewarded with separate cooking of the breast and leg-thigh pieces. Breast meat benefits from sautéing and grilling; pheasant legs are better suited to braising in stews or using in terrines and pâtés. For a truly aristocratic presentation of pheasant, the two parts can be presented in different courses, or on the same plate with different flavors and garnishing touches.

Just as *coq au vin* evolved in France using an old rooster and slow braising, an older wild pheasant demands a similar approach. On the other hand, a young farm-raised pheasant can be cooked using the same method that would be applied to a young spring chicken.

When roasting whole pheasant, the breasts may need to be barded with bacon strips, pork fat, or salt pork or rubbed with an herbal compound butter or olive oil mixture. This is not always necessary with farm-raised birds, which are bred with a small amount of fat around the breast. Many cooks like to roast pheasant on a bed of vegetables for aromatic and flavor enhancement. Test for doneness by feeling for a loose leg or by piercing the thigh with a fork; the juices should run pink.

M. F. K. Fisher argues for the preparation of pheasant in stews in order to maximize the use of the bird: "A roasted bird, or little beast, while one of the most delicious things to eat that man has invented, emerges from the oven with no accompaniment except its own few unconsumed essences, and more often than not it has shrunk some into the bargain. A stew, on the other hand, seems to make a much bigger meal, because other things are usually cooked with it and have absorbed some of its flavor, and at the same time it is making a generous amount of fine odorous sauce which can be eaten with the meat and also with rice or potatoes or the humble and almighty crust of bread." A soulful concept, indeed!

Classic Dishes

There are many traditions in pheasant cooking. Long prized in European and American kitchens, the delectable bird can be roasted and served with apples and a flamed Calvados sauce; cooked in a soup with barley, cock-a-leekie style; served regally "under glass"; stuffed with wild rice and wild mushrooms; cooked in pot pies; braised in Marsala wine or with juniper berries and gin; served in a casserole with bread and milk; or stewed with herbed dumplings.

Brillat-Savarin details a classic pheasant recipe from the 19th century that involves making a forcemeat of the flesh of woodcock with steamed beef marrow, bacon, salt, pepper, fresh herbs, and fresh truffles. This was stuffed into the cavity of the pheasant while the livers and entrails of the woodcock were ground with truffles, anchovies, bacon, and butter. This paste was then spread over bread and placed underneath the pheasant to collect its juices while the bird was roasting.

Of this dish, Brillat-Savarin commented: "A pheasant thus prepared is worthy of being served to angels themselves, if by chance they still roamed the earth as in the days of Lot . . . thus, of all the delicious things which have been brought together, not a single droplet or crumb escapes attention, and given the excellence of the dish, I believe it worthy of the most august banquet boards."

Classic Recipe

BRAISED PHEASANT IN GIN AND JUNIPER

SERVES 2

Recommended Wine: A crisp Sauvignon Blanc works well with this flavorful, but slightly austere classic.

The combination of gin and juniper berries (from which gin is made) is an ageless culinary tradition. Traditionally the dish is created by reducing white wine, water or chicken stock, onion, celery, carrots, garlic, parsley, garlic, bay, and juniper berries to a flavorful stock. A stuffing is then made with chunks of bread and the magical juniper berry–gin combination. The primary goal of the stuffing is to moisten and flavor the pheasant; it is often discarded after roasting.

Another variation on this theme involves using the gin and juniper berries to make a sauce for roasted pheasant. It is frequently combined with cream for extra richness and texture.

The special affinity that juniper berries have for game is highlighted in this dish. The trick with pheasant is to cook it so that it doesn't dry out. We bard the bird (page 17) to help ensure a moist, juicy product.

1 pheasant (2 to 3 pounds)
Salt and freshly ground black pepper to taste
Thin sheets of pork fat, or 6 to 8 slices bacon
¼ cup vegetable oil
½ cup slivered shallots
½ teaspoon juniper berries, crushed
2 bay leaves
⅔ cup high-quality gin
¼ cup dry sherry
1 cup Basic Game Bird Stock (page 40)
3 tablespoons minced fresh parsley
2 tablespoons butter (optional)

Season pheasant with salt and pepper and truss cavity closed to help maintain shape. Completely wrap bird with pork fat.

In a deep, heavy-bottomed saucepan, sauté bird in oil until golden brown on all sides. Cover and cook slowly for 35 minutes. Uncover, skim off fat, and cook until bird is tender and juices run pink when thigh is pierced with a fork, 10 to 15 minutes more.

Remove pheasant to a serving platter and cover with aluminum foil to keep warm. Skim off excess fat from pan, and add shallots, juniper berries, and bay leaves. Sauté until shallots are soft but not browned. Add gin and sherry and carefully ignite. When flame dies out, add stock and reduce quickly over high heat to a light sauce consistency. Whisk in parsley and butter, if desired.

Remove and discard trussing strings from pheasant. Carve bird into serving pieces. Pour sauce over and serve immediately.

GRILLED PHEASANT WITH APPLE AND SUN-DRIED CHERRY RELISH
Served with Cabbage Salad

SERVES 2

Recommended Wine: The sweet-tart fruit flavors of the relish are complemented by the cherry-tinged fruit of a Pinot Noir or a lively, young Chardonnay.

Pheasant, perfectly cooked on the grill, is a real delight and a nice diversion from the more typical roasting, braising, and sautéing methods. The smoky flavor of a mesquite barbecue lends just the right touch to this warm-weather dish.

The key to success is a gentle marinade, frequent basting, and separate cooking times for the leg-thigh pieces and the breasts. By all means, try to find sun-dried cherries, as they make a wonderful accompaniment; dried currants, however, will work just fine. The red cabbage salad is an extra treat on the plate.

1 pheasant (2 to 3 pounds)

MARINADE
½ cup kirsch, Calvados, or regular brandy
6 juniper berries, crushed
1 teaspoon minced fresh tarragon, or ¼ teaspoon dried tarragon
2 teaspoons fresh lemon juice
¼ teaspoon freshly grated lemon zest
1 tablespoon olive oil
½ teaspoon salt
½ teaspoon freshly ground white pepper

APPLE AND SUN-DRIED CHERRY RELISH
½ cup sun-dried cherries or dried currants
¼ cup brandy
½ cup sliced red onion
¼ cup diced, peeled red apple
1 tablespoon olive oil
1 teaspoon honey
2 teaspoons balsamic vinegar
1 tablespoon unsalted butter or olive oil
Cabbage Salad (recipe follows)

Cut pheasant into breast and leg-thigh pieces. Reserve wings and back for use in stock or soup. To make marinade, whisk together all ingredients. Place pheasant in marinade for 3 to 4 hours at room temperature, or overnight in the refrigerator.

To make relish, soak cherries or currants in kirsch for about 30 minutes to plump them. In a small skillet, sauté onion and apple in oil for 5 minutes. Add cherries and kirsch, honey, and vinegar.

Continue to simmer for 3 to 5 minutes, stirring continuously. Remove from heat and cool to room temperature.

Prepare a fire in a charcoal grill with mesquite charcoal. Remove pheasant from marinade and pat dry. Strain marinade and use for making salad. In a sauté pan, brown pheasant pieces in oil for 2 to 3 minutes per side. Grill pheasant legs, skin side down only, over hot coals for about 5 to 7 minutes per side. Grill breasts, skin side down, for 4 to 5 minutes per side. Meat should be tender and juicy. Cover pheasant with aluminum foil and let rest in a warm place.

To serve, slice breast on the bias and fan slices. Place leg-thigh pieces next to breast and spoon some of the relish on the side. Serve wth Cabbage Salad.

CABBAGE SALAD

SERVES 2

Strained marinade from pheasant
1 tablespoon red wine vinegar
½ pound red cabbage, finely shredded
2 ounces crumbled goat cheese, at room temperature
½ pound bacon, diced and browned

Combine marinade and vinegar. In a small sauté pan, reduce marinade over high heat for 3 to 5 minutes. Add cabbage and sauté for 30 seconds. Remove cabbage from pan, place alongside pheasant, and top with goat cheese and bacon.

GRILLED PHEASANT SALAD WITH CITRUS-APPLE CREAM AND PECANS

SERVES 2

Recommended Wine: This elegant, apple-tinged dish is nicely complemented by a crisp Chardonnay.

For those who tend to think of pheasant as something only to be eaten in the fall, this salad is a good example of the countless opportunities for multiseason delight. Tim Anderson of Goodfellow's in Minneapolis has discovered a subtle combination of fresh ingredients that underscores the pheasant. Anderson's elegant creation uses the breasts only. If working with a whole pheasant, we like to embellish the dish with the leg-thigh pieces as well, although their texture is different.

MARINADE

1 cup apple cider
2 cloves garlic, crushed
¼ cup sugar
¼ cup fresh lemon juice
1 tablespoon kosher salt

2 pheasant breasts, plus leg-thigh pieces, if desired

CITRUS CREAM

1 cup apple cider, or as needed
Juice from 1 lemon
½ cup fresh orange juice
¾ cup sour cream

1 tablespoon vegetable oil
Salt to taste
About ¼ pound mixed salad greens
1 apple, cored and very thinly sliced
1 cup pecan halves, toasted

To make marinade, combine apple cider, garlic, sugar, lemon juice, and salt in a small saucepan and mix thoroughly. Bring to a boil, then remove from heat, cool, and chill. When chilled, pour over pheasant breasts and marinate for 4 hours at room temperature.

To make citrus cream, combine 1 cup apple cider and citrus juices in a saucepan and reduce over high heat until 6 tablespoons remain. Fold the reduced juice into the sour cream. If too thick, thin with a small amount of apple cider.

Prepare a fire in a charcoal grill. Remove pheasant from marinade, reserving marinade, and pat dry with paper towels. Rub pheasant breasts with oil and sprinkle with salt. Grill breasts, skin side down, over hot coals for 5 minutes, basting frequently with marinade. Turn and grill on other side for 3 to 5 minutes. Leg-thigh pieces, if used, will require about 7 to 8 minutes additional cooking time to reach proper doneness; do not overcook.

Divide salad greens between 2 plates. Slice the breasts thinly on the bias. Alternating them, arrange pheasant and apple slices on top of salad in spoke design. Sprinkle with pecan halves and drizzle salad and pheasant meat with citrus cream. If used, serve leg-thigh pieces to the side of the salad.

PHEASANT WITH CHORIZO AND BLUE CORN-BREAD STUFFING

SERVES 4

Recommended Wine: A Fumé Blanc or Sauvignon Blanc with crisp acidity and good fruit will bolster the spicy flavors found in the cornbread stuffing and the natural succulence of the pheasant.

This evolutionary recipe started with talented Texan chef Stephan Pyles and was adapted by Mark Miller for his popular Coyote Cafe in Santa Fe, New Mexico, and then adapted again by us for this book.

We find the combination of spicy chorizo sausage, blue cornbread, and serrano chilies in the stuffing to be a vivid example of the best Southwest cooking has to offer and surprisingly well suited to pheasant's mild flavor. Miller likes to serve this as a holiday dish; we like it almost any time of year.

BLUE CORNBREAD

¼ pound butter, melted
1 cup blue cornmeal
¼ cup whole-wheat flour
¾ cup unbleached white flour
2 teaspoons baking powder
½ teaspoon baking soda
1 egg
¾ teaspoon salt
1½ cups buttermilk

STUFFING

¾ pound chorizo or spicy pork or Italian sausage
2 tablespoons butter
¾ cup chopped yellow onion
¾ cup diced celery
1 tablespoon minced, seeded fresh serrano chili pepper
1 teaspoon minced garlic
4 cups coarsely crumbled corn bread
1 teaspoon chopped fresh thyme, or ½ teaspoon dried thyme
1 teaspoon dried sage
½ cup loosely packed fresh cilantro leaves, chopped
¼ cup half-and-half
1 egg, beaten
Freshly ground black pepper to taste

¼ cup clarified butter, or as needed
2 pheasants (2 to 3 pounds each), at room temperature
6 slices bacon

First, make cornbread. Preheat oven to 425° F. Grease an 8-inch-square pan. In a food processor, combine all ingredients except buttermilk and blend for about 3 seconds. Scrape down sides of the bowl, add buttermilk, and blend for 5 seconds; again scrape down sides of bowl.

Transfer mixture to prepared pan and bake in preheated oven for 30 minutes, or until center is firm and edges draw away from sides of pan. Do not overcook or cornbread will dry out and toughen. Turn onto rack and cool to room temperature. Use right away, or cover fully with plastic wrap to preserve moisture.

To make stuffing, crumble chorizo and place in a skillet. Cook until browned, about 5 minutes. Drain and set aside. Melt butter in the same skillet and add onion, celery, chilies, and garlic. Sauté over medium-high heat for 2 to 3 minutes, then transfer to a large bowl. Crumble enough of the reserved cornbread to measure 4 cups and add to onion mixture. Add reserved chorizo, thyme, sage, and cilantro. Toss well and moisten with half-and-half and egg. Add pepper and mix well.

Preheat oven to 400° F. In a large ovenproof pan or skillet, heat ¼ cup clarified butter over medium-high heat until almost smoking. Quickly sear each pheasant until golden brown, 1 to 2 minutes per side. Remove pheasants from pan and let cool. Fill each pheasant cavity with stuffing and truss cavity closed (page 37), placing 2 bacon slices under the string of each pheasant, crossed, over the breast and one slice across the back, also under the string. Any leftover stuffing can be baked separately or frozen for another use.

Place pheasant on a baking sheet or in an ovenproof pan. Roast until crispy but moist and juices run light pink when thigh is pierced with a fork, 30 to 40 minutes or until thermometer registers 160° F.

To serve, cut each pheasant in half and serve on a bed of cornbread stuffing, or carve breast meat off pheasant and serve with leg-thigh pieces on top of stuffing.

BRAISED PHEASANT WITH POLENTA

SERVES 2 TO 4

This very rustic pheasant dish was created by Lidia Bastianich of New York City's Felidia Restaurant. It has its roots in traditional Italian cooking and can be enjoyed the year around. If desired, the pheasant may be cooked 2 days in advance and reheated just before serving.

POLENTA

4 cups water
2 teaspoons salt
1 tablespoon unsalted butter
1 bay leaf

Recommended Wine: A hearty
Zinfandel will provide rustic emphasis for this delicious dish.

1½ cups polenta or coarse cornmeal

1 pheasant (2 to 3 pounds), cut into 6 serving pieces
Salt and freshly ground black pepper to taste
¼ cup extra-virgin olive oil
1 large yellow onion, chopped
2 slices bacon, chopped
1 teaspoon dried rosemary
4 whole cloves
2 bay leaves
4 teaspoons tomato paste
1 cup dry white wine
2½ cups chicken stock or Basic Game Bird stock (page 40)
5 tablespoons unsalted butter
2 tablespoons freshly grated Parmesan cheese

To make polenta, lightly butter an 8-inch-square baking pan
and set aside. In a large, heavy-bottomed saucepan, combine
water, salt, butter, and bay leaf. Bring to a simmer over moderate
heat. Add the cornmeal, sifting it through the fingers of one
hand, stirring constantly with a wooden spoon. When all cornmeal has been added, reduce heat to moderately low. Cook, stirring frequently, until polenta is thick and smooth and pulls away
from the sides of the saucepan, 8 to 10 minutes. Remove bay
leaf. Pour polenta into the prepared pan and set aside to cool.

Lightly season pheasant pieces with salt and pepper. In a large
skillet, heat oil. Add onion, bacon, rosemary, cloves, and bay
leaves and cook over moderate heat, stirring occasionally until
onion softens, about 5 minutes. Add pheasant pieces and cook,
turning once, until golden, about 5 minutes per side. Drain off
any remaining fat.

Stir in tomato paste until evenly distributed; then stir in wine,
scraping up any browned bits from the bottom of skillet. Add
stock and bring to a boil. Reduce heat to low and simmer, partially
covered, until pheasant is tender, 12 to 15 minutes for breast
pieces. Remove breasts. Transfer to a plate. Keep warm. Continue cooking leg-thigh pieces for an additional 20 to 25 minutes.
With a slotted spoon, transfer leg-thigh pieces to a plate, cover,
and keep warm.

Increase heat to high and boil liquid until reduced to 1 cup,
about 10 minutes. Sauce can be strained through a fine sieve, if
desired, for a more uniform consistency, or served as is for a more
rustic presentation. Season with salt and pepper and return pheasant to sauce.

Turn polenta out of pan and cut into squares measuring about 2 inches. In a large, heavy skillet, melt butter over moderate heat. Add polenta squares. Cook, turning carefully once or twice with a spatula, until polenta is heated through and lightly browned, about 5 minutes. Keep warm on a baking sheet if not serving immediately. There will be enough polenta squares for leftovers, composed salads, or first courses. The squares are particularly good when brushed with a little olive oil and grilled.

Arrange pheasant pieces on individual plates and place one of the polenta squares on the side of each serving. Spoon sauce over pheasant. Sprinkle cheese on top.

PHEASANT WITH BLACK OLIVE SAUCE
Served with Parsnip Purée with Saffron

SERVES 4

Recommended Wine: A robust Zinfandel heartily echoes the intensity of the black olive sauce.

Brian Whitmer, the extraordinarily talented chef at the Pacific Edge restaurant at the Highlands Inn on the Big Sur coastline in Carmel, has created one of the most spectacular game dishes that we can recall. The intensity of the black olives and the Zinfandel sauce is beautifully complemented by the clean, fresh taste of the Parsnip Purée.

1 recipe Basic Liquid Game Marinade (see page 27)
2 pheasants (2 to 3 pounds each), cut into pieces with bones reserved (see page 19)

SAUCE

2 tablespoons olive oil
1 medium onion (skin on), quartered
½ bulb garlic (skin on), cut cross-wise
1 750ml bottle Zinfandel or hearty red wine
6 cups chicken stock or Basic Game Bird Stock (see page 40)
3 ounces pitted black olives (Kalamata preferred)
1 medium tomato, peeled, seeded, and coarsely chopped
Salt and freshly ground black pepper to taste
⅓ cup chopped fresh parsley
2 tablespoons olive oil

Parsnip Purée with Saffron (see page 141)

Prepare marinade, using 2½ cups of the Zinfandel for the red wine. Marinate boned pheasant in the refrigerator for 24 to 48 hours.

To make sauce, crack reserved pheasant bones. In a saucepan over medium heat, bring oil to a gentle simmer. Add pheasant bones and saute for 8 to 10 minutes, until golden brown all over. Add onion and garlic and continue to cook for 6 to 8 minutes. Strain excess oil from pan.

Deglaze pan with wine, stirring with a wooden spoon to loosen food particles. Reduce heat to medium and simmer approximately 15 minutes, until wine evaporates to a thin layer. Add stock, bring to a boil, then lower heat to medium and reduce until it reaches a light sauce consistency, approximately 35 to 40 minutes. Add black olives and tomatoes and simmer sauce vigorously for 4 to 5 minutes to intensify. Season with salt and pepper. Swirl in parsley. Keep warm.

Preheat oven to 400° F. Remove pheasant from marinade and pat dry with paper towels. Season with salt and pepper. In an oven-proof saucepan, sear pheasant skin-side down in 2 tablespoons olive oil until golden brown, about 3 to 4 minutes. Turn and continue cooking on the other side, approximately 4 to 5 minutes. Transfer pheasant, still in pan, to the oven and cook for 8 to 10 minutes. Remove breasts before the leg-thigh pieces, while still springy and juicy, and keep warm. Do not overcook.

To serve, slice breasts on an angle. Place a large dollop of Parsnip Purée in the middle of a warm plate and arrange a sliced breast and leg-thigh piece on either side. Drizzle sauce over pheasant and around plate.

GRILLED BREAST OF PHEASANT WITH TROPICAL FRUIT VINAIGRETTE

SERVES 6

Recommended Wine: A slightly spicy Gewürztraminer accents the tropical flavors of the dish.

The yogurt marinade adds an interesting flavor note to this simple but delicious recipe for pheasant breasts (the leg-thigh pieces should be reserved for another occasion). The combination of tropical fruits and pheasant takes the bird slightly out of its normal context, which is what we like about the dish.

1 recipe Basic Yogurt Marinade (page 27)
3 large half pheasant breasts

VINAIGRETTE

2 tablespoons minced green onion
1 cup diced, peeled mango or papaya
¼ cup raspberry vinegar
¼ cup corn oil or peanut oil
2 tablespoons minced fresh mint
Salt and freshly ground white pepper to taste

2 tablespoons olive oil (for wilting greens)
4 cups young greens, such as spinach, mustard, kale, and arugula
Salt and freshly ground black pepper to taste
Cut-up tropical fruits for garnish
Sautéed slivered wild mushrooms for garnish (optional)

Prepare marinade and marinate pheasant, refrigerated, for 6 hours.

Combine all ingredients for vinaigrette and allow to sit for at least 2 hours for flavors to develop.

Prepare a fire in a charcoal grill. Remove pheasant from marinade and pat dry with paper towels. Grill pheasant over hot coals until just done and juicy, about 4 minutes per side.

Meanwhile, in a large skillet, heat oil and quickly sauté greens until just wilted. Season to taste and divide among individual plates.

Arrange pheasant breasts on top of greens and drizzle vinaigrette over. Garnish with tropical fruits and sautéed wild mushrooms, if desired.

STUFFED PHEASANT WITH ORANGE AND GINGER BUTTER SAUCE

SERVES 8

Recommended Wine: A crisp Chardonnay matches both the texture and the orange- and ginger-tinged flavors of the butter sauce.

Guinea fowl, sometimes called African pheasant, are similar enough in size and taste that they can be used interchangeably with pheasant. This dish was created by Jeff Madura, the very talented young chef at John Ash & Company restaurant in Santa Rosa, California. The pheasant or guinea fowl breasts and leg-thigh pieces are cooked separately and are punctuated by the orange-ginger flavors of the sauce. This is an elegant and thoroughly satisfying presentation.

¼ cup slivered shallots
2 tablespoons minced garlic
2 ounces dried porcini mushrooms, rinsed well, soaked in 2 cups warm water with big pinch sugar for 30 minutes, drained, and julienned
4 tablespoons clarified butter or light olive oil
1 cup chicken stock or Basic Game Bird Stock (page 40)
2 large eggs, beaten
1 tablespoon finely chopped fresh parsley
1 tablespoon finely chopped fresh thyme
1 tablespoon finely chopped fresh chives
½ cup coarsely chopped pecans

½ cup pistachios
½ cup coarsely chopped walnuts
Salt and freshly ground white pepper to taste
4 pheasants or guinea fowl (2 to 3 pounds each)

SAUCE

3 tablespoons minced shallots or green onions
½ cup sliced fresh mushrooms
6 tablespoons unsalted butter
2½ cups chicken stock or Basic Game Bird Stock (page 40)
⅔ cup dry white wine
1 tablespoon fresh lemon juice
2 tablespoons minced fresh ginger
⅔ cup heavy cream
Zest and juice of 2 medium oranges
Salt and freshly ground white pepper to taste

Lightly sautéed fresh wild mushrooms for garnish

In a skillet, sauté shallots, garlic, and mushrooms in butter until lightly colored. Add stock and reduce over medium-high heat until most of the moisture is evaporated. Cool. Stir in eggs, parsley, thyme, chives, pecans, pistachios, and walnuts. Season with salt and pepper.

Remove legs from the pheasant and remove thigh bone out to create a pocket. Season legs lightly with salt and pepper and stuff with a tablespoon of the nut mixture. Fold meat over to enclose stuffing, then wrap in aluminum foil to hold shape. Bake remaining stuffing at 400° F for 25 minutes and reserve for another use.

Remove breast from bone and split in half. Remove skin and any fat. Gently pound breasts between layers of waxed paper to ¼-inch thickness. Season lightly with salt and pepper and roll up a tablespoon or so of the nut mixture inside each breast. Enclose in plastic wrap and carefully tie ends closed to form sausage shape.

Preheat oven to 400° F. To make sauce, in a heavy, 2-quart saucepan, sauté shallots and mushrooms in 1 tablespoon of butter until golden brown. Add stock, wine, lemon juice, and ginger and cook over high heat until reduced by half.

Add cream and reduce again to a light sauce consistency. Strain, add orange zest and juice, and season with salt and pepper. (This sauce will hold for a couple of hours in a warm spot near the stove or in a thermos if made in advance.)

Place legs on rack in a roasting pan and roast in preheated oven for 15 to 18 minutes. While legs are cooking, poach breasts in their plastic wrappers in simmering water for 8 to 10 minutes. Remove plastic and foil wraps and place a breast and leg portion on 8 warm serving plates. Garnish with mushrooms and surround with butter sauce.

PHEASANT SOUP WITH BARLEY AND LEEKS

SERVES 4

Recommended Wine: The hearty flavors of this soup are nicely matched by a robust Zinfandel.

A hearty soup for a cold fall or winter supper always seems like the right ticket. Although pheasant is called for here, other game birds can be used equally well. The key to this recipe is to save the tender breasts and grill or broil them just before adding to the soup.

1 large pheasant (about 3 pounds)
2 tablespoons olive oil
Salt and freshly ground black pepper to taste
¼ pound pancetta or bacon, chopped
3 cups sliced leeks
1 cup finely diced carrot
½ cup slivered celery
1 cup diced, seeded ripe tomatoes
1 cup hearty red wine
5 cups chicken stock or Basic Game Bird Stock (page 40)
2 bay leaves
1 tablespoon minced fresh savory, or 2 teaspoons dried savory
⅔ cup barley
1 tablespoon balsamic vinegar
Chopped fresh basil and/or flat-leaf parsley for garnish
Lightly sautéed fresh wild mushrooms for garnish (optional)

Remove breasts from pheasant. Coat breasts lightly with oil and season with salt and pepper.

In a heavy-bottomed stockpot, sauté bacon until crisp. Remove with a slotted utensil and drain on paper towels. Chop pheasant carcass into 6 pieces, add to stockpot, and brown lightly. Remove and set aside. Add leeks and sauté slowly until they just begin to color. Add carrot and celery and sauté for 3 minutes longer. Add tomatoes, wine, stock, bay leaves, savory, and browned pheasant carcass pieces. Simmer slowly for 30 minutes, skimming any fat that rises to surface. Add barley and simmer for another 30 minutes. Remove pheasant carcass and pull off any meat; discard skin and bones. Return meat to pot.

Prepare a fire in a charcoal grill. Grill breasts, skin side down, until medium-rare, 4 to 5 minutes per side. Meanwhile, reheat soup and season with vinegar, salt, and pepper. Allow breasts to sit for 1 or 2 minutes, then slice thinly. Ladle soup into warm bowls and place sliced breast meat on top. Garnish with reserved pancetta, chopped basil, and wild mushrooms, if used.

QUAIL

One of the smallest and loveliest of the upland game birds, quail have long been a hunter's favorite. In the wild, they can often be sighted migrating in bevies of a hundred or more birds. Many of us have also encountered a covey of quail scurrying along the side of the road or in rolling fields. But the true pleasure of quail, for the cook and the eater, is on the plate, for it is one of the most succulent and sweetest of all game birds.

Favored in many cultures, from the British and Scottish to the varied tables of the Mediterranean and the Orient, quail is prized for its medium-colored flesh and delicate flavor. In fact, culinary lore tells us that at one time quail were offered as hostess presents among housewives, and were held in very high esteem.

One of the more unusual characteristics of wild quail is that they are monogamous, a fact that caused the sixteenth-century physician, Antoine Mizauld, to comment: "Husbands who love their wives, wives who want to be loved by their husbands, have only to take a pair of quails, from which you will extract the two hearts, to wear them on your persons, the husband that of the male, the wife that of the female, and you can count on getting along well together."

Contemporary interest in quail focuses more on their taste than on their promise of marital fidelity. Quail are raised nowadays in many parts of the country, but they are particularly plentiful in California, New Jersey, North and South Carolina, Mississippi, Georgia, and Texas.

There are four basic types of quail, with the *coturnix* from Japan the most popular commercial bird. The native American bobwhite (known for its identifiable whistle) is one of the most cherished. The pharaoh quail is another popular variety that is often available. Much confusion exists because quail are called partridge in the southern part of the United States.

As they are quite tiny, quail are most often savored by nibbling the juicy meat right off the bone. This is a ritual we particularly enjoy when they are served hot off the grill and the smoky flavor permeates the skin and meat to create a sublime sensory treat. In fact, one of our fondest gustatory recollections is of eating bobwhite quail that had been marinated, grilled on a grapevine shoot, and then served whole on the grapevine. The enjoyment of this preparation was like a scene out of *Tom Jones,* with each tender, flavorful morsel providing immeasurable sensual pleasure.

Brillat-Savarin would probably agree, although he had his biases about proper preparation. He wrote, "The quail is of all game . . . the most delicate and the most agreeable. . . . You show your ignorance whenever you serve it otherwise than roasted or *en papillote,* for its savor is extremely volatile and every time the animal is put in contact with liquid, it dissolves, evaporates and perishes."

Brillat-Savarin offered further insight into quail appreciation: "How to eat a small bird? Not many persons know how to eat a small bird: here is the method, as it was privily revealed to me by Chanon Carcot, a born gourmand, who became a perfect gastronome some thirty years before the word was coined. Take a plump birdlet by the beak, sprinkle him with salt, remove the gizzard, thrust him boldly into your mouth, bite him off close to your fingers, and chew manfully; there is plenty of juice to wet the whole organ, and you will taste a delight unknown to the herd."

Shopping for Quail

Quail, one of the most widely available of all game birds, are stocked in many poultry departments. Markets that don't carry them can order them easily, given a few days advance notice. While quail can be found fresh, they are, more often than not, frozen. They vary in size from 4 to 8 ounces, with most running around 5 ounces. Look for well-cleaned birds with glossy skin. Typically, 2 birds are required per person for a main course and 1 bird per person for a salad course.

Cooking and serving whole quail avoids the annoying, time-consuming task of deboning the tiny birds, a task that we find better relegated to the butcher. Some quail are boned mechanically, a process that can sometimes change the flavor of the meat. Therefore, we recommend having the butcher debone them whenever possible. When a recipe in this section calls for boneless quail, it means the backbone and breast bones have been removed, leaving only the bones in the wings and leg-thigh sections.

Cooking Tips

Whether wild or domestic, the firm, light flesh of quail is particularly adaptable to different flavors and a variety of cooking methods. In addition, quail has very little internal fat, thus it is a nutritional meat. It is one of the few game birds where the flavor does not vary substantially between the wild and farm-raised fowl.

Like all other game birds, quail need to be cooked carefully to avoid overcooking, as the flesh can dry out. They are, however, slightly more forgiving than squab and other game birds to overcooking. When plans call for grilling, sautéing, or broiling, quail takes well to marinating for flavor enhancement. Cook skin side down first, then turn once. The birds are done when their juices run pink.

When serving whole quail, urge your guests to eat the legs and thighs as finger food; it is simply too frustrating to try to cut the meat off of birds as small as quail.

Classic Dishes

One of the grand traditions of Europe was serving quail on toast, a practice that involved presenting the whole bird on a big slab of country bread to absorb the tasty cooking juices. A more elegant and courtly preparation was quail in aspic, often served with *foie gras* or truffles.

In the southwest of France, quail are wrapped in oiled grape leaves and grilled over vine cuttings. They are also skewered and grilled over heavy pans filled with country bread that has been rubbed with garlic. The bread is then toasted over hot embers until it is crusty.

The movie *Babette's Feast* also comes to mind. *Cailles en sarcophages*, prepared by the earnest Babette for her reticent guests, were the cornerstone of her sumptuous feast.

Traditional American methods of preparing quail include frying them in oil (probably the most widely prepared version) and serving them with a gravy, marinating them in oil and garlic and grilling, or stuffing them with cornbread, grits, or scrapple.

One of the favored methods of cooking quail is smoking, and they can often be purchased this way. Smoked quail seem literally to explode with flavor, particularly when served in salads with such bitter greens as frisée, mâche, and radicchio and a tart, fruit-based vinaigrette to offset the smoky flavors.

Classic Recipe

ROAST QUAIL WITH PANCETTA AND FRESH HERBS

SERVES 6

Recommended Wine: A crisp Sauvignon Blanc is a superb contrast to this delectable dish.

This easy-to-prepare dish features pancetta, an unsmoked bacon that is cured with pepper and spices. It has a unique flavor and should not be overcooked. In Italy, where it originates, it's sometimes eaten raw like prosciutto, its close cousin. You should be able to find pancetta at any good supermarket delicatessen.

12 quail
6 tablespoons light olive oil
Salt and freshly ground black pepper to taste
16 thin slices pancetta
½ cup thinly sliced shallots, leeks, or green onion
½ cup thinly sliced fresh shiitake, oyster, and/or chanterelle mushrooms
½ cup dry white wine
Sea salt and freshly ground white pepper to taste
½ teaspoon minced fresh thyme leaves
½ teaspoon fresh marjoram leaves
½ teaspoon fresh savory leaves
2 teaspoons chopped fresh chives
2 tablespoons balsamic vinegar
½ cup chicken stock or Basic Game Bird Stock (page 40)

Preheat oven to 400° F. Rub skin of quail with 2 tablespoons of the oil. Tuck wings behind back and lightly season quail inside and out with salt and black pepper. Mince 4 slices of the pancetta and add to sauté pan with 2 tablespoons of the oil. Heat, add shallots and mushrooms, and sauté until very lightly browned. Add wine and cook until liquid evaporates. Season with sea salt and white pepper. Let cool and stir in thyme, marjoram, savory, and chives.

Stuff quail cavities with mushroom mixture and skewer shut if necessary. In a sauté pan, lightly brown quail with remaining 2 tablespoons oil. Place a slice of pancetta on the breast of each quail, and set quail on a rack in a roasting pan.

Roast quail until just done, 6 to 8 minutes. Be careful not to overcook. Remove quail and keep warm on a serving platter. Add vinegar and stock to pan juices and reduce slightly on stove top. Drizzle over quail and serve immediately.

COFFEE-AND-SPICE-RUBBED QUAIL WITH VANILLA-SCENTED SAUCE

SERVES 6

Recommended Wine: This dish works equally well with a barrel-fermented Chardonnay or with a Zinfandel or Cabernet Sauvignon. The secret to the match is the vanilla sauce, which ties the dish to the vanilla-like quality found in wine aged in good French oak barrels. This is a food-and-wine tour de force!

Here is an exotic, dazzling combination of flavors that reminds us of the tropics. The idea for this dish came from a friend who had recently returned from Brazil and couldn't stop talking about the intoxicating aromas of spice and vanilla encountered there. The recipe works well with other delicate-fleshed game birds, such as pheasant, squab, or duck breasts. We think this particular dish is one of the most interesting and unusual in the book, partly because vanilla, often thought of only as a dessert flavoring, is the heart of the butter sauce. The effect is sublime.

1 tablespoon white sesame seed
12 black peppercorns
20 coriander seed
3 whole cloves
2 juniper berries
½-inch-piece cinnamon stick
1 bay leaf
3 tablespoons freshly and finely ground dark roast coffee
1 teaspoon kosher salt
2 teaspoons sugar
12 boneless quail

SAUCE

3 tablespoons unsalted butter
3 tablespoons chopped shallots
½ cup sliced fresh mushrooms
3 cups chicken stock or Basic Game Bird Stock (page 40)
1 cup dry white wine (preferably Chardonnay)
⅔ cup heavy cream
3-inch-piece vanilla bean, split lengthwise, or 2 teaspoons vanilla extract
Fresh lemon juice to taste
Salt and fresh ground white pepper to taste

3 tablespoons light olive oil
Baby greens or spinach leaves wilted in olive oil for garnish

Preheat oven to 300° F. On a baking sheet, arrange the sesame seed, peppercorns, coriander seed, cloves, juniper berries, and cinnamon in separate piles. Toast until sesame seeds are golden colored, about 25 minutes. Using a mortar and pestle or spice grinder, finely grind the toasted spices along with bay leaf. Add coffee, salt, and sugar and continue grinding until well pulverized.

Lightly rub spice mixture over skin of quail. Reserve excess marinade and freeze for another use. Cover and refrigerate for 2 to 3 hours.

To make sauce, heat 2 tablespoons of the butter and sauté the shallots and mushrooms until lightly browned. Add stock and wine and cook over medium-high heat until reduced by half.

Add cream and vanilla bean and reduce over medium-high heat to a light sauce consistency; strain. Remove vanilla bean, and scrape soft center into strained sauce. Whisk in remaining tablespoon of butter. Correct seasoning with drops of lemon juice, salt, and pepper. Hold sauce in a warm-water bath until serving time, up to 2 hours.

In a sauté pan, heat oil and cook quail, in batches if necessary, until medium-rare but still juicy and quite pink, about 2½ minutes per side. If cooking in batches, keep warm until all quail are cooked.

Serve two quail per person in a pool of vanilla-scented sauce. Garnish with wilted baby greens or spinach leaves.

BROILED QUAIL WITH MUSTARD BUTTER SERVED ON FRENCH BREAD

SERVES 4

Recommended Wine: A crisp, young Chardonnay is a perfect companion to this mustard-based dish.

Back in the early seventies, an extraordinary series called Foods of the World was published by Time-Life Books. One of our favorite recipes was included in the volume called *American Cooking: The Eastern Heartland.* This is an adaptation of that wonderful recipe.

½ **pound unsalted butter, melted**
8 **thin rounds French bread**
3 **tablespoons Dijon-style mustard**
2 **teaspoons wild honey**
1 **tablespoon roasted garlic purée (page 31)**
2 **teaspoons fresh lemon juice**
8 **boneless quail**
Salt and freshly ground black pepper to taste
¼ **cup dry white wine**
½ **cup chicken stock or Basic Game Bird Stock (page 40)**
1 **bunch watercress, trimmed, for garnish**

In a skillet, melt 3 tablespoons of the butter and sauté bread rounds on both sides until golden brown. Set aside.

Combine remaining butter, mustard, honey, garlic, and lemon juice and slather over quail. Season quail lightly with salt and pepper. Marinate for 2 hours at room temperature.

Preheat broiler to highest heat. Remove quail from marinade, reserving marinade. Place birds, breast side down, in a broiler pan. Tuck wings behind back and tuck legs into cavity. Broil birds for 3 to 4 minutes. Turn over, paint with marinade mixture, and broil until golden brown but still juicy, 3 to 4 minutes longer. Remove and keep warm.

Add wine, stock, and remaining marinade to pan juices, transfer to stove top, and reduce over high heat to a light sauce consistency, stirring constantly. Taste and adjust seasoning.

To serve, place sautéed bread rounds on warm plates and arrange birds on top. Surround with watercress sprigs. Drizzle reduced pan juices over and serve immediately.

FRIED MARINATED QUAIL WITH PEACH SAUCE
Served with Cinnamon-Scented Couscous and Cabbage with Pancetta

SERVES 2 TO 4

Recommended Wine: The peach flavors of this sauce play nicely off a lush California Chardonnay with a tropical-fruit character.

Fried quail reaches new heights in this recipe. To accomplish this transcendence, we've borrowed unmercifully from two of our culinary heroes. The quail and peach sauce concept and the cabbage and pancetta idea come from Wolfgang Puck of Spago and Chinois fame in Los Angeles; the cinnamony couscous is derived from Anne Rosenzweig, the talented chef of Arcadia in New York. We use succulent bobwhite quail in our preparation, although any type of quail is satisfactory. One quail per person will suffice if the side courses are prepared. Otherwise, plan on 2 quail per person.

MARINADE

2 tablespoons olive oil
3 tablespoons sherry
1 teaspoon chopped fresh thyme, or ¼ teaspoon dried thyme
2 teaspoons chopped fresh ginger
1 tablespoon chopped shallots
2 tablespoons thinly sliced green onions, white part only
Salt and freshly ground white pepper to taste

4 boneless quail
¼ cup cornstarch
½ cup water

SAUCE

1 teaspoon chopped crystallized ginger
2 teaspoons chopped shallots
⅓ cup white wine
¾ cup chicken stock or Basic Game Bird Stock (page 40)

½ teaspoon ground cinnamon
¾ cup fresh or thawed, frozen puréed peaches
Salt and freshly ground black pepper to taste
2 tablespoons butter (optional)

Peanut oil for frying

Combine all ingredients for marinade and marinate quail, refrigerated, for 2 to 4 hours. Remove quail from marinade and pat dry. Mix cornstarch and water in a medium-sized mixing bowl. Dip quail in cornstarch mixture until evenly coated. Set aside on a cake rack.

To make sauce, place ginger, shallots, and wine in a saucepan and reduce over high heat until 1 tablespoon of liquid remains. Add stock and cinnamon and reduce to about ⅓ cup. Add peach purée and simmer for 10 minutes. Season with salt and pepper. Swirl in butter, if desired. Keep warm until ready to serve.

To cook quail, pour oil to a depth of at least 1 inch into a heavy-bottomed frying pan or wok. Heat oil to 350° F. Cook quail, skin side down, for 2 to 3 minutes. Turn and cook until tender but still juicy, 2 to 3 minutes longer. Remove and drain on paper towels.

To serve, divide couscous evenly among serving plates. Place quail on couscous and spoon peach sauce over. Arrange cabbage decoratively on the side.

CINNAMON-SCENTED COUSCOUS

SERVES 2 TO 4

1½ cups chicken stock
1 tablespoon ground cinnamon
1 tablespoon olive oil or butter
1 cup couscous
⅔ cup minced green onions

In a saucepan, bring stock, cinnamon, and oil to a boil. Place couscous in a mixing bowl and pour boiling stock over it. Stir thoroughly and let stand, covered, for 3 to 4 minutes to allow couscous to absorb stock. Stir in onions.

CABBAGE WITH PANCETTA

SERVES 2 TO 4

1 tablespoon olive oil
3 ounces pancetta, diced
2 tablespoons balsamic vinegar
2 tablespoons red wine
½ head cabbage, thinly sliced
Salt and freshly ground black pepper to taste

In a sauté pan, heat oil and sauté pancetta for 2 to 3 minutes. Deglaze pan with vinegar and wine and bring to a boil. Reduce heat and simmer for 2 to 3 minutes. Add cabbage and cook until just wilted, 3 to 4 minutes. Season with salt and pepper.

SAUTÉED QUAIL WITH COUNTRY HAM, BLACK-EYED PEAS, AND RED PEPPERS WITH BASIL VINAIGRETTE

SERVES 2

Recommended Wine: A crisp, fruity Sauvignon Blanc makes a wonderful addition to this bevy of southern flavors and helps emphasize the roasted pepper and herbal components.

This recipe was inspired by Elizabeth Terry, a genteel cook whose restaurant, Elizabeth's on 37th in Savannah, Georgia, reflects a new sensibility toward contemporary southern cuisine. This adaptation relies on keeping the composed salad fresh and crisp-tasting. Terry likes to serve her version of this dish with a garnish of deep-fried julienned turnip greens.

⅓ cup dried black-eyed peas
Salt to taste
1 tablespoon olive oil
¼ pound country ham, diced (preferably dry-cured)
1 red bell pepper, roasted, peeled, seeded, and diced
1 medium tomato, seeded and chopped
1 green onion, thinly sliced
½ teaspoon minced fresh thyme, or ¼ teaspoon dried thyme
4 fresh sage leaves
2 whole quail
Freshly ground black pepper to taste
2 tablespoons butter or olive oil

VINAIGRETTE

2 tablespoons red wine vinegar
¾ teaspoon Dijon-style mustard
¼ cup finely chopped purple (or green) basil
¼ cup olive oil
Salt and freshly ground black pepper to taste

About ¼ pound mixed salad greens, such as arugula, spinach, and/or kale

Place black-eyed peas in a bowl, add water to cover by at least ½ inch, and soak for 6 to 8 hours; drain. Place beans in a saucepan, add water to cover, and salt lightly. Bring to a boil and cook until just tender, 20 to 25 minutes. Do not overcook; drain.

In a sauté pan, heat oil and sauté ham with drained peas for 3 to 5 minutes. Remove from heat and add roasted pepper, tomato, green onion, and thyme; mix thoroughly. Let stand at room temperature.

Place sage leaves under the skin of quail and season birds lightly with salt and pepper. In a nonstick skillet, heat 2 tablespoons oil and sauté quail, skin side down, for 4 to 5 minutes. Turn and sauté until tender but still juicy, about 3 minutes. Set aside.

To make vinaigrette, in a small bowl, whisk together vinegar, mustard, and basil. Slowly drizzle in oil, whisking constantly. Season with salt and pepper.

Divide black-eyed pea mixture between 2 serving plates. Divide mixed greens evenly between plates. Place quail on greens and drizzle everything with vinaigrette.

GRILLED QUAIL SALAD WITH GRILLED PLUMS AND PROSCIUTTO WITH BLACK MUSCAT VINAIGRETTE

SERVES 4 AS A FIRST COURSE, OR 2 AS AN ENTRÉE

Chefs Nancy Oakes and Pamela Student of San Francisco's L'Avenue work magic with game birds of all kinds. This is one of our favorite dishes; the combination of smoky, sweet, and tart flavors is extremely appealing. If plums are difficult to find or not in season, figs can be substituted with equal success. Port or other sweet red wines will work nicely in the vinaigrette if Black Muscat can't be found.

This dish can be prepared as an entrée without the salad, using the vinaigrette as a sauce. It can also be prepared in the oven with whole quail; sauté the plums (or figs), wrap in prosciutto, and place inside the cavity of the quail before roasting. Remove fruit from cavity and use as a garnish.

MARINADE

¼ cup olive oil
2 teaspoons chopped fresh sage, or 1 teaspoon dried sage
¼ teaspoon freshly ground black pepper
¼ teaspoon kosher salt

4 boneless quail

Recommended Wine: The tart-sweet Black Muscat vinaigrette demands a high acid, young Zinfandel or even Pinot Noir to play off this lively component.

VINAIGRETTE

1 cup Black Muscat wine or port
3 teaspoons finely chopped shallots
3 tablespoons red wine vinegar
1 tablespoon balsamic vinegar
½ cup olive oil
Salt and freshly ground black pepper to taste

NUTS

2 cups water
½ cup walnut halves
2 tablespoons olive oil
1 teaspoon sugar
¼ teaspoon kosher salt

4 pitted plums or figs, halved
Olive oil for brushing on fruit
4 thin slices prosciutto
½ pound mixed baby lettuces
3 ounces Roquefort, Gorgonzola, or American blue cheese, crumbled

Combine all ingredients for marinade and marinate quail, refrigerated, for at least 2 hours.

To make vinaigrette, combine wine and shallots in a saucepan and reduce over high heat to a syrup. Remove from heat and add both vinegars. Cool mixture and whisk in oil in a slow, steady stream. Season with salt and pepper. Whisk again prior to serving.

To prepare nuts, preheat oven to 400° F. Bring water to a boil. Add walnuts, remove from heat, and let stand for 5 minutes. Drain and place on a baking sheet. Bake for 10 minutes. Remove from oven. Heat oil in a sauté pan. Add walnuts, sprinkle with sugar and salt, and cook over moderate heat until coated, about 3 minutes. Set aside.

Prepare a fire in a charcoal grill. Wipe excess marinade off quail and grill over hot coals for 4 to 5 minutes. Brush fruit with a little oil. Turn quail, place fruit on grill, and continue cooking until quail is nicely browned and fruit is warmed through, about 3 to 5 minutes. Wrap fruit in prosciutto slices.

Divide lettuces evenly among plates. Top with walnuts, cheese, and wrapped figs. Place quail alongside lettuces and top both with vinaigrette.

WARM QUAIL SALAD YERBA BUENA

SERVES 4 AS A FIRST COURSE, OR 2 AS AN ENTRÉE

Recommended Wine: The refreshing minty-citric quality of this quail salad is underscored by a refreshing Johannisberg Riesling, chilled for warm-weather enjoyment.

Chef Peter DeMarais from San Francisco's Cafe Majestic enjoys adapting old San Francisco recipes as part of his contemporary repertoire. This very appealing warm weather salad is easy to prepare. The refreshing mint essence underscores the flavors. An added bonus is that this dish, which is low in fat and high in vitamins A and C, won top honors at a cancer-prevention recipe contest.

MARINADE

¼ cup sherry wine vinegar
½ medium yellow onion, sliced
4 tablespoons fresh mint sprigs
1 tablespoon cracked white peppercorns
Pinch salt

4 boneless quail

VINAIGRETTE

4 tablespoons chopped fresh mint
1 tablespoon chopped shallots
¼ cup sherry wine vinegar
6 tablespoons pink grapefruit juice
Dash green or white crème de menthe
1 tablespoon honey
¼ cup low-fat plain yogurt
1 tablespoon walnut oil
Salt, freshly ground white pepper, and pinch ground cloves to taste

GARNISHES

1 head limestone lettuce
Few leaves radicchio
1 ruby grapefruit, peeled and sectioned
Fresh mint sprigs
3 or 4 red or golden cherry tomatoes, quartered

Combine all ingredients for marinade and marinate quail, refrigerated, for at least 2 hours.

To make vinaigrette, combine mint, shallots, vinegar, grapefruit juice, crème de menthe, and honey in a small saucepan and place over low heat for 3 to 5 minutes. Remove from heat and let cool. Mix together yogurt and walnut oil in a medium-sized mixing bowl. Whisk mint mixture into oil-yogurt mixture and season with salt, pepper, and cloves.

Prepare a fire in a charcoal grill, preheat oven to 450° F, or preheat broiler. Wipe excess marinade off quail and grill over hot coals 4 to 5 minutes. Turn and continue cooking until nicely browned, 2 to 3 minutes longer. Alternatively, roast in preheated oven for 7 to 9 minutes or place under broiler for 3 to 4 minutes per side.

Divide lettuces evenly on plates. Garnish with grapefruit sections, mint sprigs, and tomato. Top with quail and drizzle with vinaigrette.

MOLASSES-GRILLED QUAIL ON COLD BLACK AND WHITE CHILI

SERVES 12

Recommended Wine: The spiciness and hint of sweetness in this dish require a lighter-style, fruity Gamay Beaujolais or lighter-style Zinfandel to contrast the spicy, sweet elements in the dish.

The vivacious and talented Anne Rosenzweig from Arcadia in New York City assimilates many different cultures into her cooking. Here she creates an extremely tasty dish that features the sweetness of glazed quail with a spicy chili that is served cold—an interesting twist that makes for enjoyable warm-weather eating. This recipe can be halved with success. The quail may be roasted in the oven, instead of grilled.

MARINADE

1 cup fresh orange juice
1 tablespoon chopped fresh ginger
2 tablespoons chopped garlic
3 tablespoons cracked black pepper
¼ cup molasses
1 cup sliced onions
1 cup sliced carrots
¼ cup vegetable oil
Salt and freshly ground black pepper to taste

12 boneless quail

CHILI

1 pound dried black turtle beans
1 pound dried white lima beans
Salt to taste
2 carrots, peeled and chopped
½ medium-sized yellow onion, chopped
1½ cups diced red onion
¼ cup fresh lemon juice or lime juice
1½ cups thinly sliced green onion
1½ cups diced, seeded tomato
1½ cups diced, seeded red bell pepper
½ cup chopped fresh chives
½ cup chopped fresh parsley
6 tablespoons chili powder
2 teaspoons ground cinnamon
½ teaspoon cayenne pepper, or to taste
1 tablespoon ground coriander
Olive oil and red wine vinegar or balsamic vinegar to taste

Chopped fresh parsley or coriander for garnish

Combine all ingredients for marinade and marinate quail, refrigerated, overnight.

To make chili, place turtle beans and lima beans in a large bowl, add water to cover by ½ inch, and soak overnight; drain. In a large, heavy-bottomed saucepan, place beans and cover with lightly salted water by 1 inch. Add carrots and yellow onion and bring to a boil. Cook for 30 to 40 minutes, or until just tender. Do not overcook. Drain beans, place in a large bowl, and cool. Mix in all remaining chili ingredients, adding just enough oil and vinegar for moisture and flavor. The chili can be made 1 to 2 days in advance and refrigerated; bring to room temperature before serving.

Prepare a fire in a charcoal grill. Wipe excess marinade off quail and grill over hot coals for 4 to 5 minutes. Turn and continue cooking until nicely browned, 2 to 3 minutes longer.

Place chili on plate and top with quail. Garnish with parsley.

GRILLED QUAIL WITH WARM GOAT CHEESE AND TOMATILLO-JALAPEÑO CHUTNEY
Served with Marinated Black Beans

SERVES 4 AS A FIRST COURSE,
OR 2 AS AN ENTRÉE

Recommended Wine: A crisp, dry Sauvignon Blanc cuts through the spicy chutney and black beans and mirrors the tart goat cheese.

Stephan Pyles of Dallas's Routh Street Cafe/Baby Routh works wonders with the bounty of Texas game. He creates some fabulous flavor combinations, including this wonderful first course that can also be served as a main course.

CHUTNEY

1 pound tomatillos, husks discarded and quartered
2 small red bell peppers, seeded, deribbed, and thinly sliced
1 small green bell pepper, seeded, deribbed, and thinly sliced
8 green onions, thinly sliced
4 small fresh jalapeño chili peppers, seeded and minced
⅔ cup red wine vinegar
½ cup fresh corn kernels
¼ cup firmly packed light brown sugar
1 tablespoon chopped fresh cilantro
1 teaspoon kosher salt
1 clove garlic, minced
¼ teaspoon cayenne pepper
¼ teaspoon ground cumin

In a large, heavy-bottomed saucepan, bring all ingredients for chutney to a boil, stirring frequently. Reduce heat and boil gently, stirring occasionally until thick, 30 to 35 minutes. Remove from heat and let cool completely. Cover and refrigerate until ready to serve. (The chutney can be prepared 5 days in advance.)

GOAT CHEESE

4 rounds goat cheese (2 ounces each)
2 tablespoons olive oil
¼ cup dry corn bread or regular bread crumbs

4 boneless quail
2 tablespoons olive oil or clarified butter
Salt and freshly ground black pepper to taste
Marinated Black Beans (recipe follows)

To prepare goat cheese, moisten cheese rounds with oil and coat with bread crumbs. Refrigerate for at least 30 minutes. About 15 minutes before serving, preheat oven to 350° F.

Prepare an aromatic fire in a charcoal grill. Brush quail with oil, season with salt and pepper, and grill over hot coals for 4 to 5 minutes. Turn and continue cooking until nicely browned, 2 to 3 minutes longer.

Meanwhile, place cheese on a baking sheet and bake in oven for approximately 3 minutes. To serve, arrange cheese on a plate with grilled quail, a large dollop of chutney, and a portion of black beans.

MARINATED BLACK BEANS

MAKES 1½ CUPS

1 cup cooked black beans
1 small clove garlic, minced
1 fresh serrano chile, seeded and minced
2 teaspoons chopped fresh cilantro
¼ cup diced, peeled, and seeded ripe tomato
2 green onions, white part only, thinly sliced
6 tablespoons herb-flavored vinaigrette
2 tablespoons diced avocado
Salt to taste

In a mixing bowl, combine all ingredients, except salt and avocado, and marinate for 30 minutes or longer. Stir in avocado and season with salt.

ROAST QUAIL STUFFED WITH GREEN ONION CORNBREAD AND PECANS ON A BED OF LENTILS

SERVES 4

Recommended Wine: A medium-bodied Pinot Noir or Zinfandel works beautifully with this delicious fall preparation.

This tradition-bound recipe is the creation of Frank Stitt, whose Highlands Grill in Birmingham, Alabama, excels in contemporary interpretations of southern classics. The stuffing can be used for squab, duck, or goose with equal success, and is ideally suited for the holiday table.

CORNBREAD

3 tablespoons vegetable shortening or bacon drippings
1 cup all-purpose flour
1 tablespoon baking powder
2 teaspoons sugar
1 teaspoon salt
2 cups stone-ground yellow cornmeal
2 cups milk
2 eggs, beaten
⅓ cup chopped green onions

LENTILS

1 tablespoon vegetable oil
1 carrot, finely chopped
½ medium-sized yellow onion, finely chopped
1 stalk celery, trimmed and finely chopped
1 cup lentils
1 sprig fresh thyme
1 bay leaf
Salt to taste
Extra-virgin olive oil and red-wine vinegar to taste

4 quail
Salt and freshly ground black pepper to taste
1 tablespoon butter

STUFFING

Reserved ⅔ cup crumbled corn bread
¼ cup pecans, toasted and chopped
3 tablespoons minced fresh parsley
1 shallot, finely minced
½ clove garlic, finely minced
½ teaspoon chopped fresh thyme, or ¼ teaspoon dried thyme

1 bunch watercress, trimmed
Pecan halves for garnish
Vinaigrette to taste

To make cornbread, preheat oven to 425° F. Grease a heavy 10-inch skillet (preferably cast iron) with shortening. Place skillet in oven while preparing batter.

In a medium-sized bowl, sift together flour, baking powder, sugar, and salt. Mix in cornmeal. Add milk and eggs and stir to blend. Remove skillet from oven, add green onions, and stir until beginning to soften, about 1 minute. Add onions and shortening to batter and stir to blend. Pour batter into skillet. Bake in preheated oven until golden brown and springy to the touch, about 20 minutes. Let cool, then crumble enough to measure ⅔ cup; set aside to use for making stuffing. Reserve remaining corn-bread for another use.

To make lentils, in a medium-sized saucepan, heat oil and sauté carrot, onion, and celery until lightly colored. Add lentils, thyme, and bay leaf. Cover with lightly salted water to cover lentils by 1 inch. Bring to a simmer and cook gently until just tender, about 15 to 20 minutes. Drain and toss with olive oil and vinegar. Season with salt.

Preheat oven 450°F. Season quail with salt and pepper and rub with butter.

To make stuffing, combine all ingredients and mix well. Fill cavity of each quail with stuffing and truss closed, if necessary (page 37). Place quail on rack in roasting pan and roast until nicely browned, about 9 to 10 minutes.

To serve, make a bed of lentils on each serving plate. Place quail on lentils and surround with watercress sprigs. Garnish with pecan halves. Drizzle vinaigrette over watercress to coat lightly.

GRILLED QUAIL WITH SPICY CAPONATA AND MANGO RELISH

SERVES 8

Recommended Wine: A full-flavored Zinfandel or Petite Sirah are needed to balance the intense flavors of the spicy caponata.

Ralph Tingle from California's wine country likes to mingle sweet and spicy flavors. This tongue-tingling creation juxtaposes these two tastes beautifully and perfectly offsets the smoky quail. Other tropical fruits such as papaya, kiwi, or pineapple can be substituted if the short-season mango is not available. The *caponata*, a Mediterranean-inspired eggplant dish, is best when made a day ahead. The dish can be halved or quartered as needed.

MARINADE
1 cup chopped mixed fresh herbs such as basil, oregano, thyme, and/or sage
½ cup olive oil
⅓ cup balsamic vinegar
Freshly ground black pepper to taste

16 boneless quail

RELISH
2 cups diced, peeled ripe mango or papaya (½-inch cubes)
1 small red onion, finely chopped
¼ cup julienned fresh basil
⅓ cup walnut oil
¼ cup rice wine vinegar
Juice of 1 lime
Sea salt and freshly cracked white pepper to taste

CAPONATA

3 medium eggplants, trimmed and cut into ¾-inch cubes
2 tablespoons kosher salt or sea salt
¼ cup extra-virgin olive oil
1 medium-sized yellow onion, chopped
2 stalks celery, trimmed and chopped
2 shallots, finely chopped
4 cloves garlic, finely chopped
4 ripe tomatoes, peeled, seeded, and finely chopped
10 Kalamata or niçoise olives, pitted and coarsely chopped
1½ tablespoons drained capers
4 to 5 anchovy fillets, chopped
1½ teaspoons red-pepper flakes
1 tablespoon chopped fresh oregano
2 tablespoons chopped fresh basil
1 tablespoon balsamic vinegar
Freshly ground black pepper to taste

Combine all ingredients for marinade and marinate quail, refrigerated, 2 to 3 hours or overnight.

To make relish, combine all ingredients and mix thoroughly. Let rest for at least 1 hour before serving. Serve at room temperature.

To make caponata, toss eggplant with salt and spread out cubes on paper towels for 30 minutes; rinse and pat dry.

In a large saucepan, heat oil and sauté onion until translucent. Remove onion with a slotted utensil and set aside. Add eggplant to saucepan and sauté in oil remaining in pan until golden brown, 6 to 8 minutes. Remove eggplant with slotted utensil and set aside.

Add celery, shallots, and garlic to pan and sauté for 2 to 3 minutes. Return reserved onions and eggplant to pan along with all remaining ingredients. Simmer for 10 to 15 minutes, stirring occasionally. Adjust seasonings. (This can be served warm or at room temperature.)

Prepare a fire in a charcoal grill. Wipe excess marinade off quail and grill quail, skin side down, over hot coals for 4 to 5 minutes. Turn and continue cooking until nicely browned, 2 to 3 minutes.

Serve quail on bed of caponata with mango relish on side.

GRILLED QUAIL WITH JICAMA-ORANGE RELISH

SERVES 2

Recommended Wine: A Chardonnay or off-dry Chenin Blanc or Semillon poses enough acidity to complement the zesty relish.

Anyone who reads this whole book will notice the name Stephan Pyles mentioned frequently. His interest and ability with game cooking is legendary, and we enjoy cooking his recipes immensely. In this dish, grilled quail is counterpointed by a lively citrus-based relish. Pyles likes to serve this dish with Sweet Potato Pancakes (page 245). The extra pancakes may be frozen.

RELISH

½ pound jicama, peeled and cut into ¼-inch dice
½ small ripe mango or papaya, peeled and cut into ¼-inch dice
1 large navel orange, peeled, sectioned, and cut into ¼-inch dice
3 tablespoons fresh orange juice
2 tablespoons finely diced, peeled, and seeded cucumber
1 tablespoon finely diced red bell pepper
1 tablespoon finely diced yellow bell pepper
1 tablespoon chopped yellow onion
½ fresh serrano chili pepper, seeded and minced
1 teaspoon chopped fresh mint
2 tablespoons fresh lime juice
Salt to taste

4 boneless quail
1 tablespoon vegetable oil
Salt and freshly ground black pepper to taste

Fresh mint sprigs for garnish

To make relish, in a medium nonreactive bowl, combine all ingredients. Toss well, taste, and adjust seasonings. Cover and let rest for 1 hour at cool room temperature or for up to 4 hours in the refrigerator before serving.

Prepare a fire in charcoal grill or preheat broiler. Brush quail with oil and season with salt and pepper. Grill quail, skin side down, 4 to 5 minutes. Turn and continue cooking until nicely browned, 2 to 3 minutes. Alternatively, place skin side up on a baking sheet and broil until crisp on outside but pink inside, 3 to 4 minutes. Turn and continue broiling for 2 to 3 minutes.

Place a dollop of relish on plates and top with quail. Save remaining relish for another use. Garnish with mint sprigs.

QUAIL PIE

SERVES 6

Recommended Wine: A lush Merlot would be the ideal accompaniment for this delicious pie.

This dish evolved from the children's rhyme "birds baked in a pie." It's very much in the tradition of English meat pies, but we've used filo dough for the crust to lighten it.

12 quail
¼ cup olive oil
2 cups sliced yellow onion
1 cup finely diced carrot
1 cup thinly sliced celery
½ cup thinly sliced fennel bulb
3 cups chicken stock or Basic Game Bird Stock (page 40)
¼ cup thick tomato purée
1 cup hearty red wine
3 tablespoons red wine vinegar
1 teaspoon juniper berries, crushed
2 cups quartered fresh shiitake or other flavorful mushrooms
½ cup clarified butter
Salt and freshly ground black pepper to taste
1 cup golden raisins
6 sheets filo dough (see Note)

Remove breasts from quail and reserve. Split the carcasses and brown in oil in a heavy-bottomed saucepan. Remove carcasses with a slotted spoon and add onion, carrot, celery, and fennel. Sauté until lightly colored. Return carcasses to pan and add stock, tomato purée, wine, vinegar, and juniper berries. Cover and simmer until meat is very tender, 15 to 20 minutes.

Remove quail carcasses and pick off all meat. Set meat aside. Discard bones and skin. Skim off fat from onion mixture and reduce over moderate heat to a "marmalade" consistency, or until most of the liquid has evaporated.

While mixture is reducing, sauté mushrooms in 2 tablespoons of the clarified butter until golden brown. Season with salt and pepper. When onion mixture has reduced, add mushrooms. Stir in reserved quail meat and raisins and adjust seasoning.

Preheat oven to 375° F. Melt remaining clarified butter. Lightly butter a 6-cup soufflé dish with melted butter. Lay 1 sheet of filo over the bottom and sides of the dish and lightly paint with butter. Continue layering filo, brushing each sheet with butter, so that the bottom and sides of dish are completely covered. The excess should hang over the sides of the dish. Fill bottom of dish with the quail-onion mixture.

Slice reserved breasts in half lengthwise and arrange evenly on top of mixture. Gently press breast pieces down into mixture.

Carefully fold filo over top, painting each layer with a little butter. Place in preheated oven and bake until filo is crisp and brown, about 30 minutes. Remove from oven and allow to sit for 10 minutes.

To serve, cut into wedges and serve warm or at room temperature.

NOTE: Filo pastry dries out quickly, making it difficult to work with. Keep the filo sheets covered with plastic wrap until you are ready to use them.

RABBIT AND HARE

*R*abbit, for all the mythology and fantasy that it conjures up, is one of the most widely available of all game animals, and is prized by a wide variety of cultures for its versatile culinary nature. Whether marinated in red wine, herbs, and soy and grilled over mesquite, or braised in a pot with onions, fresh vegetables, and olives, mild-flavored rabbit meat adapts beautifully to different cooking treatments and flavorings.

Wild hare, which is known to America as the jackrabbit or snowshoe rabbit, is fancied by avid sportsmen, but it requires significantly different cooking treatment than its domestic cousin. Younger hares take well to marinating and roasting rare; older ones need to be braised or stewed. Many hare devotees like to lard hare with strips of pork fat seasoned with herbs and Cognac. The rich dark meat, when prepared properly, is extremely flavorful with a slightly earthy taste.

As an alternative to chicken, to which it is often compared, rabbit offers a lean, slightly sweet meat with a closely textured flesh that has virtually no fat and is very high in protein. In short, rabbit is the ultimate health food meat, offering perhaps the fewest calories per pound of any meat available. An added benefit is that rabbits are commonly raised without the use of hormones or steroids to promote growth.

Interestingly, rabbit is one of the most controversial game animals. Some people adhere to a strongly protective attitude toward the lovely little creatures, prompted in part by images of spunky Bugs Bunny, delightful Peter Cottontail, frisky Thumper, and the benevolent Easter bunny. To those people, we offer both our sincere understanding and our sympathy, since they will not experience this versatile culinary treasure.

Shopping for Rabbit

Domestic rabbits are bred extensively in America today, and they can be readily found in poultry sections of better markets around the country. If not immediately available, most stores can easily order rabbit with some advance notice. Smaller fryers, which weigh up to 3 pounds, and slightly larger roasters or stewers, which weigh between 4 and 6 pounds, are the two principal sizes available. Some specialty suppliers also provide loins, legs, and saddle cuts only.

Wild hare, unfortunately, is quite difficult to find. Specialty game supplies sometimes provide wild blue hare—whole, in saddle cuts, and in fillets. Prices are considerably more expensive than rabbit due to market scarcity.

Cooking Tips

When handling uncooked *wild* rabbits or hares, gloves should always be worn because of the potential danger of tularemia infection, an uncommon disease that is nevertheless well worth being cautious about. Cooking wild rabbits kills these bacteria. This is not a problem with domestic rabbits.

Using a sharp, small knife or poultry shears, remove all organs from the cavity of the rabbit, reserving the liver and kidneys for use in pâtés, terrines, or salads. Trim all fat from the cavity, legs, and backbone, and cut into pieces (see drawing on page 22). Reserve carcass for use in stocks. Some cooks find the forelegs of the rabbit too small for cooking and use them instead for making stocks. Remove any small protruding bones from the remaining parts of the rabbit and rinse rabbit thoroughly with water.

Like other types of game, cooking rabbit involves a few special tricks that virtually guarantee moist, flavorful meat instead of the stringy, dry meat that some people have experienced. Rabbit loin is best suited to either fast grilling or sautéing; the legs and thighs are better handled with long simmering (braising) in liquid. The best compromise is to braise the two together, although we certainly don't want to discourage grilling or sautéing as suitable, even wonderful methods of cooking rabbit.

Many knowing rabbit connoisseurs and hunters prize simple fried rabbit. Frying can easily dry out the meat, however, so care must be taken. Rabbit on the grill is a supremely fine taste, preferably after it has been marinated; the marinade can then serve as the basting liquid to keep the meat moist. Any of these methods produce extraordinary satisfaction; the choice depends on your taste, and perhaps the season of the year and where you wish to do your cooking.

Classic Dishes

Probably the best known of all rabbit dishes is the German classic called *hasenpfeffer*, in which the rabbit is first marinated in vinegar, herbs, and spices, then browned, and finally braised in its marinade. There are innumerable variations on *hasenpfeffer*, but all feature vinegar prominently.

The Spanish are very fond of rabbit as well. Rabbit in almond sauce with copious amounts of garlic is quite common in Spanish cooking. The nutty almond flavor complements rabbit well.

Finally, rabbit with paprika is a classic combination that has evolved in many Eastern European cuisines. The bright flavor of paprika, in combination with sour cream, is a perfect foil for the succulent meat of rabbit.

Classic Recipe

BRAISED RABBIT WITH APPLES AND BACON

SERVES 4

Recommended Wine: The apple-tinged flavors of this dish match nicely with a well balanced Chardonnay.

Frank Stitt of the Highlands Grill in Birmingham, Alabama, loves to cook rabbit. He ensures quality by buying them at a nearby farm where they are raised. While you may not have this option, the fresher the rabbit you can buy, the better. The long braising in wine develops rich flavors.

MARINADE

2 large carrots, peeled and sliced
1 large yellow onion, sliced
2 shallots, sliced
2 cloves garlic, sliced
5 black peppercorns, crushed
4 juniper berries, crushed
1 sprig fresh thyme, or ¼ teaspoon dried thyme
1 sprig fresh basil, or ¼ teaspoon dried basil
1 cup dry white wine
2 tablespoons olive oil

2 rabbits, cut into serving pieces (page 22)
¼ pound bacon, finely diced
Flour for dredging
2 tablespoons olive oil
¼ cup Calvados or other apple brandy
1 cup chicken stock or Basic Game Bird Stock (page 40)
½ cup cream
Salt and freshly ground black pepper to taste

2 Granny Smith or other tart green apples, peeled, cored, and cut into ½-inch wedges
2 tablespoons unsalted butter
Chopped fresh parsley or basil for garnish

To make marinade, in a large bowl combine all ingredients for marinade. Add rabbit pieces and marinate, refrigerated, overnight.

Preheat oven to 325° F. In a large ovenproof skillet, cook bacon over moderate heat until crisp, about 10 minutes. With a slotted utensil, transfer bacon to paper towels to drain. Set aside. Reserve fat in skillet.

Remove rabbit pieces from marinade, reserving marinade, and pat dry with paper towels. Strain marinade; reserve liquid and vegetables separately. Dredge rabbit pieces in flour, shaking off excess. Add oil to skillet with bacon fat and heat over medium-high heat. Add rabbit pieces and cook, turning once, until golden brown, about 4 minutes per side. Add Calvados, heat for a moment, and then carefully ignite. When the flames die out, transfer the rabbit to a plate.

Add reserved marinade vegetables to skillet and cook over moderate heat, stirring occasionally, until softened, about 10 minutes. Add reserved marinade liquid and stock and bring to a simmer. Return rabbit to skillet, cover, and simmer gently until rabbit is tender, about 40 minutes.

Transfer rabbit pieces to a serving platter and keep warm. Skim off fat from surface of liquid remaining in skillet, then boil over high heat until reduced by half, about 5 minutes. Add cream and any juices from rabbit that have collected on platter. Simmer until sauce thickens slightly. Season with salt and pepper.

While sauce is cooking, in another large sauté pan, sauté apple wedges in butter until lightly browned. Keep warm.

To serve, place rabbit on warm plates, spoon sauce over, and garnish with apple slices, bacon, and parsley.

FETTUCINE WITH BRAISED RABBIT, SUN-DRIED TOMATOES, AND HERBS

SERVES 4

Recommended Wine: A young Zinfandel adds robust character to this hearty Italian-style dish.

In this recipe, we braise the rabbit slowly until the meat literally falls off the bones. We then add enough stock to make a sauce for fresh pasta. This approach works equally well with such game birds as wild turkey and guinea fowl, especially if you happen to get a more "mature" bird. Good-quality (preferably fresh) pasta is a must!

1 large rabbit, cut into quarters (page 22)
Salt and freshly ground black pepper to taste
⅓ cup olive oil
½ pound fresh chanterelle or shiitake mushrooms, stemmed and sliced
1 cup sliced yellow onion
3 tablespoons slivered garlic
½ cup diced, peeled carrots
½ cup thinly sliced celery
¼ cup sun-dried tomatoes in oil, drained
2 cups hearty red wine
2 cups diced, seeded ripe tomatoes
1 teaspoon minced fresh thyme or ½ teaspoon dried thyme
1 teaspoon minced fresh sage or ½ teaspoon dried sage
4 cups chicken stock or Basic Game Bird Stock (page 40)
⅓ cup chopped fresh parsley (preferably flat-leaf)
¼ cup chopped, fresh basil, or 1 tablespoon chopped fresh mint
1 pound fresh fettuccine or ½ pound dried fettuccine
Fresh basil or mint sprigs and small wedge Asiago or Parmesan cheese for garnish

Season rabbit pieces liberally with salt and pepper. In a large, heavy-bottomed saucepan, heat oil and quickly brown rabbit. Remove and set aside. Add mushrooms, onion, garlic, carrots, and celery, in batches if necessary, and sauté until very lightly browned.

Return rabbit to pan and add sun-dried tomatoes, wine, to-matoes, thyme, sage, and stock and bring to a simmer. Cover and simmer until rabbit is tender and begins to pull away from the bones easily, 45 to 50 minutes. Remove rabbit, separate meat from bones, discard bones, and cut meat into bite-sized pieces. Add meat back to pan with the vegetables and warm through. Taste and adjust seasonings. Strain and reserve the vegetables. Return the strained sauce to the pot and reduce over high heat for approximately 10 minutes. Stir in parsley and basil just before serving.

Meanwhile, bring a large pot of water to a boil, add salt to taste and pasta. Cook pasta until just tender, drain, and toss with rabbit sauce. Garnish with basil sprigs. With a vegetable peeler or sharp knife, shave thin pieces of cheese over the top.

BRAISED SWEET AND SOUR RABBIT

SERVES 4

Recommended Wine: A rich California Cabernet Sauvignon or Petite Sirah with its chocolatey overtones complements the complex flavors of this dish.

This rustic, flavorful stew is good hot or at room temperature on a warm summer day. As with all stews, it seems to taste better the next day, after the flavors have married. The dish is particularly good with the optional chocolate and candied orange peel.

MARINADE

2 cups hearty red wine
½ cup chopped yellow onion
½ cup chopped carrot
2 whole cloves
2 sprigs fresh parsley
1 bay leaf
1 teaspoon minced fresh thyme, or ½ teaspoon dried thyme
6 black peppercorns
½ teaspoon salt

1 rabbit, cut into serving pieces (page 22)

4 tablespoons olive oil
3 ounces salt pork, diced (optional)
1½ cups sliced yellow onion
1 tablespoon flour
1 cup chicken stock or Basic Game Bird Stock (page 40)
2 tablespoons sugar
½ cup red wine vinegar
⅓ cup golden raisins
1 tablespoon grated unsweetened chocolate (optional)
1 tablespoon candied orange peel (optional)
Salt and freshly ground black pepper to taste
¼ cup pine nuts, lightly toasted

Combine all ingredients for marinade in a saucepan and bring to a boil. Remove from heat, let cool, and pour over rabbit. Marinate for 2 to 3 hours at room temperature.

In a large ovenproof saucepan, heat together 2 tablespoons of the oil and salt pork, if used. Add onion and sauté until very lightly browned. With a slotted utensil, remove onion from pan and set aside.

Remove rabbit from marinade, reserving marinade. Pat rabbit dry with paper towels and lightly dust with flour. Brown in oil remaining in saucepan. Return onions to pan and then strain marinade liquid over rabbit. Bring to a boil, reduce heat, and simmer, uncovered, for 20 minutes. Liquid will have mostly evaporated. Add enough stock to cover rabbit barely. Cover pan and simmer slowly until rabbit is tender, about 20 minutes.

While rabbit is cooking, combine sugar and vinegar in a small saucepan and place over moderate-high heat until sugar has dissolved. Add raisins and chocolate and orange peel, if used, and cook for 1 minute. Remove from heat and set aside.

When rabbit is done, remove from pan to a serving platter and keep warm. Reduce liquid in pot to a light sauce consistency. Add raisin mixture and cook momentarily, whisking to make a smooth sauce. Season with salt and pepper. Pour over rabbit and top with pine nuts.

BRAISED RABBIT WITH PRUNES

SERVES 2 TO 3

Recommended Wine: A sturdy Cabernet Sauvignon will stand up to the hearty texture of the stew. If the sauce is finished with white wine and cream, a rich Chardonnay works wonders.

The combination of sweet prunes and rabbit in this classic dish is divine. The dish can be enriched by adding 1 cup heavy cream or crème fraîche and 2 tablespoons Dijon-style mustard to the sauce with the fruit preserves. If finishing with cream, use a dry white wine instead of a red wine. The dish goes particularly well with polenta (page 156).

2 cups Basic Liquid Game Marinade (page 27)
1 rabbit, with liver and giblets, cut into serving pieces (page 22)

2 tablespoons oil
¼ pound bacon
1 cup pearl onions
½ pound fresh small button mushrooms
Salt and freshly ground white pepper to taste
¾ pound pitted dried prunes
1 tablespoon flour
2 tablespoons raspberry vinegar
2 tablespoons red currant preserves or apple preserves (optional)

Prepare marinade and marinate rabbit, refrigerated, 4 to 6 hours or overnight.

In a heavy-bottomed saucepan, heat oil and sauté bacon, pearl onions, and mushrooms until lightly browned. Remove and set aside.

Remove rabbit from marinade, reserving marinade. Pat rabbit dry with paper towels. Season rabbit pieces with salt and pepper and sauté in oil remaining in pan until lightly browned. Remove rabbit from pan and set aside. Stir flour into oil remaining in pan and cook slowly for 3 to 4 minutes. Strain marinade into the pan. Return bacon and rabbit to pan and bring to a boil. Reduce heat, cover, and simmer for 25 minutes. Add pearl onions, mushrooms, and prunes and simmer until rabbit is tender, about 20 minutes. Season with salt and pepper.

Remove rabbit, vegetables, and prunes to a deep serving dish and keep warm. Chop reserved liver and other giblets finely and add to sauce along with vinegar and preserves. Reduce over medium heat to a light sauce consistency. Pour sauce over rabbit and serve immediately.

DEVILED RABBIT SAUTÉ

SERVES 4

Recommended Wine: A rich, oaky Chardonnay with a buttery texture highlights the creamy mustard sauce beautifully.

Mustard has a special affinity for game, we think, and this recipe showcases the interaction admirably. When Dijon-style mustard is used in cooking, it loses a lot of its "sharp" character and mellows into a luscious, rich flavor. The "deviled" reference in this case refers to the mustard-chili components in the dish. Serve with baby vegetables and sautéed spinach.

1½ cups Basic Liquid Game Marinade (page 27)
1 rabbit, cut into serving pieces (page 22)
¼ cup clarified butter or vegetable oil

MUSTARD COATING
¼ cup olive oil
2 tablespoons chopped shallots or green onion
1 tablespoon chopped garlic
1 tablespoon brown sugar
⅔ cup Dijon-style mustard

½ cup fresh white bread crumbs, tossed with olive oil to coat lightly

MUSTARD CREAM SAUCE

3 tablespoons unsalted butter
2 tablespoons minced shallots
1 cup chicken stock or Basic Game Bird Stock (page 40)
⅓ cup dry white wine
2 tablespoons Dijon-style mustard
½ cup heavy cream
2 teaspoons yellow mustard seed, lightly toasted
Drops of fresh lemon juice
Salt and freshly ground white pepper to taste

Lightly steamed baby vegetables and sautéed spinach or baby Swiss chard for garnish

Prepare marinade and marinate rabbit, refrigerated, for 24 to 36 hours.

Remove rabbit from marinade and pat dry with paper towels. In a large skillet, melt clarified butter and sauté rabbit over moderate heat until evenly browned. Remove from heat and let cool.

Preheat oven to 400° F. In a food processor or blender, combine all coating ingredients and blend until smooth. Spread mustard coating evenly over browned rabbit. Sprinkle lightly with bread crumbs and place in preheated oven for 10 minutes. Remove loin pieces, turn oven down to 350° F, and continue cooking until leg-thigh pieces are tender and coating is browned, 8 to 10 minutes longer.

To make sauce, in a small saucepan, heat 1 tablespoon of the butter and sauté shallots until soft, not brown. Add stock, wine, and mustard and reduce over medium-high heat by half. Add cream and reduce to a light sauce consistency. Cut remaining 2 tablespoons butter into bits and whisk into sauce along with mustard seed. Season with lemon juice, salt, and pepper. Keep warm until ready to serve.

To serve, spoon a pool of mustard sauce on each warm serving plate and arrange rabbit pieces on top. Garnish with steamed baby vegetables and sautéed spinach.

BRAISED RABBIT WITH WILD MUSHROOMS AND SOFT POLENTA WITH GORGONZOLA CHEESE

SERVES 2 TO 3

Recommended Wine: Cabernet Sauvignon will mirror its use in the preparation of the sauce and will bolster the hearty quality of the dish.

Charles Saunders, our old friend and the former chef at Sonoma Mission Inn in Northern California, created this wonderful dish. Saunders spent a number of years in Italy and this recipe, with its soulful flavors, shows that influence. The polenta and Gorgonzola are perfect companions for this comfort dish.

6 rabbit hind legs (reserve loins for another use)
Salt and freshly ground black pepper to taste
Flour for dredging
2 tablespoons olive oil

SAUCE

1 cup roughly chopped yellow onion
½ cup roughly chopped carrot
½ cup roughly chopped celery
2 tablespoons olive oil
6 cloves garlic
½ cup roughly chopped, seeded tomato
2 tablespoons chopped fresh rosemary, or 1 teaspoon dried rosemary
1 tablespoon chopped fresh thyme, or ½ tablespoon dried thyme
2 cups Cabernet Sauvignon
4 cups chicken stock or Basic Game Bird Stock (page 40)
Salt and freshly ground black pepper to taste
¼ recipe polenta (page 156)

MUSHROOMS

1 tablespoon olive oil
1½ cups mixed fresh wild mushrooms (shiitake, oyster, and morel), sliced
1 tablespoon dried porcini, soaked in warm water for 30 minutes, drained, and chopped
½ teaspoon finely chopped garlic
1 cup reserved rabbit sauce
½ cup chopped, seeded tomato
1 teaspoon chopped fresh basil, or ½ teaspoon dried basil
¼ cup extra-virgin olive oil

6 ounces Gorgonzola, cut into 6 cubes
Fresh basil leaves for garnish

Preheat oven to 300° F. Season rabbit legs with salt and pepper and dredge in flour. In an ovenproof saucepan over medium heat, sear rabbit legs in oil. Remove rabbit and set aside.

To make sauce, place onion, carrot, and celery in same pan. Sauté in 2 tablespoons oil until vegetables are caramelized. Add garlic, tomato, rosemary, and thyme. Deglaze with wine and reduce over high heat by one third.

Return rabbit to pan and add stock; season with salt and pepper. Cover and place in preheated oven until tender, about 1 hour. Remove rabbit and reduce liquid over high heat to a light sauce consistency. Strain sauce and reserve. Measure 1 cup for adding to mushrooms; set aside.

To prepare mushrooms, in a sauté pan, heat oil over moderate heat. Add fresh and dried mushrooms and garlic and sauté for 2 minutes. Add reserved rabbit sauce, tomato, and basil. Stir in olive oil. Set aside.

Preheat broiler. Meanwhile, prepare polenta according to instructions in recipe, but do not pour into pan to cool. Keep warm. Place a serving of polenta on each of 6 flameproof serving plates and make a well in center. Fill with sautéed mushrooms. Place a cube of Gorgonzola atop each serving of polenta and mushrooms and warm under broiler. Remove plates from broiler and arrange a rabbit leg on each plate. Spoon reserved sauce over each leg. Garnish with basil leaves.

GRILLED RABBIT WITH PEANUT-CHILI SAUCE
Served with Spaghetti Squash

SERVES 2

The smoky flavors of the grilled rabbit combine perfectly with the spicy peanut-chili dipping sauce. The dish seems to convert even the most skeptical to the wonderful world of rabbit. To be truly savored, you should pick up the rabbit pieces, dip them in the sauce, and eat them with your fingers. Messy and delicious!

MARINADE

¼ cup peanut or olive oil
⅓ cup soy sauce
⅓ cup dry sherry
⅓ cup chopped yellow onion
¾ teaspoon dry mustard
1 teaspoon chopped fresh tarragon, or ½ teaspoon dried tarragon
1 teaspoon slivered garlic

1 rabbit, cut into serving pieces (page 22)

Recommended Wine: A crisp Sauvignon Blanc with a fresh, fruity character is an excellent counterpoint to this lively dish, while a youthful, spicy Zinfandel matches its spicy flavors.

PEANUT-CHILI SAUCE

⅓ cup dry sherry
¼ cup half-and-half or heavy cream
3 tablespoons creamy peanut butter
3 to 4 tablespoons bottled chili sauce or chili salsa
1½ teaspoons fresh lime juice
Salt and freshly ground black pepper to taste

Spaghetti Squash (recipe follows)

Combine all ingredients for marinade and marinate rabbit, refrigerated, for 4 to 6 hours or overnight.

Prepare a fire in a charcoal grill. Remove rabbit from marinade and pat dry with paper towels. Grill over hot coals, turning once and basting frequently with the marinade, 8 to 10 minutes. Check the loin pieces for doneness. Remove and keep warm. Baste the legs again and continue cooking until done, about 5 to 7 minutes longer. Leg meat should remain moist and just pull away from the bone.

To make sauce, combine sherry, cream, and peanut butter in a small, heavy saucepan and bring to a gentle simmer. Add chili sauce and lime juice and continue simmering, stirring frequently, until sauce thickens, 8 to 10 minutes. Season with salt and pepper.

Divide squash between serving plates. Place rabbit on top of squash and serve sauce on the side for dipping.

SPAGHETTI SQUASH

MAKES 2 CUPS

1 to 1½ pounds spaghetti squash
2 tablespoons butter
2 tablespoons honey
½ teaspoon freshly grated nutmeg
Salt and freshly ground black pepper to taste

Preheat oven to 350° F. Cut spaghetti squash in half lengthwise and scoop out seeds. Butter cavities of squash and season with honey, nutmeg, salt, and pepper. Place on a baking sheet and cover squash lightly with foil. Bake in preheated oven until meat of squash is just cooked through, 45 to 50 minutes. Remove from oven and lift out flesh with a fork. It will resemble long strands of spaghetti. (This squash can be baked in advance and reheated quickly with a little butter or oil.)

RABBIT STEW WITH OLIVES AND FENNEL

SERVES 4

Recommended Wine: The robust flavors of this dish require a big Zinfandel or Petite Sirah to cut through the layers of spicy, olive-tinged flavors.

Kelly Mills, the talented chef of the Four Seasons Clift Hotel in San Francisco, inspired this dish. Mills is known for his healthful approach to cooking, and this dish exemplifies his style well. We've changed the wine from white to red and added olives, capers, and additional herbs and spices to Mills's original concept. The rabbit meat falls off the bone when cooked in this manner, and the dish absolutely bursts with hearty flavors. Chunks of French bread and orzo pasta lightly tossed with olive oil are nice accompaniments.

3 tablespoons olive oil
2 rabbits, cut into serving pieces (page 22)
1 cup sliced sweet or red onion
¾ cup sliced fennel (about 2 bulbs)
4 cloves garlic, minced
½ cup red wine
3 tablespoons tomato paste
½ cup chicken stock or Basic Game Bird Stock (page 40), or more as needed
2 jars (9 ounces each) green olives (preferably Spanish), pitted and sliced
1 cup Kalamata or niçoise olives, pitted and sliced
1½ teaspoons drained capers
1 cup diced, seeded tomato
1 teaspoon chopped fresh oregano, or ½ teaspoon dried oregano
1 teaspoon chopped fresh thyme, or ½ teaspoon dried thyme
1 teaspoon paprika
2 tablespoons chopped fresh parsley
Salt and fresh ground black pepper to taste

Preheat oven to 350° F. In a large, heavy-bottomed, oven-proof saucepan, heat olive oil and brown rabbit pieces. Remove rabbit and set aside. Add onion, fennel, and garlic, and cook until onion is translucent; be careful not to burn garlic. Add wine and tomato paste and boil until wine is reduced by half. Return rabbit to pan and add ½ cup stock, olives, capers, tomato, oregano, thyme, and paprika. Cover and bake in preheated oven for 1½ hours. If liquid reduces too much, add more stock.

Remove pan from oven and lift out rabbit pieces. Let cool, then pull meat off bones and dice into smaller chunks, if necessary. Return meat to pan and stir in parsley. Season with salt and pepper. Reheat before serving. (This dish can be made 2 days in advance, refrigerated, and then reheated just before serving.)

Spoon stew onto plates and serve very hot.

CAJUN-STYLE RABBIT TERRINE
Served with Apple-Ginger Chutney

MAKES ONE 3-POUND TERRINE
SERVES 10 TO 12

Recommended Wine: The rich, slightly fatty texture of the rabbit terrine requires a lighter-style Gewürztraminer or Johannisberg Riesling with a hint of sweetness as contrast.

Chef John Folse of Lafitte's Landing in the bayou country of Louisiana is extremely proud of the Acadians, who introduced Cajun cooking to Louisiana. Wild game played an extremely important role with these early settlers, who were people of considerable stamina, strength, and courage. They created their daily feasts from the plentiful nearby forests and swamp floor of the Mississippi River. Rabbits were part of their bounty; this classic preparation can be prepared with wild or domestic rabbit. The chutney can be made in advance.

2 rabbits, cut into serving pieces with meat cut from bones (page 22)
1 pound pork butt, cubed
1½ pounds bacon, sliced
½ pound pork fat, chopped
½ teaspoon salt, plus salt to taste
3 tablespoons cracked black pepper
2 teaspoons dried thyme
Pinch dried sage
Pinch ground allspice
2 bay leaves
½ cup plus 2 tablespoons Cognac
¼ pound butter
¼ cup finely diced yellow onion
¼ cup finely diced celery
¼ cup finely diced green onion
1 tablespoon minced garlic
½ cup finely diced fresh mushrooms
1 cup finely diced andouille or other spicy sausage (about 1 pound)
¼ cup port
1½ cups Basic Game Bird Stock (preferably from rabbit bones; page 40), chilled
2 eggs
Cornichons
Apple-Ginger Chutney (page 123)

Combine rabbit, pork butt, ½ pound of the bacon, pork fat, ½ teaspoon salt, 1 tablespoon of the pepper, 1 teaspoon of the thyme, sage, allspice, bay leaves, and ½ cup Cognac in a mixing bowl. Using your hands, mix well to coat meat thoroughly. Let stand at room temperature 3 to 4 hours or refrigerate overnight.

In a heavy-bottomed saucepan, melt butter over medium high heat. Add yellow onion, celery, green onion, garlic, remaining 2 tablespoons pepper, and mushrooms and sauté until vegetables are wilted, 3 to 5 minutes. Add sausage and sauté for 2 to 3 minutes, then remove pan from heat.

Add remaining 2 tablespoons Cognac, port, stock, and remaining 1 teaspoon thyme and return to heat. Place over high heat until reduced by half. Remove from heat and set aside to cool.

Preheat oven to 350° F. Remove meats from marinade. Using a meat grinder, grind all meats and fat, except rabbit loins, twice; reserve loins. (The pulse mode of a food processor may also be used if a meat grinder is not available.) Once ground, add eggs and reserved vegetables and mix well. (Meat may be tested for proper flavor by panfrying a 1-inch patty in butter.)

Completely line the inside surface of a 2-quart terrine mold with remaining 1 pound bacon. Allow bacon to overhang the terrine. Fill mold halfway with meat mixture, pressing it down into all corners. Place rabbit loins down center of mold, then top with remaining meat mixture, filling terrine to top. Cover top completely with overhanging bacon.

Cover terrine mold with aluminum foil and place mold in baking pan. Add water to baking pan to reach halfway up sides of mold. Bake in preheated oven until juices run clear when top is pierced, about 1 hour. Remove from oven, weight the top with canned goods or a brick, and cool.

To serve, slice thinly and serve with cornichons and chutney.

RABBIT AND VEGETABLE POT PIE

SERVES 8

Recommended Wine: A full-bodied Chardonnay will stand up nicely to the hearty flavors and creamy texture of this delicious pot pie.

Here the humble, traditional chicken pot pie has been updated with the use of fresh vegetables and rabbit. Chef Waldy Malouf of Manhattan's fashionable Hudson River Club has put together a new American classic. You will need 8 individual, 2-cup oven-proof casseroles to serve these pies.

½ cup extra-virgin olive oil
Flour for dredging
3 rabbits, cut into serving pieces (page 22)
5 large shallots, minced
3 cloves garlic, minced
16 small pearl onions
1 pound mixed fresh wild mushrooms such as shiitake and chanterelle, julienned
½ pound fresh domestic mushrooms, sliced
1 cup julienned carrot

1 cup peeled julienned turnip
1 cup sliced celery
¼ cup tomato paste
3 tablespoons chopped fresh tarragon, or 1½ tablespoons dried tarragon
4 cups dry white wine
½ cup brandy
8 cups chicken stock or Basic Game Bird Stock (page 40)
Bouquet garni of parsley stems, thyme sprigs, 1 bay leaf, 6 peppercorns, and 2 cloves, tied in cheesecloth
4 ripe tomatoes, peeled, quartered, and seeded
1½ cups shelled fresh green peas
2 tablespoons cornstarch dissolved in ¼ cup water
Salt and freshly ground black pepper to taste
2 pounds puff pastry (see Note)
2 eggs, beaten with pinch salt

Preheat oven to 350° F. Heat oil in a large sauté pan. Lightly flour rabbit pieces and brown in batches in oil. Remove rabbit and set aside. In same pan, lightly brown shallots, garlic, and onions in oil remaining in pan. Add mushrooms, carrot, turnip, and celery, and cook for 1 minute. Stir in tomato paste and tarragon. Add wine and brandy and simmer for 5 minutes to reduce.

Transfer to an ovenproof 10-quart stockpot. Add stock, bouquet garni, tomatoes, and browned rabbit and bring to a boil. Cover and cook in preheated oven for 45 minutes. Remove from oven and let cool to room temperature.

Remove rabbit and vegetables to a platter, reserving all liquid in pot; discard bouquet garni. Debone rabbit, keeping pieces of meat as large as possible. Divide meat among 8 individual, 2-cup casseroles. Distribute cooked vegetables and raw peas evenly among casseroles.

Strain cooking liquid through a fine sieve into a pot. Reduce over high heat to about 4 cups. Strain liquid again, return to pot, and whisk in cornstarch mixture, 1 teaspoon at a time. Cook until sauce is very thick. Season with salt and pepper. Divide sauce among casseroles. (Casseroles can be prepared up to this point and then refrigerated overnight.)

To finish pot pies, preheat oven to 425° F. Roll out puff pastry ⅛-inch thick. Cut into rounds 1 inch larger in diameter than casseroles. Place pastry rounds on tops of casseroles and crimp to sides; brush pastry with beaten eggs.

Bake in preheated oven until pastry is golden brown, about 30 minutes.

NOTE: Ready-made puff pastry is available frozen at gourmet food shops and well-stocked supermarkets. Thaw in wrapper in refrigerator.

RABBIT ESCABECHE

SERVES 2 TO 4

Recommended Wine: A slightly chilled, fruity Gamay Beaujolais or lighter-style Zinfandel will combat the heat and tartness of this heady dish.

Chef Felipe Rojas-Lombardi of New York City's The Ballroom handles game with a distinctive Spanish–South American touch. The tartness of the vinegar, the heat of the chilies, and the sweet aromas of the various spices create multilayered flavors.

½ cup all-purpose flour
2 tablespoons kosher salt
1 tablespoon paprika
½ teaspoon cayenne pepper
1 rabbit, cut into serving pieces (page 22)
1 cup olive oil
6 to 8 large cloves garlic
2 bay leaves
4 to 6 fresh serrano chili peppers, seeded and julienned
½ teaspoon coriander seed
1 teaspoon juniper berries, crushed
1 cinnamon stick (6 inches), halved lengthwise
10 sprigs fresh thyme, or 1½ teaspoons dried thyme
1 medium yellow onion, chopped
2 tablespoons tomato paste
3 cups sherry wine vinegar
2 cups red wine
1 cup chicken stock or Basic Game Bird Stock (page 40)
Salt and freshly ground black pepper to taste
½ pound pearl onions

Preheat oven to 350° F. In a medium-sized bowl, combine flour, 1 tablespoon of the salt, paprika, and cayenne pepper. Mix well. Dredge rabbit pieces in this mixture and place them in a single layer on a baking pan.

In a large skillet, heat oil until very hot. Quickly fry rabbit pieces until golden brown on all sides, 6 to 8 minutes. Remove rabbit and set aside. Carefully strain oil through a cheesecloth-lined sieve. Pour strained oil into an earthenware, ovenproof pot large enough to hold rabbit and all liquid called for in recipe.

Heat oil in pot, add garlic cloves, and sauté until garlic is golden. Add bay leaves, chili peppers, coriander seed, juniper berries, cinnamon stick, and thyme. Stir and cook for 2 minutes.

Stir in onion and tomato paste and cook until onion becomes translucent. Add vinegar, wine, and stock. Bring to a boil, lower heat slightly, and reduce to about 3 cups liquid. Season with salt and pepper. Add rabbit pieces.

Cover pot and bake in preheated oven for 1 hour. About 15 minutes before rabbit is done, add onions. Remove pot from oven and serve right from the pot either warm or at room temperature.

RABBIT WITH BOURBON AND PEARL ONIONS
Served with Corn Cakes

SERVES 4

Recommended Wine: A lighter-bodied Pinot Noir or Gamay Beaujolais offsets the full-flavored sauce and enhances the grilled loin.

In this rabbit preparation by Frank Stitt of Birmingham, Alabama's Highlands Grill, the rabbit is cooked two ways. The loin is coated with olive oil and herbs and grilled (or sautéed) to capture the succulent flavors of the tender meat. The chewier legs are braised in bourbon with pearl onions for a heartier taste. The two preparations are served together on the same plate. We like this dish with Corn Cakes.

MARINADE

¼ cup olive oil
2 shallots, chopped
2 cloves garlic, crushed
3 sprigs fresh basil
1 carrot, peeled and finely chopped
Salt and freshly ground black pepper to taste

2 rabbits, cut into serving pieces (page 22)
2 tablespoons vegetable oil
1 large yellow onion, finely chopped
1 carrot, peeled and finely chopped
1 celery stalk, trimmed and finely chopped
½ cup bourbon (preferably Jack Daniels)
¾ cup fruity white wine (preferably Johannisberg Riesling or Gewürztraminer)
2 cups chicken stock or Basic Game Bird Stock (page 40)
4 sprigs fresh thyme
2 bay leaves
1 cup pearl onions
Pinch sugar
3 tablespoons butter
2 tablespoon extra-virgin olive oil

⅓ cup chopped fresh basil, or 2 tablespoons dried basil
Corn Cakes (recipe follows)

Combine all ingredients for marinade and marinate rabbit, refrigerated, for 2 hours or overnight. Remove rabbit from marinade and pat dry with paper towels. Drain and reserve vegetables from marinade for later use.

Preheat oven to 325° F. In a large, heavy skillet, heat oil. Add rabbit legs and brown on all sides. Remove rabbit and set aside. Add onion, carrot, celery, and reserved vegetables from marinade to skillet and cook until just softened. Add bourbon, wine, stock, thyme, and bay leaves and bring to a simmer. Place rabbit legs in an earthenware casserole just large enough to hold legs and vegetable-stock mixture. Pour vegetable-stock mixture over rabbit, cover casserole, and place in preheated oven for 1 hour and 15 minutes. Remove from oven and place legs on a plate; keep warm.

Transfer vegetables and liquid in casserole to a saucepan. Place over medium-high heat and reduce by half, skimming off any fat that accumulates on surface. Strain. In a blender or food processor, purée strained vegetables and return purée to saucepan.

Meanwhile, in another small saucepan, combine pearl onions and sugar with water to cover barely. Bring to a boil, reduce heat, and simmer until tender, 5 to 7 minutes. Drain and toss with 1 tablespoon of the butter; keep warm.

To cook reserved rabbit loins, prepare a fire in a charcoal grill. Grill loins over hot coals, turning once, until just done, 3 to 4 minutes per side.

Just before serving, swirl remaining 2 tablespoons butter into warm puréed vegetable sauce. Season with salt and pepper. To serve, place sauce on one half of each serving plate. Top with leg. Slice loin and place on other half of plate; drizzle with oil and sprinkle with basil. Place pearl onions and Corn Cakes in center of plate.

CORN CAKES

SERVES 4

1 tablespoon butter
½ cup minced green onion
¼ cup dry white wine
4 eggs
¾ cup half-and-half
¼ cup plus 1 tablespoon cornmeal
⅓ cup flour
½ teaspoon salt
Pinch freshly ground white pepper
¼ teaspoon chopped fresh thyme, basil, or oregano, or ⅛
teaspoon dried thyme, basil, or oregano
1½ teaspoons sugar
1½ teaspoons honey
¼ teaspoon baking powder
1 tablespoon chopped red or green bell pepper
2½ cups fresh corn kernels
¼ cup clarified butter

In a small saucepan, melt 1 tablespoon butter and sauté onion until soft. Add wine and reduce over medium-high heat to 1 teaspoon. Remove from heat and cool to room temperature.

In a mixing bowl, combine cooled reduced wine mixture with all remaining ingredients, except corn and clarified butter, and beat until mixture is smooth. Stir in corn. Sauté a small amount, taste, and adjust seasoning.

In a large skillet, melt clarified butter. Drop corn mixture by dollops into skillet and sauté until lightly browned on both sides. Cook cakes in batches to avoid overcrowding the pan.

RABBIT COOKED TWO WAYS
Served with Minted White Beans

SERVES 8 TO 10

Ralph Tingle, a talented chef from California's wine country, combines a host of rustic flavors for this rabbit dish. Once again, the loin of the rabbit is grilled while the legs are braised. The results are succulent, flavorful morsels that are highlighted by the texture of the beans and assertive mint.

1 recipe Basic Liquid Game Marinade (page 27)
4 rabbits, cut into serving pieces (page 22)
Salt and freshly ground black pepper to taste
Minted White Beans (recipe follows)
Fresh mint sprigs for garnish

Recommended Wine: A robust Zinfandel provides the body and intensity of fruit required to support this hearty dish.

Combine all ingredients for marinade and marinate rabbit pieces, refrigerated, for 6 to 8 hours or overnight.

Remove rabbit loins from marinade, pat dry with paper towel, and set aside. Transfer rabbit legs with marinade to a heavy-bottomed stockpot. Bring to a boil, reduce heat, and simmer gently until rabbit is tender, 1 to 1½ hours. Rabbit should be covered with liquid at all times; if necessary, add water to stock to cover. Skim off fat occasionally.

Prepare a fire in a charcoal grill. Grill loins over hot coals, turning once, until done, 3 to 4 minutes per side. Season with salt and pepper. Slice on the bias and place on top of Minted White Beans. Place braised legs alongside. Garnish with mint sprigs.

MINTED WHITE BEANS

SERVES 8 TO 10

4 cups cooked white beans
3 tablespoons finely chopped fresh mint
½ cup chopped roasted hazelnuts or pistachios
Salt and freshly ground pepper to taste

In a mixing bowl, combine all ingredients and mix thoroughly. Serve at room temperature.

RABBIT IN ALMOND SAUCE

SERVES 2 TO 4

Recommended Wine: The nutty character of the sauce is an excellent flavor match for a rich Chardonnay.

This recipe is Spanish in origin. Unfortunately, we've lost track of its true source as it has evolved in our kitchen. The almond flavors seem to have a particular affinity for the delicate rabbit meat.

1 large rabbit, cut into serving pieces (page 22)
Salt and freshly ground black pepper to taste
4 tablespoons olive oil
2 cups chopped yellow onion
2 tablespoons slivered garlic
½ pound blanched almonds
¼ cup rabbit livers or chicken livers
½ teaspoon ground cinnamon
¼ teaspoon red-pepper flakes
8 white peppercorns
2 whole cloves
½ teaspoon saffron threads
½ teaspoon kosher salt

1 cup dry white wine
1 cup chicken stock or Basic Game Bird Stock (page 40), or more as needed
2 bay leaves
¼ cup dry sherry (preferably Spanish)
Minced fresh parsley and lightly toasted sliced almonds for garnish

Season rabbit with salt and pepper and set aside.

Heat 2 tablespoons of the oil in a sauté pan over moderate heat and sauté onion, garlic, blanched almonds, and livers until lightly colored. Remove from heat and place in a blender or food processor along with cinnamon, pepper flakes, peppercorns, cloves, saffron, and ½ teaspoon kosher salt. Purée until smooth, scraping down sides of container; set aside.

Add remaining 2 tablespoons oil to sauté pan and lightly brown rabbit pieces. Add wine, 1 cup stock, bay leaves, and puréed almond mixture. Cover and simmer very slowly until rabbit is tender, about 1 hour. Add additional stock if sauce begins to dry out.

To serve, arrange rabbit pieces on a warm platter. Add sherry to sauté pan with cooking liquid, simmer briefly, and adjust seasoning. Whisk to smooth sauce and then pour over rabbit. Garnish with parsley and almonds.

SQUAB

*N*ibbling on the succulent, dark flesh of a freshly grilled marinated squab is for us a culinary delight. Gentle gnawing on the tiny bones appeals to our most basic, primordial instincts. Served rare, the meat of squab is a heady delicacy, both earthy and elegant. Squab's mildly gamy flavor, which is considerably stronger than the flavor of a Cornish game hen, is slightly reminiscent of beef and liver.

M. F. K. Fisher in *How to Cook a Wolf* gives us the proper perspective on squab, which were known as pigeons at the time: "And pigeons, those gentle flitting creatures, with the soft voices and their miraculous wings in flight, have always meant peace, and refreshment to sad humans. Perhaps it is an old wives' tale; perhaps it is part of our appetites . . . whatever the reason, a roasted pigeon is and long has been the most heartening dish to set before a man bowed down with grief or loneliness. In the same way it can reassure a timid lover, or comfort a woman weak from childbirth. It is not easy to find pigeons, these days. Most of the ones you know about in the city are working for the government. . . . By far the easiest way to make a pigeon cry "Come, eat me!" is to buy it, all cleaned and trussed, from a merchant . . . eating a roasted pigeon is one of the few things that can be done all by yourself and in sordid surroundings with complete impunity and a positive reaction of well-being."

The inimitable Mary Frances goes on to describe her favorite method for roasting pigeon—a nourishing, comforting covered-pot rendition that includes lemon and parsley in the cavity, followed by a brief simmer in bacon fat, and slow braising in red wine, cider, beer, orange juice, or tomato juice. In this version, the bird is served on toast with bacon and Belgian endive or celery hearts, and is savored with a fruity, young Beaujolais. This, it seems, is the truest expression of comfort food!

Squab, as we know it today, is an invention of the farm-raised game industry. The original passenger pigeon was driven into extinction from a population that reached almost ten million at one point in time. This new industry has burgeoned, particularly in Northern California. These young, nonflying pigeons (actually rock doves that have not yet developed feathers) are raised in pens on grain diets until they are about a month old, at which time they are prepared for the marketplace.

One of their interesting traits is that the male pigeon will peck on the neck of the female if she won't mate with him. This rather unusual pecking instinct seems to ensure constant gratification for the male. His amorous nature notwithstanding, the male pigeon does take a very active role in the care of his young, perhaps as compensation for his sexual exploits.

Shopping for Squab

Commercially raised squab is a relatively uniform product that is handled and packaged efficiently. Most squab weigh from 12 to 16 ounces and will serve 1 person for a main course; for salads, they can be halved and will serve 2 people. Unfortunately, these delicate birds are somewhat expensive.

Squab can often be purchased with all but the leg and thigh bones and wing joint removed. If you are deboning squab at home, save the carcass for stocks or consommés (see page 19 for boning instructions). The flavor derived from bones, which are first roasted and then crushed, can be a wonderful flavor addition to poultry or game stocks. Always reserve the livers and giblets; they can be used in pâtés or terrines or added to vinaigrettes for salads using squab.

Cooking Tips

Farm-raised birds bear only minor resemblance to the wild doves (mourning and whitewing doves) and wood pigeons that have been hunted for centuries. These wild birds, as well as woodcock, snipe, thrush, grouse, ptarmigan, and chukar partridge, exist on a diet of nuts, berries, and insects, whereas domestic squab are raised on grains and corn. Cooking methods also vary greatly, since wild doves and pigeons have virtually no fat under their skin, and squab are bred with a small amount of fat. Squab are also larger than wild doves or wood pigeons, therefore cooking times will vary significantly.

The wild birds are considerably less tender than domestic squab, and they have the reputation of being somewhat difficult to cook because of their leanness. The meat can easily become dry and stringy although, when cooked properly, they are extremely flavorful. The game hunter typically must hang the catch and then bard the breasts with bacon fat or salt pork during cooking to preserve moistness. Sometimes a milk marinade is necessary to reduce gaminess, a quality desired by some but disdained by others. These steps are not required with domestic squab.

In order to preserve the flavor and texture of farm-raised squab meat, the bird should be served rare to medium-rare with juices running pink. This means the flesh should remain rosy and moist. As the breast meat begins to turn from pink to brown, the flavor of the bird develops a "livery" taste and loses much of its natural appeal.

Squab can be roasted, broiled, grilled, or sautéed with equally good results, and they can be cooked with the bone in or deboned. When grilling, broiling, or sautéing, it helps to remove the backbone and flatten the bird so that the heat will evenly penetrate the surface. A salt-and-pepper rub is effective in bringing out the natural flavor of the bird. The bird should always be placed skin side down to start, so that the thin layer of fat can help baste the meat internally and prevent it from drying out. Basting with a cooking or marinating liquid is also effective. Once the bird is turned, it need not be cooked for long.

If roasting whole squab, herbs such as thyme or sage; crushed, toasted juniper berries; and pancetta can be placed in the cavity for a welcome aromatic and flavor contribution. Allow grilled, roasted, or broiled birds to stand at room temperature under foil to settle their juices for 5 minutes before serving.

Before serving whole birds with a sauce, cut tiny slits under the legs and thighs and in the breast to release juices. If you do this, the sauce will not become diluted by the juices. If using squab in a salad, use the juices as part of a fruit-based or balsamic vinaigrette for a delicious presentation.

If the birds are boned, the breast meat can be sliced and fanned out on the plate when served. Slice the breast meat thinly on an angle without carving all the way through to the bottom, then gently spread the slices out in an oval shape to highlight the pink, succulent meat. Serve the leg-thigh piece next to the fanned breast.

Classic Dishes

The popularity of squab (or pigeon) peaked in the 18th and 19th centuries, when there was a plentiful supply. They regularly appeared as part of the banquet fare of the day. Traditional recipes for wild game birds call for brief grilling, spit roasting, panfrying, braising in wine (often Madeira, sherry, or Marsala), baking in casseroles and pies, or serving on toast. Most of these classic recipes are quite simple, and are relatively interchangeable among game birds, with cooking times varying slightly depending on the size of the bird. For many years, squab under glass was an elegant and famous presentation at Boston's Locke-Ober restaurant.

Squab is also highly prized by the Chinese, who mince it and wrap the meat with hoisin sauce in lettuce leaves, by Moroccans whose *bastilla* (pigeon pie) is a signature dish of their cuisine, and throughout the countries of the Mediterranean, where squab is eaten with great regularity in a variety of preparations. Only in England, where it is thought to be a pest, has the pigeon fallen from culinary favor.

Classic Recipe

MINCED SQUAB, CHINESE STYLE

SERVES 6 AS A FIRST COURSE, OR 2 AS AN ENTRÉE

Recommended Wine: A slightly sweet Gewürztraminer or Johannisberg Riesling is required to offset the spicy, slightly sweet quality of this dish.

This preparation of squab wrapped in lettuce leaves appears on the menus of many Chinese restaurants, both in the United States and in China, where it is often served as a first course. In this version, offered by Hugh Carpenter of Chopstix in Los Angeles, diced shrimp is mixed with the squab for added flavor interest. We've never once served this dish when all the wrapped "bundles" weren't devoured immediately!

8 dried Chinese black mushrooms (see Note)
10 fresh water chestnuts, peeled and finely diced, or 1 medium carrot, peeled and finely diced
1 red bell pepper, seeded, deveined, and finely diced
2 green onions, finely diced
½ cup pine nuts
1 squab
2 teaspoons dry sherry or dry white wine
1 teaspoon dark soy sauce
1 teaspoon finely minced fresh ginger
½ teaspoon plus 1 tablespoon cornstarch
½ teaspoon plus 2 tablespoons peanut oil
½ pound shrimp in the shell
3 heads iceberg lettuce
Peanut oil for deep-frying
2 ounces rice stick noodles (see Note)
1 tablespoon water

SAUCE
2 tablespoons dry sherry or dry white wine
1 tablespoon soy sauce
1 tablespoon oyster sauce (see Note)
1 tablespoon sesame oil (see Note)
½ teaspoon sugar
¼ teaspoon chili sauce (see Note)

Soak dried mushrooms in hot water to cover until soft, about 20 minutes. Discard stems and finely dice caps. Combine with water chestnuts, red pepper, and onions. Refrigerate until ready to cook.

Preheat oven to 325° F. Toast pine nuts in preheated oven until they are lightly golden, about 8 minutes. Set aside.

Bone squab and chop meat coarsely. Place in a mixing bowl and add sherry, soy sauce, ginger, ½ teaspoon cornstarch, and ½ teaspoon peanut oil. Mix well. Shell and devein shrimp, then cut crosswise into very thin slices. Add to squab mixture and refrigerate until ready to cook.

Cut top third off each head of lettuce; reserve tops for another use. Carefully separate leaves; you should end up with about 18 round lettuce cups, each about 3 to 5 inches across. Refrigerate leaf cups.

In a wok or deep saucepan, pour in peanut oil to a depth of about 2 inches and heat to 375° F, or until a rice-stick noodle puffs up within about 4 seconds of being dropped in oil. Cook noodles, a small handful at a time, in oil. As noodles puff up, flip them over with chopsticks, tongs, or a fork and cook for about 10 seconds longer. With a slotted utensil, remove to paper towels to drain. Place cooked rice sticks in a paper bag and store at room temperature until ready to use.

In a small bowl, combine all ingredients for sauce and set aside.

When ready to finish dish, dissolve remaining 1 tablespoon cornstarch in water; set aside.

Place wok over high heat. When it is very hot, add remaining 2 tablespoons peanut oil. Tilt wok so that oil coats inside completely. When oil just begins to smoke, add squab-shrimp mixture. Stir-fry until shrimp turn white, about 2 minutes.

Add water chestnut mixture and stir-fry for about 1 minute. Add pine nuts and sauce and bring to a gentle boil. Stir in just enough of the cornstarch mixture for the sauce to glaze the food lightly.

Serve at once by spooning inside lettuce cups. Break rice sticks into small pieces and distribute evenly among lettuce cups. The lettuce leaf can be rolled around squab mixture like a taco, and then eaten out of hand.

NOTE: These ingredients can be found in Asian markets.

SQUAB ROASTED ON THE SPIT
Served with Grilled Eggplant and White Corn Salsa

SERVES 6

Recommended Wine: A Petite Sirah or Zinfandel echoes the rustic flavors of this wonderfully earthy dish.

Based loosely on a memorable Easter dinner we had in northern Greece, this simple recipe works nicely with any small bird, including quail and partridge. If a spit is not available, the squab can be cooked on a grill and turned often, using the same method. The accompaniments are obviously optional, but they turn the dish into something very special.

6 squab, with giblets
⅓ cup tarragon vinegar or other herb vinegar
½ cup olive oil
Salt and freshly ground black pepper to taste
6 fresh sage leaves, plus 1 tablespoon chopped fresh sage
1 cup red wine
1 large lemon, sliced
12 Kalamata or niçoise olives, pitted
Grilled Eggplant (recipe follows)
White Corn Salsa (recipe follows)

Rub squab with a bit of the vinegar inside and out. Brush with some of the oil and season liberally with salt and pepper. Place giblets back in each bird along with 1 sage leaf. Thread birds on a spit, if available.

In the bottom of the grill, directly beneath the spit or the area of the grill where you will cook the squab, place a shallow drip pan. Put wine, remaining vinegar, chopped sage, lemon, and olives in pan. Lay fire using the indirect-heat method (page 33). Spit roast or grill birds, turning them slowly and occasionally brushing with remaining oil. As the mixture heats, the vapor will rise and add flavor to the birds.

When birds are done, about 15 to 20 minutes for rare to medium-rare, remove them from spit or grill and cut them in half. Remove giblets and chop finely. Keep birds warm.

Transfer drippings from drip pan to small saucepan, add giblets, and cook briskly on top of stove for 3 minutes to concentrate flavors. Season with salt and pepper and pour over squab halves.

To serve, place squab on one side of the plate. Spoon a generous portion of salsa on the other side of the plate and place grilled eggplant on top of salsa. Reserve leftover salsa for another occasion.

GRILLED EGGPLANT

SERVES 6

2 tablespoons roasted garlic purée (page 31)
3 tablespoons minced fresh basil, or 1½ tablespoons dried basil
¼ cup olive oil
½ teaspoon kosher salt
¼ teaspoon freshly ground black pepper
6 small Japanese eggplants (about 1 pound), sliced in half lengthwise

Whisk together garlic, basil, oil, and salt and pepper and paint the cut sides of the eggplant with the mixture. Place over medium-hot coals and grill for 4 to 5 minutes. Turn and continue to grill until flesh is tender. Can be served hot or at room temperature.

WHITE CORN SALSA

MAKES 6 CUPS

3½ cups fresh white corn kernels
¾ cup diced red bell pepper
½ cup diced sweet red onion
½ cup loosely packed fresh basil or cilantro leaves, minced
1 teaspoon minced, seeded fresh serrano or jalapeño chili pepper
¼ cup rice wine vinegar
1 tablespoon fresh lemon juice
1 tablespoon honey
¼ cup olive oil
Kosher salt and freshly ground white pepper to taste

Combine all ingredients and let stand for at least 1 hour before serving. Adjust balance as necessary.

HOME-SMOKED SQUAB WITH AN ORIENTAL TOUCH

SERVES 4

This recipe features an interesting technique that works well with most game birds. It is delicious served hot, or better yet at room temperature as part of a summer buffet. It combines both a marinade and a basting sauce.

MARINADE

Grated zest of 1 lemon
Grated zest of 1 orange
½ cup light soy sauce
⅓ cup oyster sauce (see Note)
1 teaspoon minced fresh ginger

Recommended Wine: A slightly sweet Gewürztraminer is the perfect companion to the smoky-spicy-salty flavors of the squab.

2 cloves garlic, minced
1 tablespoon chopped fresh cilantro
½ teaspoon freshly ground black pepper
1 bay leaf
2 tablespoons honey

4 squab, left whole or halved with backbones removed

SAUCE
2 teaspoons vegetable oil
1 teaspoon minced garlic
1 teaspoon minced fresh ginger
¼ teaspoon red-pepper flakes
3 shallots, minced
1 tablespoon soy sauce
1 teaspoon red wine vinegar
2 tablespoons brown sugar
1½ tablespoons water
2 teaspoons sesame oil (see Note)

Combine ingredients for marinade in a blender or food processor and blend well. Marinate squab, refrigerated, for 6 hours. Remove squab from marinade, reserving marinade, and pat dry with paper towels.

In a kettle barbecue, use indirect-heat method (page 33) and barbecue and smoke hens, with vents nearly closed, for about 1 hour. Baste every 15 minutes with marinade. Add a few hot coals after 30 minutes to maintain even heat.

Meanwhile, make sauce. Combine all ingredients, except sesame oil, in a saucepan and bring to a boil. Reduce heat and simmer for 5 minutes. Remove from heat, let cool, and stir in oil.

Squab are done when juices run clear when thigh is pierced with a fork. Remove squab from grill, brush thoroughly with sauce, and serve.

NOTE: These ingredients can be found in Asian markets and well-stocked supermarkets.

BREAST OF SQUAB WITH BLACK-EYED PEA PILAF

SERVES 6

Recommended Wine: A complex Pinot Noir offers the body and flavors to support this interesting dish.

This is a simple but lovely dish loosely based on one we had in Tennessee at an old friend's cabin in the mountains. He did it with squirrel, which has a pretty strong flavor (no doubt an acquired taste!). Squab, we're sure, has broader appeal.

6 boneless squab breasts, with skin left on (page 19)
Salt and freshly ground black pepper
4 tablespoons unsalted butter or olive oil
1½ cups thinly sliced onion
¾ cup bulgur (cracked wheat)
¼ cup diced high-quality smoked ham
⅓ cup thinly sliced fresh shiitake or other fresh mushrooms
1½ cups chicken stock or Basic Game Bird Stock (page 40)
2 cups shelled fresh black-eyed peas, or drained, canned or thawed, frozen peas if fresh are unavailable
½ cup pine nuts, lightly toasted
¼ cup minced fresh parsley (preferably flat-leaf)
2 teaspoons finely grated lemon zest

Season squab breasts lightly with salt and pepper. Add 2 tablespoons of the butter to an ovenproof sauté pan and brown lightly. Remove squab breasts and set aside. Discard fat in pan and add remaining 2 tablespoons butter to pan. Add onion and sauté slowly until soft but not browned.

Add bulgur, ham, and shiitakes. Sauté 3 minutes longer, stirring occasionally. Add stock, cover, and simmer for 5 minutes. Add black-eyed peas and gently stir in. Place squab breasts on top, cover pan, and simmer until liquid is absorbed, about 10 minutes. Set aside off heat, covered, for 5 minutes.

In a small bowl, mix together pine nuts, parsley, and lemon zest. Divide squab and black-eyed pea pilaf among individual serving plates. Sprinkle pine-nut mixture over and serve immediately.

WHOLE SQUAB BRAISED IN CIDER WITH APPLES, CHESTNUTS, AND RED CABBAGE

SERVES 4

Although this rustic dish is good anytime, it seems especially appropriate in fall and winter. The recipe works equally well with rabbit or quail; adjust the cooking time accordingly.

4 squab
Salt and freshly ground black pepper to taste
4 tablespoons olive oil, rendered bacon fat, or rendered duck fat
3 cups sliced yellow onion
2 tablespoons slivered garlic
¼ cup slivered shallots
3 cups finely shredded red cabbage

Recommended Wine: A toasty Chardonnay emphasizes the richness of this dish, while a full-flavored, dry rosé contrasts with that same quality. Either wine is an excellent choice.

4 medium-sized tart apples, peeled and cut into ¼-inch wedges (about 2 cups)
1½ cups chicken stock or Basic Game Bird Stock (page 40)
1 cup dry white wine
3 cups natural apple cider
3 tablespoons raspberry vinegar or black currant vinegar
⅔ cup whole fresh chestnuts, peeled, (page 47), or unsweetened drained, canned chestnuts
2 teaspoons chopped fresh rosemary, or 1 teaspoon dried rosemary
Sautéed apple slices and fresh rosemary sprigs for garnish

Preheat oven to 400° F. Season squab with salt and pepper. In an ovenproof saucepan, heat oil and quickly brown squab. Remove squab and set aside. Add onion, garlic, and shallots to pan and sauté until lightly colored, about 7 minutes. Add cabbage, apples, stock, wine, apple cider, and vinegar and bring to a boil. Remove from heat.

Remove 1 to 2 cups of the vegetable mixture with a slotted utensil, draining well, and loosely stuff into squab cavities. Arrange squab on top of vegetable mixture remaining in pan and add chestnuts and rosemary. Bring mixture to a simmer, cover tightly, and bake in preheated oven until the squab is just cooked (juices should run light pink when thigh joint is pierced), about 15 minutes.

Remove squab and keep warm. Strain out braising vegetables and reserve. Return cooking liquid to pan and reduce over high heat to a light sauce consistency. Taste and adjust seasoning. Return vegetables and squab to pan and reheat briefly.

To serve, arrange vegetables and squab on warm plates. Garnish with apple slices and rosemary sprigs.

GRILLED SQUAB WITH MIXED GREENS AND CUMIN-CORIANDER VINAIGRETTE
Served with Couscous with Raisins

SERVES 2 AS ENTRÉE, OR 4 AS A SALAD COURSE

For this dish, we adapted a specialty from talented Alfred Portale, the chef at Gotham Bar & Grill in New York City. We're particularly fond of the juxtaposition of the rich, hearty squab with a vinaigrette laced with *harissa*, a spicy purée of red peppers from North Africa. Portale serves the dish as a main course with a side of couscous and a touch of *harissa* added to amplify further the North African theme. If served as a salad course, the couscous is not required. And if you don't feel like firing up the grill, the squab can be sautéed.

Recommended Wine: A hearty
Zinfandel or full-bodied Fumé
Blanc or Semillon is required to
balance the intense flavors of this
dish.

2 boneless squab, breasts and leg-thigh pieces separated
1 tablespoon olive oil
Salt and freshly ground black pepper to taste

VINAIGRETTE

¼ cup fresh lemon juice
⅓ teaspoon salt
¼ teaspoon freshly ground white pepper
½ teaspoon ground cumin
½ clove garlic, finely minced
½ teaspoon *harissa* (see Note)
⅔ cup extra-virgin olive oil

3 small heads mixed lettuces such as red leaf, Bibb, and
frisée (about ¼ pound)
Spicy Couscous with Raisins (recipe follows)

Combine all ingredients for vinaigrette, except oil, and whisk
thoroughly. Whisk in oil in a slow, steady stream. Taste and
adjust seasoning. Set aside.

Rub squab with oil, salt, and pepper and let stand at room
temperature for 2 to 3 hours.

Prepare a fire in a charcoal grill. Pat squab pieces dry with
paper towels and grill, skin side down, over hot coals for 5 to 7
minutes. Turn, and continue cooking until done, 3 to 5 minutes.
Legs should be cooked slightly longer than breasts, which should
be medium-rare. Keep warm.

To serve, toss lettuces with most of the vinaigrette. Divide
lettuces on individual serving plates and top with squab pieces.
Spoon remaining vinaigrette over top. Place couscous around
edges of greens.

COUSCOUS WITH RAISINS

¼ cup couscous
¾ cup chicken stock
1 tablespoon butter
¼ cup golden raisins
1 tablespoon *harissa*
Salt and freshly ground black pepper to taste

Place couscous in a small bowl. In a small saucepan, heat
chicken stock and butter to boiling and pour over couscous. Stir

in raisins and *harissa*, cover, and let stand for 10 minutes. Season with salt and pepper.

NOTE: *Harissa*, made from chilies, garlic, and oil, can be found in jars and cans in shops carrying North African and Middle Eastern foods.

TAMARIND-GLAZED GRILLED SQUAB
Served with Southern Sauté

SERVES 4

Recommended Wine: A spicy, fruity Pinot Noir offers the right character to cut through the tartness of the tamarind glaze and the spiciness of the andouille sausage.

The "East meets South" concept makes for a delicious dish. The combination of the eastern-influenced, tamarind-glazed squab and the decidely southern concoction of baby greens, white corn, andouille sausage, and roasted red peppers sets off sparks on the taste buds. The dish can also be prepared with quail instead of squab.

The tamarind glaze is from our friend, Mark Malicki, a talented chef from the Northern California wine country. For his creation Malicki grills whole quail on long grapevine cuttings. The bird is served whole on the grapevine shoot and is eaten *Tom Jones* style.

4 boneless squab (see page 19)
Olive oil for brushing on squab
Salt and freshly ground black pepper

TAMARIND GLAZE

1 tablespoon minced garlic
1 tablespoon minced shallots
1 tablespoon minced fresh ginger
1 tablespoon olive oil or butter
3 tablespoons sugar
3 tablespoons fish sauce (see Note)
6 tablespoons water
1½ tablespoons tamarind concentrate (see Note), mixed with 1½ tablespoons water
3 tablespoons fresh lime juice

Southern Sauté (recipe follows)

Brush squab with oil and season with salt and pepper. Marinate, refrigerated, for 3 to 4 hours.

To make glaze, in a skillet, sauté garlic, shallots, and ginger in oil for 2 to 3 minutes; set aside. Combine sugar and fish sauce in a pot and bring to a boil. Add water, tamarind-water mixture, and lime juice and reduce over high heat by one third. Stir in reserved garlic mixture.

Prepare a fire in a charcoal grill. Grill squab, skin side down, over hot coals for 5 to 7 minutes. Brush with tamarind glaze, turn, brush top with glaze, and cook until done, 3 to 5 minutes. Be careful not to overcook.

To serve, place squab on individual serving plates and serve greens alongside, garnished with radishes.

SOUTHERN SAUTÉ

SERVES 4

2 ears of white corn, husked
¼ pound andouille (or other spicy sausage), thinly sliced
1 teaspoon olive oil, or more as needed
1 shallot, chopped
2 tablespoons balsamic vinegar
2 red bell peppers, roasted, peeled, seeded, deveined, and diced
½ pound collard, turnip, or mustard greens, leaves cut in half crosswise, briefly blanched, and drained
8 radishes, thinly sliced, for garnish

With a serrated knife, cut corn kernels off cob; set aside. In a large, nonstick sauté pan over medium-high heat, sauté andouille in 1 teaspoon oil for 7 minutes, stirring frequently. Add shallot and sauté for 2 minutes. Deglaze pan with vinegar, scraping up browned bits. Add corn, red peppers, and greens and sauté until greens are just wilted, 3 to 4 minutes. Add a small amount of oil if greens begin to stick. When serving greens, garnish with radishes. Don't overcook; the greens should have a fresh, crunchy appeal.

NOTE: Fish sauce and tamarind concentrate can be found in Asian markets.

SAUTÉED SQUAB WITH BLOOD ORANGE–CUMIN SAUCE
Served with Spiced Couscous

SERVES 8

Recommended Wine: A full-bodied, citrusy Chardonnay will highlight the citrus character of this multi-dimensional sauce; a young Pinot Noir will serve the mildly gamy flavor of the squab well. Either wine is an excellent choice.

Chefs Nancy Oakes and Pamela Student of San Francisco's L'Avenue have created a beautiful Middle Eastern–influenced dish. The rich flavor of dark squab meat combines well with many different fruits, particularly citrus. Blood oranges are a particularly tasty and vivid complement to the sauce, giving it a deep orange tint and intense flavor.

SAUCE

7 blood oranges
1 teaspoon whole cumin seed
½ teaspoon coriander seed
2 teaspoons olive oil
3 shallots, sliced
3 cloves garlic
⅔ cup dry white or red wine
1 tablespoon Champagne vinegar or white wine vinegar
½ teaspoon black peppercorns
4 cups chicken stock or Basic Game Bird Stock (page 40)
2 tablespoons butter
Salt, freshly ground black pepper, and honey to taste

4 boneless squab (page 19)
Salt and freshly ground pepper to taste
Flour for dredging
2 teaspoons peanut oil
Spiced Couscous (recipe follows)

To make sauce, zest 2 of the oranges and juice these along with the remaining 5 oranges. Set aside zest and juice. In a dry sauté pan over medium heat, roast cumin and coriander seed until toasted, about 2 minutes. Grind half the seed in a mortar with a pestle or in a spice grinder; reserve remaining whole seed.

In a saucepan, heat oil. Add shallots and garlic cloves and sauté until lightly browned. Add wine, vinegar, peppercorns, and whole cumin and coriander seed, and reduce over medium-high heat to a glaze. Add reserved orange juice and reduce by half. Add stock and reduce to a light sauce consistency.

Strain sauce and return to pan. Whisk in butter. Stir in reserved ground cumin and coriander, reserved orange zest, and salt and pepper. Keep warm.

Season squabs with salt and pepper and let rest for 15 to 30 minutes. Dredge squab lightly in flour; shake off excess. Heat oil in a large skillet. When hot, place squab skin side down in pan, and sauté until golden brown, 5 to 7 minutes. Turn and continue to cook for 2 to 3 minutes. Do not overcook.

To assemble, mound couscous in center of plate. Spoon sauce around couscous and arrange squab, skin side up, on sauce.

SPICED COUSCOUS

SERVES 8

1 medium onion, diced
2 tablespoons olive oil
2 teaspoons minced garlic
¼ teaspoon ground cumin
¼ teaspoon ground coriander
⅛ teaspoon ground allspice
1½ cups water or chicken stock
½ teaspoon ground cinnamon
½ teaspoon salt
1½ cups couscous
¼ cup dried currants
¼ cup toasted pine nuts, lightly toasted
Salt and freshly ground black pepper to taste

In medium-sized, heavy saucepan, sauté onion in oil until lightly brown and tender. Add garlic, cumin, coriander, and allspice and sauté lightly until spices become aromatic. Add water, cinnamon, and salt and bring to a boil. Slowly stir in couscous with a fork. Add currants and pine nuts. Turn off heat, cover, and let stand 15 minutes. Fluff the couscous with a fork and season with salt and pepper.

DRUNKEN PIGEONS

SERVES 4

Chef Peter DeMarais of San Francisco's Cafe Majestic developed this dish from a recipe he found in a 1903 Landmark Club cookbook. Originally the dish was marinated in red wine with tomatoes and raisins. DeMarais has changed the sauce to include bourbon and port and has added blood oranges for zest. Wild rice is the perfect textural accompaniment to the bold flavors of this mouth-watering dish.

4 squab
Olive oil, for sautéing, plus 1 tablespoon olive oil
1½ cups chicken stock or Basic Game Bird Stock (page 40)
1 carrot, peeled and sliced
½ medium yellow onion, chopped

Recommended Wine: The complex flavors of this dish invite a full-bodied, ripe Cabernet Sauvignon or Zinfandel to complete the experience.

2 teaspoons plus pinch minced fresh thyme
1 bay leaf
2 tablespoons chopped shallots
⅓ cup chopped fresh mushrooms
Salt and freshly ground black pepper to taste
½ cup bourbon
½ cup port
Zest of 3 blood oranges, chopped
2 tomatoes, peeled, seeded, and chopped
½ cup golden raisins
1 tablespoon butter (optional)
Salt and freshly ground black pepper to taste
3 blood oranges, sectioned, for garnish

Bone squab according to instructions on page 19. Chop carcasses. In a large, heavy-bottomed pot, heat oil and sauté carcasses until browned. Add stock, carrot, onion, 1 teaspoon of the thyme, and bay leaf and simmer for 30 minutes. Strain and reserve liquid.

In a saucepan, sauté shallots and mushrooms in oil with pinch thyme, salt, and pepper. Add bourbon and port and reduce over medium-high heat by half. Add reserved liquid and reduce over high heat to slightly less than 1 cup. Add orange zest, tomatoes, and raisins and simmer approximately 10 minutes to form a light sauce consistency. Whisk in butter, if desired, to finish. Season with salt and pepper.

Prepare a fire in a charcoal grill. Rub squab breasts and leg-thigh pieces with 1 tablespoon oil, remaining 1 teaspoon thyme, salt, and pepper. Grill, skin side down, over hot coals for 5 to 7 minutes. Turn and grill until medium-rare, 3 to 5 minutes. (The squab pieces can also be panfried and finished skin side up in a hot oven.) Do not overcook.

Serve squab topped with sauce. Garnish with blood-orange sections.

WILD TURKEY

*T*he taste of wild turkey is so different from domestic turkey that it's worth the special search to find it. It has a more intense gamy flavor (somewhere between domestic turkey and squab), darker meat, and a different body configuration, with longer legs and a broader breast than the domestic bird.

There is considerable dispute about the origin of the turkey. Both the Greeks and Romans make mention of it (although some seem to think they may have been guinea fowl), and one was reportedly cooked for Charlemagne's wedding.

According to one account, the French brought turkeys to France from India at the end of the seventeenth century. Other accounts believe they arrived in Europe from the Americas, most likely Mexico, with early Spanish explorers. In an effort to settle the claim to turkeys, Alexander Dumas noted "as a result of the general belief that the followers of Loyola brought the turkey back from America, some cheap wits have got into the habit of calling turkeys 'Jesuits.' Contrary to vulgar belief, we do not owe the turkey to the Jesuits since the order was not founded by Ignatius of Loyola until 1534. Turkeys have just as much right to resent being called Jesuits as the Jesuits would if they were called turkeys. . . ." Despite the controversy, most scholars agree that the turkey was a uniquely North American bird.

Clearly the king of game birds, its regal size made turkeys the prize quarry of colonial America. There were so many turkeys in the colonies that the forests resounded with their calls. In fact, it's said that all turkeys have a distinctly different voice, and can recognize when others are calling.

Turkeys were a prime source of meat in the 1600s and 1700s in the United States, when they were hunted almost to extinction. They proved to be so easily domesticated that even on game farms, wild turkeys raised for eventual release would often hang around the farmer's chickens, and normally were so friendly that they were easy prey.

It was so easy to develop new breeds of domestic turkeys that we've almost lost the original "wild" turkey. It's very likely that the original domestic turkeys in the United States were actually brought back from Europe, first cousins to their American ancestors.

Shopping for Wild Turkey

Although wild turkeys are still relatively scarce, they are available from specialty game-bird suppliers. Fresh, of course, is preferred to frozen; they can often be purchased fresh during the Thanksgiving and Christmas season. If you find a whole wild turkey, look at the feet as a sign of its age (this applies to most other game birds, too). They should be soft, clean, and even colored. Rough, old-looking feet are a sign of an older, tougher bird.

The preferred types of farm-raised wild turkeys are the bronze and the Merriam, a native to the Colorado Plains, New Mexico, and Arizona that exhibits excellent flavor and a juicy flesh. There is some resurgence of turkeys in the wild, especially in the Pacific Northwest and Canada. Many of these come from domesticated stock that appear to be evolving back to their original roots.

Allow 1–1½ pounds of turkey per person.

Cooking Tips

In the recipe section that follows, the recipes can be used with both "wild" and domestic turkeys. If you are cooking the whole bird, slow roasting is preferred. We find that roasting the breast separately from the rest of the bird yields a good result, since the breast tends to cook more rapidly than the legs and thighs. Basting frequently with butter or oil is highly recommended.

Most home cooks prefer to roast a stuffed whole wild turkey for the drama of the presentation. Still other turkey enthusiasts swear by spit roasting, in which the rotating bird can be basted with butter, herbs, wine, lemon juice, and turkey drippings. There are a number of techniques that help ensure good results with wild turkey: barding the breasts with bacon or salt pork prior to roasting, covering only the breasts with aluminum foil, and basting the whole bird with butter or oil and cooking liquid.

As with most modern game, the cooking times quoted in many cookbooks are too long and will result in a dried out, tough, stringy mess if used for wild turkey. For a whole, wild turkey the usual 20 minutes per pound should be reduced to 12 to 14 minutes per pound at 325°F. With an instant-read thermometer, internal temperature should be 150° to 160°F when the bird comes out of the oven. The juices should run clear, rather than pink. Let the bird rest under foil for 15 to 30 minutes before carving to allow the meat to absorb the juices. Carving a wild turkey is different from carving a domestic bird; the meat is much denser and has the texture of steak rather than of fowl.

Classic Dishes

At no time is turkey more prevalent and widely revered than at Thanksgiving, the most American of all holidays. Our patriotism and patronage to this distinctly native bird becomes symbolic when we re-create the early meals of our pilgrim forefathers with feasts of genuine reverance.

Noted San Francisco columnist and humorist Herb Caen has wittily observed of domesticated turkey and the Thanksgiving ritual: "Take away the turkey, and what have you got for Thanksgiving? Well, a house that doesn't smell for one thing. . . . The turkey is such a wonderful bird, overall, that the incredible firepower of its bouquet is a small price to pay. Actually, a turkey is a bargain no matter what you pay. It is the gift that keeps on giving until you can hardly stand it. . . . The Great American Turkey was designed for ingestion to the point of indigestion, and it fills its role admirably. . . . In Pilgrim times, the American turkey was a lean, lithe sporty bird that flew like the wind. . . . Were Ben Franklin around today, he wouldn't recognize him, for that matter. Through the marvels of science, it has developed breasts that rival Dolly Parton's. . . . The legs look like those on an East German Olympic runner, but without the steroids . . . . The reason that Franklin was right about turkey is that it's the most democratic of birds, serving the needs of the rich and poor alike. A turkey doesn't care who's eating it, or where. It's a giving bird that's there for the taking, from now to infinity. It's like an artichoke. When you've finished an artichoke, there's more in your plate than when you started. Actually, you can never finish a turkey. It'll finish you first."

Classic Recipe

ROAST TURKEY WITH THREE STUFFINGS

SERVES 8 TO 10

Whether wild or domestic, turkey has become America's traditional fare for the holidays. If you can find a wild turkey, you'll experience much richer flavor and firmer texture than is the case with its domestic counterpart, although this recipe will work for either.

The special stuffing for this recipe goes into the neck cavity, while the body cavity is left empty. We agree with James Beard that "stuffings" are much better baked separately, so that they get crisp around the edges and retain a light rather than soggy texture, which often happens when they're baked in the bird. All of these stuffings work well with other smaller game birds or goose. They are designed to work collectively or individually, depending on the extent of your meal and your prep time.

BASIC STUFFING FOR NECK CAVITY

1 cup finely diced yellow onion
4 tablespoons butter
½ pound fresh mushrooms, finely diced
1 pound lean ground pork
¼ pound high-quality smoked ham, diced
1 teaspoon kosher salt
½ teaspoon freshly ground white pepper
1 teaspoon minced fresh thyme, or ½ teaspoon dried thyme
2 tablespoons minced fresh parsley
¼ cup Madeira or port

1 wild or domestic turkey (12 to 14 pounds), with giblets
Salt and freshly ground black pepper to taste

To make stuffing for neck, in a small skillet, sauté onion in 2 tablespoons of the butter until soft but not browned. Remove onion and set aside. Sauté mushrooms in remaining 2 tablespoons butter until lightly browned. In a mixing bowl, combine onion and mushrooms with all remaining ingredients. Stuff the neck cavity of the turkey and skewer or truss closed (page 37). Reserve giblets for using in cornbread stuffing, if making.

Preheat oven to 325°F. Season turkey inside and out with salt and pepper. Set breast side down on a rack in a roasting pan. Place turkey in preheated oven for 1 hour. Turn breast side up, baste with pan juices, and continue cooking for 2½ hours (12 to 14 minutes per pound) or until thermometer registers 160°F. Remove turkey and cover with aluminum foil for 20 minutes before carving.

If desired, bake the 2 additional stuffings in their separate dishes during last 1½ hours that the turkey is roasting. To serve, carve turkey and attractively mound each of the 3 stuffings (or just one) alongside.

CORNBREAD AND OYSTER STUFFING

MAKES 6 CUPS

CORNBREAD

4 tablespoons light vegetable oil
1¼ cups yellow cornmeal
¾ cup all-purpose flour
1 teaspoon sugar
½ teaspoon salt
1 tablespoon baking powder
1 cup buttermilk
1 large egg, beaten
¼ cup minced green onion

1½ cups chopped leeks, white part only
6 tablespoons butter
1½ cups (12 ounces) fresh shucked oysters, drained and roughly chopped
2 cups finely diced fresh mushrooms
2 eggs, lightly beaten
1 cup walnuts, lightly toasted and chopped
1 teaspoon minced fresh thyme, or ½ teaspoon dried thyme
1 tablespoon minced fresh sage, or ½ tablespoon dried sage
1 teaspoon fennel seed
2 teaspoons kosher salt
½ teaspoon freshly ground white pepper
½ teaspoon freshly grated nutmeg
Cooked giblets from turkey, diced (optional)

To make cornbread, preheat oven to 450°F. Place 2 tablespoons of the oil in a 9-inch cast-iron skillet and place in oven for about 5 minutes.

In a mixing bowl, sift together cornmeal, flour, sugar, salt, and baking powder. Stir in buttermilk, egg, green onion, and remaining 2 tablespoons oil. Stir until just mixed; do not overmix.

Pour batter into heated skillet. It will sizzle. Return skillet to oven and reduce heat to 400°F. Bake until bread has pulled away from the edges and is golden brown, 20 to 25 minutes. Remove from oven and let cool. Cut cornbread into ½-inch dice to measure 7 cups; set aside. Reserve remaining cornbread for another use.

Preheat oven to 325°F. In a large skillet, sauté leeks in 2 tablespoons of the butter until soft. Add oysters and sauté until they just begin to plump, about 1 minute. Remove leeks and oysters from skillet and set aside. In same pan, sauté mushrooms in remaining 4 tablespoons butter over high heat until golden brown. In a large mixing bowl, combine leeks, oysters, and mushrooms with all remaining ingredients, including reserved 7 cups corn bread, and toss to combine. Mixture should be moist but loose.

Place in an ovenproof casserole and bake in oven, covered, until the edges are lightly browned and slightly crisp, 1 to 1½ hours. Remove cover for the last 15 to 20 minutes of cooking. Makes enough to stuff an 18- to 22-pound turkey, if desired.

SAUSAGE, APPLE, AND APRICOT STUFFING

MAKES 8 CUPS

2 cups finely chopped yellow onion
1 cup chopped celery
6 tablespoons butter
1 pound chorizo or other spicy sausage, cut into ¼-inch dice
8 cups wheatberry or other whole-grain bread, cut into ½-inch cubes and toasted in oven
1 cup diced, peeled tart apples
1 cup diced dried apricots
½ cup minced fresh parsley
2 teaspoons minced fresh oregano, or 1 teaspoon dried oregano
½ to 1 cup chicken stock or Basic Game Bird Stock (page 40)

Preheat oven to 325°F. In a large skillet, sauté onion and celery in butter until onion is translucent. Add sausage and sauté 5 minutes. In a large mixing bowl, combine onion mixture with all remaining ingredients except for stock. Gradually add stock until mixture is moist but still light and loose.

Place stuffing in a lightly buttered ovenproof casserole and bake in oven, covered, until the edges are lightly browned and slightly crisp, 1 to 1½ hours. Remove cover for the last 15 to 20 minutes of cooking. Makes enough to stuff an 18- to 20-pound turkey, if desired.

YUCATÁN STUFFED WILD TURKEY

SERVES 8 TO 10

Recommended Wine: The spicy flavors of this tantalizing stuffing call for a well-chilled Gewürztraminer or Gamay Beaujolais to calm the spice.

The complexity of this Mexican fiesta dish by Mark Miller may intimidate some and relegate its use to a special holiday meal. But the dish is so spectacular that we would urge more widespread use when a little extra cooking time is available. Miller is legendary for his full-flavored fare at the Coyote Cafe in Santa Fe, New Mexico; this dish exemplifies his approach. The gamy flavor and superior texture of the wild turkey over a domestic bird argues for its use.

1 cup dried black beans
7½ cups water
3 tablespoons puréed chipotle chili peppers in adobo (see Note)
1 bay leaf
⅔ cup long-grain white rice
3 dried cascabel chili peppers (see Note), or 2 dried Chinese chili peppers with seeds
2 tablespoons achiote seeds
1 bunch fresh marjoram or oregano, large stems removed
2 cups fresh orange juice
2 tablespoons fresh lime juice
Salt and freshly ground black pepper to taste
2 tablespoons olive oil
1 pound medium shrimp, peeled and deveined
1 medium onion, finely diced
1 small carrot, peeled and finely diced
1 medium red bell pepper, seeded, deveined, and finely diced
1 pint (16 ounces) shucked fresh oysters with their liquor (about 20)
⅓ cup unroasted green pumpkin seeds (see Note)
½ cup chopped fresh cilantro
1 teaspoon finely chopped orange zest
1 wild or domestic turkey (12 to 14 pounds)

Soak beans overnight in water to cover; drain.

In a medium-sized saucepan, combine black beans with 4½ cups of the water, 1 tablespoon of the chipotle purée, and bay leaf. Bring to a simmer over moderately low heat and cook until tender, about 1½ hours. Drain the beans and let cool; discard bay leaf.

Put rice and 2 cups of the water in a small saucepan. Bring to a boil, reduce heat, and cook, covered, until tender, about 15 minutes. Fluff up rice, let cool, and set aside.

In another small saucepan, combine cascabel chilies, achiote seeds, and remaining 1 cup water. Cook over medium-high heat until achiote seeds are soft and no liquid remains, 5 to 10 minutes.

Transfer chilies and seeds to a blender; add marjoram, orange juice, and lime juice. Purée for 10 seconds. Strain through a wire-mesh sieve. Season with salt and black pepper; set aside.

In a large skillet, heat 1 tablespoon of the oil. Add shrimp and sauté over high heat, tossing, until just pink, about 2 minutes. Transfer shrimp to a plate and let cool. Add remaining 1 tablespoon oil to skillet and reduce heat to low. Add onion, carrot, and bell pepper and cook, covered, until tender, about 5 minutes.

In a small skillet, combine oysters and their liquor with remaining 2 tablespoons of chipotle purée. Cook over high heat until edges of oysters just begin to curl, about 2 minutes. With a slotted utensil, transfer oysters to a plate. Reduce cooking liquid over high heat to ¼ cup, about 2 minutes; it will be a thick paste. Add any liquid that drains from the cooked oysters.

Toast pumpkin seeds in a dry skillet over medium heat until they stop popping, about 5 minutes. In a large bowl, combine reserved beans, rice, shrimp, oysters and reduced paste, vegetables, pumpkin seeds, cilantro, and orange zest.

Preheat oven to 325°F. Stuff the turkey neck and cavity with bean mixture and sew up or truss closed (page 37). Place extra stuffing in an ovenproof dish with a cover.

Set the turkey in a large roasting pan and pour reserved chile-achiote purée over it. Roast turkey in preheated oven, basting every 20 minutes and adding water to the pan if the glaze starts to caramelize. Continue to roast until a thermometer registers 160°F, about 3 hours. Place extra stuffing in oven for last hour of cooking. Remove turkey from oven and cover with aluminum foil for 15 to 20 minutes before carving. Serve with stuffing on the side.

NOTE: These chili peppers and pumpkin seeds can be found in Latin American markets.

TURKEY MOLÉ

SERVES 4 GENEROUSLY

Recommended Wine: A rich, hearty Zinfandel provides matching flavor and textural intensity to this dish.

Chocolate, the key ingredient in molé, and turkey probably have the same roots. Girolamo Benzoni remarked in his *History of the New World* (1565) that Mexico had made two unique contributions to the world: "Indian fowls," or turkeys, and "cavacate," or the cocoa bean. That they should come together we suppose was predestined. The intensely flavored, spicy molé, with chocolate as its base, is the perfect foil for wild turkey.

Recipes vary according to the cook, but the key elements are heat (from chilies), sweet spice (from cinnamon, clove, raisins), and the indescribable contribution that unsweetened chocolate makes.

If you are lucky enough to get a true wild turkey, the flavor match with the molé sauce is fantastic. If you can only get the broad-breasted, domestic bird, then we'd suggest using the legs and/or thighs only in this dish, since they tend to be more flavorful and closer to wild meat in texture. The turkey can be grilled as well as sautéed in this recipe.

4 large turkey leg-thigh pieces (about ¾ pound each)
2 tablespoons olive oil
⅔ cup sliced yellow onion
3 cloves garlic, minced
1 tablespoon sesame seed, toasted
¼ teaspoon ground cinnamon
¼ teaspoon ground cloves
¼ teaspoon coriander seed, toasted and crushed
2 tablespoons ground dried ancho or mixed chili peppers
2 teaspoons chopped fresh cilantro
2–3 cups chicken stock or Basic Game Bird Stock (page 40)
3 tablespoons smooth peanut butter
2½ tablespoons tomato paste
4 tablespoons golden raisins
1 ounce unsweetened chocolate, chopped
Salt and freshly ground black pepper to taste
Roasted red bell peppers, julienned, warm tortillas, and fresh cilantro sprigs for garnish

In a large, heavy-bottomed sauté pan, brown turkey in oil until done. Remove turkey and set aside. Add onion to pan and sauté until lightly brown. Add garlic, sesame seed, cinnamon, cloves, coriander seed, ground chili, and chopped cilantro and cook over moderate heat for 5 minutes. Add stock and simmer for 10 minutes, stirring occasionally.

Pour stock mixture into a blender or food processor. Add

peanut butter, tomato paste, raisins, and chocolate and process until smooth. Return sauce to pan, add reserved turkey, and simmer covered until tender, about 35 minutes. Thin with stock if necessary.

Arrange turkey on warm platter. Whisk sauce until smooth and pour over turkey. Garnish with red peppers, tortillas, and cilantro sprigs.

VENISON

*F*or generations raised on deer hunted in the wild and driven home on the hood of the hunter's jeep, farm-raised venison is likely to be disappointing. It doesn't have the bold, gamy flavor that is associated with a wild animal that has foraged in the high pines. But for those who prefer a less assertive, milder meat, this species of venison resembles well-aged, fat-free beef or lamb, and is wholeheartedly satisfying, with a velvety texture and hints of grass, cedar, pecans, acorns, or herbs, depending on where it was raised.

Venison plays a pivotal role in our culinary heritage. Long favored in Europe for its rich flavor and versatility on the table, venison is currently regarded in America with some ambivalence. Many Americans who've experienced wild deer killed during a stressed breeding cycle, improperly dressed in the field, and not cold hung for aging view it as tough, gamy, and distasteful. While sometimes true, this is an unfortunate generalization because, properly cared for and prepared, both wild and farm-raised deer are delicacies of the highest order.

We can ascertain that deer has been eaten by man since prehistory. The earliest records indicate that deer were hunted in China and Borneo half a million years ago. Deer are referred to in Deuteronomy 14:4–5: "These are the beasts which ye shall eat . . . the hart, the roebuck, and the fallow deer." Written records from the Middle Ages also detail the prominence of deer at the feast.

White-tailed deer are thought to have existed in America for several million years. They are one of some 20 different species known to exist today worldwide. Prior to the turn of the century, venison was considered to be one of the most prized of all meats in America and was consumed with great passion in the courts of Europe as well. In the inns, taverns, restaurants, and hotels of both continents, venison was served as part of elaborate multicourse dinners, which often featured a bevy of upland birds as well as game meats.

While never threatened with extinction like the bison, restrictions have existed on the killing of deer since the late seventeenth century. These laws have successfully protected deer, and approximately six million remain in the United States. Contemporary laws still prohibit the sale of hunted deer to restaurants or commercial distributors.

As a point of reference, hunted wild venison requires the tedious (but to some, engaging) process of dressing (skinning and eviscerating) the deer and "aging" it in cool storage (usually 35° to 40°F for 7 to 10 days) to tenderize the meat. The aging process is necessary in part because the animal is often "shocked" at the moment of the kill, and the contraction and rigidity of the muscles following death—known as rigor mortis—require time for the muscles to "relax." Concurrent with the aging itself is the mellowing of venison's complex, gamy flavors. This process relates to a natural enzyme action that produces more tender meat. The practice of aging venison is also common with farm-raised venison.

The word *venison* is sometimes used as a general term for the meat of other big game—antelope, elk, caribou, reindeer, and moose. It literally translates from the Latin *venatus,* meaning "to hunt." Throughout Europe, fallow deer, which have been raised extensively in northern Europe since Roman times, and European roebuck are particularly prized, while in the United States, white-tailed deer, mule deer, and black-tailed deer are treasured by knowledgeable hunters.

Deer has undergone the greatest transformation of all game animals with regard to the farm-raised movement. The success of the farm-raised venison industries in Texas, Hawaii, Florida, Wisconsin, Mississippi, and upstate New York has led to an upsurge in interest in this distinctive, low-fat, low-cholesterol meat around the country.

Currently, approximately forty states have passed legislation allowing deer farming, and the movement is picking up steam quickly. Availability has increased accordingly, particularly in fine-dining restaurants where venison is served as an entrée or as part of a mixed grill with game sausage and small game birds.

One of the primary types of deer found in America today is the axis, native to India, but raised in Texas. Axis meat is light colored and relatively mild, and it benefits from a wide variety of cooking treatments and associated flavors, particularly fruit-based sauces. Black buck antelope is a fine-grained, dark meat that is nicely complemented by fruit sauces as well.

Sika deer, another exotic variety that is native to Manchuria, is considerably darker, redder, and gamier than axis meat, and is well suited to wine-based sauces. The differences in flavor between the free-range, "wild-harvested" axis, sika, and black buck antelope from the Broken Arrow Ranch in Texas (see page 12 for more information) and their farm-raised counterparts are due to their more varied diet, which contributes additional complexity to the meat.

New Zealand venison, an increasingly available, farm-raised red deer with a relatively mild flavor, has a bit more grassy or woodsy taste due to its diet, but the meat is similar to Texas venison in many respects and the product is extremely consistent. Broken Arrow venison is considerably more expensive at this time due to its shorter supply and more labor-intensive slaughtering and processing costs.

In Scotland and Germany, principally red deer are raised. These countries contribute only a small percentage, however, to the overall worldwide production of four thousand tons and one million animals annually.

In the United States alone, one and a half million pounds of farm-raised venison are consumed annually, with approximately 80 percent coming from New Zealand. About one hundred fifty thousand pounds of American-raised deer is currently sold annually.

Ultimately, geographic locale along with diet, muscle tone, and the age of the animal all affect the subtleties of flavor with these various farm-raised and wild-harvested deer and differentiate them from truly wild deer. To the home cook, looking for relative consistency, all these species offer excellent potential.

Beyond the fine taste and supple texture of farm-raised venison, the most significant contributing force to its worldwide success in the past decade has been its health and nutritional advantages, particularly when compared to beef. The loin cut has approximately one third the calories, one half the fat, and 15 percent less cholesterol than a similar cut of beef, according to common studies (see page 263). In terms of calories, fat, and cholesterol for a three-ounce cooked portion, venison loin is similar to broiled salmon, and is substantially lower in all of these categories than chicken breast with the skin.

The nutritional benefits are inherent in the animal itself. The muscles are lean because deer and other game animals undergo a great deal more activity than domestically raised cattle, sheep, and poultry. Venison tends to accumulate what little fat it has in concentrated places in its back and under the spine. There isn't the excessive dispersion of fat known as marbling that is found in other meats. This allows for easy removal of fatty areas prior to shipment of the product. In fact, this lack of fatty pockets between the tissues of meat is what creates challenges for the cook.

Another attractive notion is that most deer are raised without hormones, steroids, or antibiotics to stimulate growth and protect them from disease. Farm-raised venison can therefore be enjoyed as a particularly "natural" product. This is an exciting alternative to the modern technology of a large portion of the domestic beef industry.

Shopping for Venison

Farm-raised venison increasingly can be purchased fresh, but it is not often found this way. Fortunately, frozen venison is handled extremely well and is often indistinguishable from fresh venison in terms of taste. It is flash-frozen immediately after slaughtering, much in the same way that some seafood is. It is stored in Cryo-vac bags that provide an excellent seal, allowing a mellowing of the flavors, and preventing oxidation and spoilage.

A wide variety of venison cuts are available from game purveyors. The most expensive cuts are the tenderloin and boneless saddle, the source of the loin cuts that are prominently featured in the following recipes. Two slightly less-expensive cuts are the Denver leg and the hind leg. Venison can also be purchased as stew, ground patties, and saddle chops, which are like steaks.

Look for bright red meat with a healthy sheen. Older, gray meat indicates possible bacterial problems and improper handling. Remove all sinew, fatty tissue, or silverskin before cooking (farm-raised venison is typically purchased already trimmed).

Fresh venison can be frozen for up to 9 months in airtight plastic bags layered in aluminum foil. Thaw frozen venison in its original wrapper in the refrigerator; it will take 4 to 6 hours per pound. Then, refrigerate thawed meat on a covered plate (not in plastic bags) to prevent it from sweating.

Four to six ounces of boneless venison or twelve to fourteen ounces of bone-in venison are the proper serving portions.

Cooking Tips

Venison is truly the king of game meats, and is also the most misunderstood of the lot. More fine deer meat has been ruined in the ovens, skillets, and grills of our kitchens than virtually any other type of game because of lack of understanding about simple principles of cooking.

Since there is so little fat in venison, there is no grease in the meat to "baste" it while it cooks. Observing proper cooking times and using sensible methods, such as braising tougher leg cuts, will help avoid disappointment. Virtually all of these principles can be applied to similar cuts of antelope, elk, moose, and caribou. A wise and simple axiom for cooking venison: Cook it dry over high heat for a short time or slowly in moisture for a long time.

Venison often benefits from marinating, which increases tenderness and enhances flavor. In addition to red wine marinades, traditional buttermilk or yogurt marinades (page 27) draw out some of the blood and help tenderize the meat. Marinade is typically not necessary with farm-raised venison, however. Do not overmarinate; 4 to 6 hours at room temperature or overnight in the refrigerator is usually sufficient. Marinades should be viewed as a creative flavoring alternative, not as a panacea for tough, improperly handled meat.

Tender cuts, such as the loin, tenderloin, sirloin, and choice leg cuts, should be broiled, sautéed, or grilled quickly to rare-medium or rare. This meat should always remain crimson; it becomes tough and chewy when it is overcooked.

Tougher cuts of wild venison, such as the shoulder, roasts, stew meat, hind leg cuts, and round steaks, may need to be larded with pork fat or barded with fatback or bacon to prevent the meat from drying out. Again, this is typically not necessary with farm-raised venison. Many venison enthusiasts like to insert thin slivers of garlic into the meat as well. Quick searing of these cuts followed by slow roasting (225° to 250°F oven) and braising in liquid are the preferred cooking methods. These cuts need to be cooked long enough for the meat to become tender.

Ground venison is best when combined with a little ground beef or pork or beaten eggs to keep it moist when grilled. These venison burgers can be cooked without the addition of beef or pork by quickly browning them over high heat (either grill or pan), and then cooking them, covered, with a little broth or wine; avoid overcooking or they will taste "leathery." This is caused by the lack of fat in venison; the fat in any meat serves as a baste and prevents the meat from bonding together and tasting tough. These hints will help avoid this problem.

Do not leave roasted venison exposed to the air for very long, or the meat will dry out and whatever small amount of fat exists will congeal. After cooking venison, cover in foil and let rest for a few minutes before serving. Then slice the meat across the grain, and serve immediately for best results.

Serve any leftovers as sandwiches on good crusty bread or toasted English muffins. Do not attempt to reheat venison unless it is in a stew.

Classic Dishes

Traditional venison recipes in the American home included pot roasts braised in coffee and cider vinegar (a throwback to campfire cuisine), savory stews and soups laden with vegetables, venison chili, meat loafs seasoned with Worcestershire sauce or laced with Louisiana hot sauces, and prized steaks gently glazed with currant jelly, peppercorns, and herbs.

Part of the challenge for the home cook of the past was to find a way to use successfully all parts of the hunted deer, a task that the cook of farm-raised game doesn't face because of the wide variety of familiar prime cuts.

Classic Recipe

MARINATED LOIN OF VENISON WITH CHANTERELLES AND JUNIPER BERRY SAUCE

SERVES 6

Recommended Wine: This elegant preparation of venison, juniper berries, and chanterelles is beautifully highlighted by a fine, aged Pinot Noir to echo the earthy qualities of the dish.

Hubert Keller, the enormously gifted chef at San Francisco's elegant Fleur de Lys, understands game intuitively from having grown up in Alsace, where it was plentiful and cooked often. This recipe is a lighter variation on a classic that Keller has adjusted for lower calories and fat. The dish does not take an extraordinarily long time to prepare and is well worth the effort for a special occasion game dinner. Keller likes to serve it with braised red cabbage with diced red apples.

½ recipe Basic Liquid Game Marinade (page 47)
1 boneless loin of venison (3 to 4 pounds)

SAUCE

Reserved marinade
1½ teaspoons tomato paste
6 juniper berries
1 cup beef stock or Basic Game Meat Stock (page 40)
Salt and freshly ground black pepper to taste

CHANTERELLES

1 tablespoon olive oil
8 to 10 ounces fresh black or golden chanterelle mushrooms, stemmed and sliced
½ teaspoon minced garlic
½ cup heavy cream
3 egg yolks, beaten
2 tablespoons finely chopped fresh chives
Salt and freshly ground black pepper to taste

3 tablespoons olive oil

Prepare marinade and add venison to it. Refrigerate and marinate for 24 hours. Remove venison from marinade, reserving marinade, and pat dry with paper towels. Strain marinade into a saucepan. Set venison aside.

To make sauce, bring strained marinade to a boil and add

tomato paste and juniper berries. Reduce over high heat to ¾ cup. Add stock and simmer over medium heat until reduced to 1 cup. Season with salt and pepper; keep warm.

To make chanterelle mixture, place a sauté pan over medium-high heat and add oil. When oil is hot, add chanterelles and garlic and sauté for 2 minutes, stirring occasionally. Meanwhile, in a small bowl, whisk cream until stiff, then fold in egg yolks. Add chives and sautéed chanterelles. Season with salt and pepper and set aside.

Preheat broiler. Cut venison loin into 12 medallions. Season meat with salt and pepper. In a large sauté pan, heat oil and sauté venison over medium heat to medium-rare, turning once, about 2 minutes per side. Transfer meat to a baking sheet and top each medallion with some of the chanterelle mixture. Broil until topping turns golden brown, about 1½ minutes. Do not overcook.

Meanwhile, pour off excess oil from the sauté pan and deglaze pan with the reserved reduced sauce. Reduce further to a light sauce consistency and adjust seasoning.

Spoon sauce onto individual warm serving plates and place 2 venison medallions atop sauce on each plate.

ROASTED VENISON WITH SUN-DRIED CHERRIES AND BLOOD ORANGE–CABERNET SAUVIGNON SAUCE

SERVES 6

The combination of sun-dried cherries and blood oranges is a fine one. This dish is also quite successful when made with dried currants and regular oranges, if the more exotic ingredients are not available.

MARINADE-SAUCE

½ cup Cabernet Sauvignon or other dry red wine
¾ cup cranberry juice
½ cup blood or regular orange juice (about 4 blood oranges)
1 tablespoon finely chopped orange zest
1 shallot, chopped
6 juniper berries, crushed
¼ teaspoon ground mixed peppercorns (black, green, and white)
⅔ cup sun-dried cherries, dried currants, or dried cranberries
⅓ cup olive oil
2 tablespoons butter, at room temperature

1 boneless loin of venison (3 to 4 pounds)

Recommended Wine: Because of the wine used in the marinade, this dish is a natural for a full-bodied Cabernet Sauvignon. This successful marriage is further assured by the use of sun-dried cherries, which echo a hint of Cabernet-like flavors as well.

Combine all ingredients for marinade, except butter, and marinate venison, refrigerated, for 4 to 6 hours. Remove venison from marinade and pat dry with paper towels. Pour marinade into a saucepan and reserve. Set venison aside.

Preheat oven to 350°F. Place venison in roasting pan. Roast for 35 to 40 minutes or until thermometer registers 125°F. Remove roast from oven and cover with aluminum foil for 10 to 15 minutes.

To make sauce, reduce marinade over high heat by half. Swirl in butter, 1 tablespoon at a time. Strain sauce if a smooth sauce is desired, or serve complete with zest and cherries.

To serve, slice venison on bias and spoon sauce over slices.

SOUTHWEST VENISON FAJITAS WITH PAPAYA-AVOCADO SALSA

SERVES 6 TO 8

Recommended Wine: Fajitas, traditionally consumed with beer, can also be enjoyed with a hearty Zinfandel or Petite Sirah to stand up to the spiciness of the dish.

The New Zealand Farm-Raised Venison Council contributed this dish. It places venison in a context commonly dominated by beef—the humble fajita. As such, it is not only tasty, but a healthful variation on the more traditional preparation. If preferred, you may sauté the venison rather than grill it. This is an ideal lunch entrée or first course.

MARINADE

½ cup olive oil
⅓ cup fresh lime juice
2 cloves garlic, crushed
1 teaspoon red-pepper flakes
Salt and freshly ground black pepper to taste

2½ to 3 pounds venison leg meat, in one piece

SALSA

1 cup chopped yellow onion
1 cup chopped tomato
1 cup cubed papaya
½ cup cubed avocado
½ cup chopped fresh cilantro
1 fresh jalapeño pepper, seeded and minced
1 tablespoon fresh lemon juice
1 tablespoon olive oil
Salt and freshly ground black pepper to taste

8 corn tortillas

Combine all ingredients for marinade and marinate venison, refrigerated, for 3 to 5 hours, turning once. Remove venison from marinade and pat dry with paper towels.

To make salsa, combine all ingredients in a small mixing bowl and mix well.

Prepare a fire in a charcoal grill. Grill venison over hot coals to medium-rare. Cover venison with aluminum foil and let rest for a few minutes. Warm the tortillas. Slice venison ¼ inch thick. Divide venison strips evenly among tortillas and top each with some of the salsa. Reserve remaining salsa for another use.

VENISON WITH PLUM-ZINFANDEL SAUCE
Served with Sautéed Watercress and Walnuts

SERVES 4

Recommended Wine: The obvious choice of Zinfandel to complement the sauce made with Zinfandel is what we call the "cheater's way" to perfect food and wine pairing (which is to say—it works!).

Robert Palmgren of the Peppercorn Duck Club at the Hyatt Regency in Kansas City developed this dish for the New Zealand Farm-Raised Venison Council. We have adapted it slightly. The sauce is a very simple reduction of stock, plums, and Zinfandel and uses no cream or butter.

SAUCE
4 large ripe plums, pitted and coarsely chopped
1⅓ cups Zinfandel
1 cup beef stock or Basic Game Meat Stock (page 40)

1 to 1½ pounds venison leg meat, sliced into medallions ¼ inch thick
Salt and freshly ground black pepper to taste
Peanut oil, for sautéing
Sautéed Watercress and Walnuts (recipe follows)
2 plums, halved and pitted, for garnish

To make sauce, in a small saucepan, combine chopped plums, wine, and stock. Bring to a boil, reduce heat, and simmer for 20 minutes or until a light sauce consistency. Transfer to a blender or food processor, and purée. Strain and keep warm.

Season venison with salt and pepper. In a large sauté pan, heat oil over medium-high heat and sauté venison to medium-rare, turning once, about 2 minutes per side. Do not overcook.

To serve, place venison on individual warm serving plates, nap with sauce, and arrange sautéed watercress alongside. Cut each plum half into slices, but not all the way through. Garnish each plate with a plum half, fanning slices out.

SAUTÉED WATERCRESS AND WALNUTS

2 tablespoons walnut oil
1 tablespoon minced shallots
2 teaspoons raspberry vinegar or black currant vinegar
3 bunches watercress (about ¾ pound), tough stems removed
3 tablespoons walnuts, lightly toasted and slivered
Kosher salt and freshly ground black pepper to taste

In a sauté pan over moderate heat, heat oil and add shallots and vinegar. Add watercress and sauté until just beginning to wilt, about 1 minute. Remove from heat, toss with walnuts, and season to taste.

VENISON WITH JUNIPER BERRY SAUCE
Served with Chestnut and Celery Root Purées

SERVES 4 TO 6

Recommended Wine: This hearty, flavorful dish with its red wine-based sauce stands up to a full-bodied Cabernet Sauvignon or Merlot.

While venison can now be enjoyed the year around and cooked in many different ways, this classic treatment by Maine's Sam Hayward (22 Lincoln in Brunswick) showcases the traditional combination of game with chestnut and celery root purées. As such, it makes a beautiful fall and winter dish, which is complicated to prepare but worth it. The purées are adaptable to many other game dishes in this book.

1 cup Basic Liquid Game Marinade (see page 27)
1 boneless loin of venison (3 to 4 pounds), sliced into six ½-inch-thick medallions

SAUCE

2 tablespoons olive oil, or more as needed
¼ cup diced celery
¼ cup diced carrot
¼ cup sliced fresh mushrooms
2 medium shallots, chopped
1 clove garlic, minced
⅓ cup chopped, seeded tomato
1 teaspoon black peppercorns, crushed
2 cups full-bodied red wine (preferably Zinfandel or Petite Sirah)
2 cups beef stock or Basic Game Meat Stock (page 40)
12 to 16 juniper berries, crushed
Salt and freshly ground black pepper to taste
1 recipe Chestnut Purée (page 48)
Celery Root Purée (recipe follows)

Prepare marinade and place venison in it. Let rest at room temperature for 1 hour. Remove venison from marinade and pat dry with paper towels. Reserve marinade. Set venison aside.

To make sauce, add 1 tablespoon of the oil to a heavy-bottomed, 6-cup saucepan. Add celery, carrot, mushrooms, shallots, and garlic and sauté, stirring frequently, until vegetables begin to brown. Add tomato, toss for a moment, and then add peppercorns, wine, stock, and reserved marinade. Bring to a boil, lower heat, and simmer until reduced to about 1½ cups. Reserve.

In a large skillet, heat remaining 1 tablespoon oil, or more if needed, and tilt pan to coat evenly. When nearly smoking, quickly sear all sides of venison evenly. Reduce heat to medium and pan roast to just rare, 2 to 3 minutes per side. Test for doneness by gently pressing for first sign of resistance and springiness. Remove venison to a plate and keep warm. Pour off any excess fat from skillet.

To finish venison, while skillet is still hot, pour in the reserved sauce. Bring to a boil, scraping up caramelized bits in pan. Reduce over medium-high heat by one third. Strain into a small saucepan, pressing hard on the solids. Add juniper berries, bring to a boil again, reduce to a light sauce consistency, and strain. Season with salt and pepper.

To serve, place venison medallions on individual warm serving plates. Spoon sauce over venison. Serve with purées to the side of venison.

CELERY ROOT PURÉE

SERVES 4 TO 6

¾ **pound celery root, peeled and diced**
Salt to taste
Fresh lemon juice to taste
1 tablespoon butter, at room temperature
¼ cup heavy cream
Freshly ground black pepper and freshly grated nutmeg to taste

Fill a small saucepan with water and bring to a boil. Add celery root and salt, reduce heat, and simmer until cubes are easily pierced by a small knife, 10 to 12 minutes. Drain celery root thoroughly, reserving liquid, and place celery root in a food processor. Add lemon juice, butter, cream, salt, pepper, and nutmeg. Purée until smooth, adding small amounts of cooking liquid as needed to make a smooth, light mousse. Keep warm until serving.

ROASTED VENISON WITH SWEET ONION SAUCE
Served with Sweet Potato Pancakes

SERVES 6

Recommended Wine: This hearty dish requires a full-bodied Cabernet Sauvignon, Zinfandel, or Petite Sirah to accompany its deep, rich flavors.

This contribution from Stephan Pyles of Routh Street Cafe/Baby Routh in Dallas is a savory mélange of complementary flavors. This dish is extremely simple and has been a big hit on our table every time we've served it. Pyles likes to prepare the dish with antelope, but venison is far easier to obtain.

2 tablespoons oil or clarified butter
1 boneless loin of venison or antelope (3 to 4 pounds)
Salt and freshly ground black pepper to taste
2 sweet onions (preferably Vidalia), chopped
½ cup chopped carrot
½ cup chopped celery
4 cloves garlic, minced
1 cup dry red wine
2½ cups beef stock, veal stock, or Basic Game Meat Stock (page 40)
4 tablespoons butter, at room temperature
Sweet Potato Pancakes (recipe follows)

Preheat oven to 400°F. Heat oil in a heavy, ovenproof roasting pan over medium-high heat. Season venison with salt and pepper and sear on all sides in oil. Remove venison from pan. Add onions, carrot, celery, and garlic to pan and cook for 2 minutes, stirring frequently. Remove pan from fire and place venison loin on top of vegetables. Place pan in preheated oven and roast to medium-rare, 10 to 12 minutes.

Remove venison from pan and keep warm in foil. Place roasting pan over high heat on stove top, add wine, and deglaze pan. Reduce to a medium sauce consistency. Add stock and reduce by half. Strain into a saucepan, discard vegetables, and reheat sauce. Reduce further, if necessary. Whisk in butter, 1 tablespoon at a time, and adjust seasoning with salt and pepper.

To serve, slice venison on the bias, spoon sauce over top, and serve with pancakes.

SWEET POTATO PANCAKES

SERVES 6

1 large sweet potato (about 1 pound), peeled and grated
1 medium baking potato (about ½ pound), peeled and grated
½ medium yellow onion, grated
1 egg, lightly beaten
1 tablespoon fresh bread crumbs
½ teaspoon salt
½ teaspoon freshly ground black pepper

2 tablespoons pure maple syrup
Pinch freshly grated nutmeg
1½ tablespoons flour
Vegetable oil or clarified butter for cooking pancakes

Place potatoes and onion in colander; rinse with cold water and drain thoroughly. In a mixing bowl, combine potatoes and all remaining ingredients, except oil.

Divide mixture into 6 large portions and drain again. Pat each portion into a flat cake about ½-inch thick.

In a large skillet, heat oil over medium-high heat. Cook pancakes until browned, 4 to 5 minutes. Turn pancakes and cook on other side until golden brown and crispy, 4 to 5 minutes. Remove pancakes to paper towels to drain. Keep warm under aluminum foil until ready to serve.

VENISON WITH POMEGRANATES, HERBS, AND PISTACHIOS

SERVES 4

Recommended Wine: The tart flavors of pomegranate with the complexity of nuts allow an opportunity to showcase an elegant Cabernet Sauvignon, which mirrors the flavors of the sauce and showcases the venison.

The combination of pomegranates and venison is a classic marriage of fall ingredients. Chef Jimmy Schmidt of the Rattlesnake Club in Detroit embellishes this recipe with pistachios for extra flavor and texture and serves it with a gratin of root vegetables or polenta. The steaks are also good grilled over a charcoal fire.

SAUCE

1 cup veal stock, beef stock, or Basic Game Meat Stock
(page 40)
1 cup pomegranate juice or cranberry juice
1½ teaspoons juniper berries, crushed
2 medium oranges, peeled, seeded, and chopped
1 tablespoon black peppercorns
4 tablespoons unsalted butter, at room temperature

4 venison steaks, from tenderloin or sirloin (6 to 8 ounces each, trimmed weight)
2 tablespoons olive oil
Salt and freshly ground black pepper to taste
½ cup pomegranate seeds
2 tablespoons minced fresh chives
2 tablespoons fresh tarragon leaves, or other fresh herb
2 tablespoons coarsely chopped, skinned pistachios
4 sprigs fresh tarragon (or other fresh herb) for garnish
4 small clusters pomegranate seeds for garnish

To make sauce, in a medium-sized saucepan combine stock, pomegranate juice, juniper berries, oranges, and peppercorns. Bring to a simmer over medium-high heat and reduce to about ½ cup, about 15 minutes. Strain sauce and return to a simmer over medium heat. Whisk in butter, 1 tablespoon at a time. Adjust seasonings. Remove from heat; keep warm.

Preheat broiler. Rub surfaces of venison with olive oil and season with salt and pepper. Place on broiler pan and cook until well seared on both sides and medium-rare, 2 to 3 minutes per side or until a thermometer registers about 130°F. Cover with aluminum foil and let rest for a few minutes before serving.

Spoon sauce into center of serving plates. Sprinkle pomegranate seeds, chives, tarragon leaves, and pistachios over and around sauce. Slice venison on the bias and place atop sauce. Garnish with tarragon sprigs and pomegranate seeds and serve.

LOIN OF VENISON WITH LAVENDER AND PETITE SIRAH SAUCE

SERVES 8

Recommended Wine: This dish obviously calls for drinking the same wine as is used in the marinade, so make sure you buy two bottles when shopping for the wine. Petite Sirah or Zinfandel is highly recommended to supplement the gamy flavors of the venison and the aromatic presence of the lavender.

Aromatic lavender and a rich, full-bodied wine make this exotic sauce developed in concept by Ralph Tingle work beautifully. The sauce itself is quite vivid, with an intense purplish cast; more butter can be used to intensify and richen it, if desired. This simple, but elegant presentation can be accompanied with a sweet potato casserole, gratin of potatoes, or Celery Root Purée (page 244; double recipe to serve 8). It is particularly well suited to the colder months of the year.

½ cup olive oil
½ bunch fresh sage, stemmed and leaves mashed
½ bunch fresh thyme, stemmed and leaves mashed
½ bunch fresh parsley, stemmed and leaves mashed
1 yellow onion, chopped
4 carrots, peeled and chopped
4 stalks celery, trimmed and chopped
5 tablespoons dried lavender blossoms (see Note)
Kosher salt and freshly ground black pepper to taste
1 boneless loin of venison (4 to 5 pounds), cut into 16 medallions
2 cups full-bodied red wine (preferably Petite Sirah or Zinfandel)
1 shallot, chopped
4 tablespoons unsalted butter, at room temperature

Combine ¼ cup of the oil, sage, thyme, parsley, onion, carrots, celery, 2½ tablespoons of the lavender blossoms, salt, and pepper. Add venison, toss well, and marinate, refrigerated, for 4 to 6 hours or overnight.

Coat the bottom of a large, heavy skillet with remaining ¼ cup olive oil and place over medium-high heat. Remove venison from marinade and pat dry with paper towels. Sprinkle venison with salt and pepper. Sauté venison in oil, in batches, to medium-rare, turning once, about 2 minutes per side. Do not overcook. Remove venison from pan and keep warm.

Add wine, remaining 2½ tablespoons lavender, and shallot and bring to a boil, scraping up any bits on pan bottom. Lower heat and reduce to a light sauce consistency. Strain and return to pan. Whisk in butter, 1 tablespoon at a time. Taste and adjust seasoning.

Spoon sauce on individual serving plates and top with venison medallions.

NOTE: Dried lavender blossoms can be found in natural-food stores.

VENISON MEDALLIONS WITH BLACKBERRY-SAGE SAUCE
Served with Wild Mushroom–Leek Compote

SERVES 4

Dean Fearing, whose adventuresome southwestern style has helped shape the region's cooking, created the original inspiration for this adapted recipe. The magnificent blend of flavors is a perfect showcase for a prime cut of venison, and the intensity of the sauce can be heightened by the use of an excellent Zinfandel.

SAUCE

1 cup red wine (preferably Zinfandel)
1 medium shallot, chopped
1½ cups blackberries or blueberries
1 cup brown veal stock or Basic Game Meat Stock (page 40), reduced to *demi-glace*
2 tablespoons butter, at room temperature
Salt and freshly ground black pepper to taste
1 to 2 tablespoons honey
2 sprigs fresh sage, or 1 teaspoon ground sage

8 medallions from boneless loin of venison (3 ounces each)
Salt and freshly ground black pepper to taste
3 tablespoons safflower oil

Recommended Wine: This dish, with its emphasis on berries, is a natural for Zinfandel, which echoes the berry flavors and is used in the reduction for the sauce.

To make sauce, combine wine and shallots in a medium saucepan and bring to a boil. Cook until liquid is reduced to about ½ cup. Add berries and return liquid to a simmer. Cook, stirring occasionally, until berries are soft, about 15 minutes. Add *demi-glace* and bring liquid to a boil. Reduce heat, and cook, stirring occasionally, until sauce coats the back of a spoon, about 15 minutes.

Strain sauce and return to pan. Whisk in butter, 1 tablespoon at a time. Add salt, pepper, and honey. Add sage to sauce and steep for 15 to 20 minutes, or until ready to use. Keep warm. Remove sage sprigs just before serving.

Season venison with salt and pepper. In a large sauté pan, heat oil to nearly smoking. Carefully place medallions in pan and sauté for 3 minutes, being careful not to crowd pan. Turn and cook to medium-rare, about 2 minutes. Repeat as necessary to brown all medallions.

To serve, spoon sauce on warm individual serving plates. Place 2 medallions in center of each plate and nestle a small mound of compote next to each medallion.

WILD MUSHROOM–LEEK COMPOTE

SERVES 4

1 large leek, white part only, cut into 2-inch lengths and julienned
1 cup julienned fresh or reconstituted, dried wild mushrooms such as morels, shiitakes, and/or cèpes
½ cup heavy cream
Salt and freshly ground white pepper to taste
Juice of ½ lemon, or to taste

Combine leeks, mushrooms, and cream in a medium saucepan. Bring liquid to a boil, reduce heat, and cook until cream has thickened, about 5 minutes. Remove from heat and season with salt, pepper, and lemon juice. Keep warm. (The compote may be prepared several hours ahead and reheated.)

MARINATED LOIN OF VENISON ROASTED IN MUSTARD
Served with Creamy Polenta with Wild Mushrooms

SERVES 8 TO 10

Recommended Wine: A rich Cabernet Sauvignon or Merlot and a lusty companion would be the perfect accompaniment for this dish.

A red wine marinade was often used to cover the flavor of old or gamy wild venison. Today's farm-raised venison is much more delicate in flavor but can still be enhanced with a marinade. We love this dish served with creamy polenta flavored with wild mushrooms.

½ recipe Basic Liquid Game Marinade (page 27)
1 boneless loin of venison (4 to 5 pounds), well trimmed
1 tablespoon olive oil for sautéing

MUSTARD COATING

3 large cloves garlic
⅓ cup chopped green onion
⅓ cup dry white wine
1 teaspoon minced fresh sage, or ½ teaspoon dried sage
1 teaspoon minced fresh thyme, or ½ teaspoon dried thyme
1 cup Dijon-style mustard
¼ cup olive oil
1 teaspoon kosher salt or sea salt

Creamy Polenta with Wild Mushrooms (recipe follows)

Prepare marinade and place venison in it. Marinate, refrigerated, 2 to 3 hours, turning occasionally. Remove venison from marinade and pat dry with paper towels. Heat a large sauté pan over high heat and quickly sear venison in oil on all sides for 3 to 4 minutes. (If you don't have enough room in pan, cut loin in half and sear in 2 pieces.)

To make coating, combine all ingredients in a blender or food processor and quickly process until smooth. Mixture should be very thick.

Preheat oven to 375°F. Place loin in a roasting pan and cover well with coating. Roast until meat is medium-rare, 15 to 17 minutes or until thermometer registers 130°F. Cover meat with aluminum foil and let rest at least 5 minutes before slicing.

To serve, slice venison and divide among individual warm serving plates. Serve polenta alongside.

CREAMY POLENTA WITH WILD MUSHROOMS

MAKES 10 CUPS

⅓ cup olive oil
1 cup finely chopped yellow onion
1 cup coarsely chopped domestic mushrooms
2 tablespoons finely chopped garlic
1 ounce dried porcini mushrooms, soaked in 2 cups warm water for 30 minutes, drained, water reserved, and roughly chopped
1 tablespoon chopped fresh basil
1 teaspoon chopped fresh oregano
6 cups chicken stock or vegetable stock
2 cups coarse polenta or yellow cornmeal
Salt and freshly ground white pepper to taste
½ cup heavy cream
½ cup freshly grated Asiago or Parmesan cheese
½ pound fresh porcini, chanterelle, or shiitake mushrooms, sautéed in 1 tablespoon olive oil, for garnish

In a large saucepan, heat oil and sauté onion, domestic mushrooms, and garlic until soft but not browned. Add dried porcini to pan and sauté for 3 minutes. Carefully strain mushroom water to get rid of any sand and add to pan along with the basil, oregano, and stock. Bring to a boil.

With a wooden spoon, stir in polenta slowly to prevent lumps. Reduce heat and simmer for 5 to 10 minutes, stirring regularly. Polenta should be very thick and creamy and begin to pull away from sides of pan. Season with salt and pepper.

Just before serving, add cream and cheese and stir vigorously. Serve alongside venison garnished with sautéed mushrooms. Pour any leftover polenta into a pie pan, cover, and refrigerate. Grill or sauté it for another dish.

BUCKWHEAT CRÊPES WITH VENISON AND HOISIN-PLUM SAUCE

SERVES 8 AS A FIRST COURSE, OR 4 AS AN ENTRÉE

This is an unusual first course, a kind of Asian fajita, which can be made in advance. Boar or buffalo may be used in place of the venison.

MARINADE

4 large cloves garlic, minced
½ cup chopped green onion
3 tablespoons low-sodium soy sauce
1 teaspoon sesame oil (see Note)
2 tablespoons mirin (see Note) or dry sherry
1 tablespoon honey
½ cup beef stock or Basic Game Meat Stock (page 40)

1½ pounds boneless venison leg, well trimmed

Recommended Wine: A fruity ripe Zinfandel offers enough intensity to complement the unusual combination of flavors in this dish.

SAUCE

5 cups finely chopped fresh plums, or 4 cups drained, canned purple plums
⅓ cup hoisin sauce (see Note)
2 tablespoons minced fresh ginger
⅓ cup fresh lime juice
½ cup mirin, or ¼ cup dry sherry
1 tablespoon chili oil (see Note), or ½ teaspoon minced, seeded fresh serrano chili pepper

CRÊPES

4 large eggs
¼ cup milk
1¼ cups water
¾ cup buckwheat flour
¾ cup all-purpose flour
¼ pound butter, melted and cooled
½ teaspoon salt
1 teaspoon sugar
Peanut oil for cooking

2 tablespoons olive oil
¼ cup chopped green onion
½ cup fresh water chestnuts, jicama, or celery, peeled and diced
¼ cup chopped fresh cilantro
Fresh cilantro sprigs for garnish

Combine all ingredients for marinade. Cut venison into strips about 1½ inches thick and 6 inches long and add to marinade. Marinate, refrigerated, for 6 hours or overnight.

To make sauce, combine all ingredients in a nonreactive saucepan and cook over medium heat until reduced and thick, about 15 minutes. Set aside 1 cup of the sauce to use with this recipe. Refrigerate any leftover sauce for another use.

To make crêpes, combine eggs, milk, and water in a blender. With machine running, add all remaining ingredients, except peanut oil. Let batter rest for at least 1 hour. Heat an 8-inch nonstick crêpe pan over medium heat and brush with a few drops of oil. To make each crêpe, ladle in just enough batter to thinly coat oiled pan. Cook until set, about 1 minute; turn and cook on second side until set, 30 to 45 seconds. Remove to flat surface to cool. Repeat with remaining batter, adding oil to pan as needed. Crêpes may be stacked when completely cool. You should have at least 12 crêpes.

Remove venison from marinade and pat dry with paper towels. In a large sauté pan, heat oil over high heat and sauté venison until just browned but still juicy and pink inside, about 2 to 3 minutes. Cool and cut into ¼-inch-wide strips. Keep warm.

In a mixing bowl, toss venison with green onion, ½ cup of the plum sauce, water chestnuts, and chopped cilantro. Filling should be moist. Add more plum sauce, if more moisture is needed.

Cut 12 crêpes in half. Roll up each half with 2 tablespoons or so of venison mixture into a cone shape. For an entrée, serve 3 filled cones per plate. Garnish with cilantro sprigs.

NOTE: These ingredients can be found in Asian markets and well-stocked supermarkets.

BIG DOG VENISON CHILI VERDE
Served with Avocado Salsa

SERVES 8 TO 10

Recommended Wine: A hearty Zinfandel underscores the intense flavors and thick texture of this venison stew.

We originally created this dish at the famous (or infamous) Big Dog Saloon, a pseudo-Mexican bar/Western saloon owned by Fetzer Vineyards, in the hills of California's Mendocino County. The saloon had burned to the ground in a bad fire a few weeks before, and was rebuilt in about a week and a half by a hardworking crew. This dish was created as part of the opening ceremonies for the new Big Dog.

We used wild venison, which had been shot in the hills and had been hung for several days to develop flavor. It's a real winner of a chili, if we say so ourselves, and, like most chilis and stews, it's better the second day.

4 pounds lean venison stew meat, cut into 1-inch cubes
Salt and freshly ground black pepper to taste
4 tablespoons olive oil
2 cups chopped yellow onion
2 tablespoons slivered garlic
1 pound chorizo or other spicy sausage, cut into ½-inch dice (optional)
2 pounds fresh tomatillos, husks discarded and quartered, or 2 cans (16 ounces each) tomatillos, drained
1 tablespoon minced, seeded fresh serrano chili peppers
2 teaspoons fennel seed
1 teaspoon cumin seed, lightly toasted and crushed
½ teaspoon ground cinnamon

½ teaspoon ground cloves
2 large bay leaves
3 cups beef stock or Basic Game Meat Stock (page 40), or as
needed
1 cup dry white wine
⅔ cup finely chopped Swiss chard
⅓ cup chopped fresh cilantro
Salt to taste
Avocado Salsa (recipe follows)
Toasted unsalted pumpkin seeds for garnish (optional)

Season venison liberally with salt and pepper. Add 2 table-spoons of the olive oil to a heavy-bottomed, 8-quart casserole and brown meat thoroughly. Remove meat and set aside. Add remaining oil, onion, garlic, and sausage and brown lightly. Return venison to casserole and add tomatillos, chilies, fennel seed, cumin, cinnamon, cloves, bay leaves, 3 cups stock, and wine. Simmer, partially covered, until meat is tender, about 1½ hours. Stir in the Swiss chard and cilantro and simmer for 5 minutes. Adjust seasoning and add more stock if too thick. Garnish with salsa and pumpkin seeds.

AVOCADO SALSA

MAKES ABOUT 2 CUPS

1 large or 2 medium-sized ripe avocados, peeled, pitted, and cut into ¼-inch dice
1 medium-sized yellow or red tomato, seeded and cut into ¼-inch dice
¼ cup finely chopped sweet red onion
½ teaspoon minced, seeded serrano chili pepper
½ teaspoon minced garlic
1 tablespoon fresh lime juice or lemon juice
2 tablespoons chopped fresh cilantro
Big pinch sugar
Salt and freshly ground white pepper to taste

In a mixing bowl, combine all ingredients and toss gently. Refrigerate at least 1 hour before serving.

VENISON STEAK SOUP

SERVES 8 TO 10

Recommended Wine: A robust Zinfandel is well suited to this hearty soup.

This very easy, hearty soup uses venison that has been grilled and is then added at the last minute. (You may broil the steak instead, if desired.) The soup is best when made with a good venison stock, of course, but any good meat or game stock will do. Make sure the stock is as clear as possible so that you can see all the vegetables.

MARINADE

¼ cup olive oil
1 teaspoon minced garlic
¼ teaspoon hot-pepper flakes
½ teaspoon fresh thyme leaves, or ¼ teaspoon dried thyme
½ teaspoon kosher salt
2 teaspoons red wine vinegar

1½ pounds lean venison steak, at least 1-inch thick
¼ cup olive oil
2 cups sliced red onion
1 cup julienned carrot
1 cup sliced celery
2 teaspoons slivered garlic
7 cups beef stock or Basic Game Meat Stock (page 40)
2 cups hearty red wine (preferably Zinfandel or Cabernet Sauvignon)
1 cup diced, seeded tomato
1 large bay leaf
1 teaspoon fennel seed
Salt and freshly ground black pepper to taste
2 cups finely shredded red cabbage
1 cup diced, peeled parsnip
Chopped fresh chives for garnish

Combine all ingredients for marinade. Marinate steak, refrigerated, for 4 hours or overnight.

In a heavy-bottomed soup pot, heat oil and sauté onion, carrot, celery, and garlic until very lightly colored. Add stock, wine, tomato, bay leaf, and fennel seed and simmer for 45 minutes. Season with salt and pepper. Add cabbage and parsnip and simmer for 3 minutes or until parsnip is cooked.

Meanwhile, prepare a fire in a charcoal grill. Quickly grill venison steak to medium-rare, turning once, 3 to 4 minutes per side. Slice across the grain into thin, even slices. Ladle soup into warm bowls and place venison slices on top. Garnish with chives.

EXOTIC GAME ANIMALS

Alligator

Described by noted humorist and writer Calvin Trillin as "the only exotic meat I have ever run across that nobody seems to describe as tasting like chicken," alligator is a greatly misunderstood creature of the wild. In fact, we find that its taste does fall somewhere between chicken and rabbit, with perhaps a hint of frog's legs.

The laws regulating alligator have changed substantially over the years. In 1962, alligator was listed on the endangered species list. Ten years later, alligator had repropagated itself to the extent that in many parts of Louisiana and Florida it had become a nuisance on highways, in residential backyards, and even in shopping centers.

Accordingly, in 1974 the federal statutes governing alligators were rescinded and the responsibility for control and processing of the animal was returned to the states. With the growth in population of alligators has come an expansion of the hunting season, and the requirement of the hunter to tag every alligator that is killed. Currently, alligator is one of the few game animals that can be sold commercially without being raised on a farm and sold through a licensed distributor.

In cuisine, because of availability and origin, alligator recipes tend to show Creole influences. Piggybacking the interest in all things blackened in the late 1980s, many blackened alligator dishes appeared on restaurant menus in the southeastern United States, and in certain other parts of the country where the novelty of the dish far outweighed serious culinary interest.

In cooking alligator, the tenderloin, which comes from a cylindrical tube inside the tail, is the most satisfying cut.

BLACKENED ALLIGATOR STEAKS

SERVES 4

Recommended Wine: With this dish, we've tried a fruity, slightly herbaceous Sauvignon Blanc to help combat the spiciness, but we must admit that we prefer beer!

This dish should only be attempted with stoves that have excellent hooded ventilation, or in kitchens with plenty of windows. The blackening causes a tremendous amount of smoke that will trigger nearby smoke detectors.

4 alligator steaks, from the tail (about 6 ounces each)
3 tablespoons butter, melted
1 teaspoon salt
1 tablespoon paprika
1 teaspoon ground cumin
1 teaspoon cayenne pepper
½ teaspoon freshly ground black pepper
½ teaspoon freshly ground white pepper
½ teaspoon dried thyme
½ teaspoon dried oregano
½ teaspoon dried chives
1 teaspoon garlic powder

Brush steaks with 2 tablespoons of the butter. In a small bowl, combine all remaining ingredients and mix thoroughly. Dip both sides of each steak into seasoning mix. Place a dry, heavy cast-iron skillet over high heat for 5 to 7 minutes. Place steaks in pan and sear for 2 minutes; turn, brush with remaining 1 tablespoon butter, and cook for 1 to 2 minutes. (With thicker steaks, it may be necessary to finish in a moderate oven for 4 to 5 minutes.)

SCALLOPINI OF ALLIGATOR

SERVES 4

Recommended Wine: A Sauvignon Blanc with its citrus overtones emphasizes the citrus-tinged sauce.

Alligator receives a kind of Italian piccata treatment in this recipe. The sauce works nicely with thinly sliced boar and boneless breasts of game birds as well.

1 pound alligator tail meat, thinly sliced
Salt and freshly ground black pepper to taste
¼ cup olive oil
3 tablespoons slivered shallots
3 tablespoons white wine vinegar
½ cup chicken stock
2 teaspoons chopped anchovy fillet
1½ tablespoons finely chopped cornichon
1 tablespoon drained capers
2 teaspoons fresh lemon juice
1 teaspoon minced garlic
3 tablespoons minced fresh parsley

Gently pound alligator slices so that they are of even thickness. Season well with salt and pepper.

In a sauté pan, heat oil and sauté alligator slices over moderately high heat, in batches if necessary. Remove to a serving platter and keep warm.

Add all remaining ingredients to pan and quickly reduce over high heat to a light sauce consistency. Taste and adjust seasoning. Pour over alligator and serve immediately.

Antelope

Although clearly a breed apart from deer, antelope are often lumped with them from a culinary standpoint, since the animals are handled very similarly. In Texas, the black buck and nilgai antelope are raised on preserves simulating a natural, wild environment.

It's estimated that when Europeans reached California, there were as many as half a million pronghorn antelope there. Today only about 7,000 remain. In 1989 a herd of 267 pronghorn antelope was moved from Northern California to an 82,000-acre preserve owned by the Nature Conservancy on the Carrizo Plain in San Luis Obispo County, about 140 miles northwest of Los Angeles. The current preservation plan does not include farming these animals, however.

Antelope can be prepared in much the same way as venison, and can be used interchangeably with the venison recipes in this book.

Escargot

It may be a bit of a stretch to include snails as game, but we think they qualify. In the wild, snails must be purged (cleaned out) before they can be eaten. It's a relatively simple process that takes a week or so of a straight cornmeal diet.

ESCARGOTS IN GARLIC BUTTER WITH SMOKED HAM AND ANGEL HAIR PASTA

SERVES 6

Recommended Wine: A crisp, fruity Sauvignon Blanc cuts through the garlicky-tomato flavors of the sauce and provides good balancing acidity.

We've had great success with this recipe at John Ash & Company. An interesting presentation is to form 6 little mounds of pasta on each plate, top each with a snail, and spoon the sauce around them. We owe this idea to Jiro Ogue, chef at the Levante restaurant in Kobe, Japan.

GARLIC BUTTER

½ pound unsalted butter, at room temperature
¼ cup finely minced shallots
¼ cup minced garlic
½ cup dry white wine
3 tablespoons brandy
½ teaspoon kosher salt
¼ teaspoon freshly ground black pepper
4 tablespoons minced fresh parsley
2 tablespoons minced fresh basil
1 tablespoon white wine Worcestershire sauce

Salt to taste
1 pound fresh angel hair pasta
⅔ cup garlic butter (see recipe above)
36 large snails, cleaned and rinsed
2 cups ripe Roma tomatoes, seeded, pulp removed, and julienned
¼ pound dry smoked ham, julienned
3 tablespoons thinly cut green onion
¼ cup slivered fresh basil
¼ cup freshly grated Asiago or Parmesan cheese
Fresh basil sprigs, toasted pine nuts, and freshly ground black pepper for garnish

To make garlic butter, in a saucepan, melt 2 tablespoons of the butter and sauté shallots and garlic until soft but not browned. Add wine, brandy, salt, and pepper and reduce until syrupy. Remove from heat and let cool. Beat wine reduction, parsley, basil, and Worcestershire sauce into remaining butter just until combined. Refrigerate until ready to use.

Fill a large pot with water, bring to a boil, and add salt. Cook pasta in boiling water until just tender, 3 to 4 minutes; drain.

While pasta is cooking, in a sauté pan, melt reserved garlic butter and sauté snails for 2 to 3 minutes. Add tomatoes, ham, green onion, and basil and heat through. Toss snail mixture with pasta.

Arrange pasta attractively on warm individual serving plates. Sprinkle with cheese. Garnish with basil sprigs, pine nuts, and a grinding or two of black pepper.

Frog

Most people do not think of frog as a game animal, yet it is one of the most widely available edible creatures in the wild. Frog's legs are extremely tasty; they do taste like chicken, just as everyone has probably always told you, but sometimes with a slightly "fishier" taste.

In American markets, frog's legs usually come cleaned, skinned, and ready to cook. They vary greatly in size, so you should specify the size that you want. We find that smaller ones are better than larger ones, which sometimes have a stronger taste. With small legs, 6 to 8 pairs per person are sufficient for a main course; 2 to 3 pairs are enough if serving large legs.

Frog's legs are best fresh, of course. If fresh are not available, frozen ones will suffice. Although frog's legs may not be immediately visible in the poultry or seafood section of your market, they are often available on request.

FROG'S LEGS WITH PINE NUTS AND LEMON

SERVES 4

Recommended Wine: A crisp Sauvignon Blanc provides excellent acidity to emphasize this tart, herbal-tinged dish.

An Italian friend of ours, who raises frogs for the commercial market, shared this favorite recipe.

3 cups dark beer
2 tablespoons fresh thyme leaves, or 1 tablespoon dried thyme
24 pairs small frog's legs
Salt and freshly ground black pepper to taste
Flour for dredging
6 tablespoons olive oil
4 tablespoons unsalted butter
⅔ cup pine nuts
2 tablespoons fresh lemon juice
2 tablespoons slivered garlic
¼ cup minced fresh parsley
¼ cup loosely packed fresh basil leaves, minced
¼ cup drained capers

Combine beer and thyme in a bowl, add frog's legs, and marinate for 1 hour at room temperature. Remove frog's legs and pat dry with paper towels. Season with salt and pepper and dredge in flour.

Heat oil in a sauté pan and sauté legs until golden brown and tender, about 8 minutes. Remove to paper towels to drain; keep warm.

In a separate sauté pan, melt butter and sauté pine nuts until lightly golden. Add lemon juice, garlic, parsley, basil, and capers and cook for 2 minutes. Taste and adjust seasoning.

Arrange frog's legs on individual warm serving plates and pour sauce over them. Serve immediately.

Rattlesnake

Rattlesnake is a quintessential part of campfire cuisine. It is not widely available to even the curious game cook, but is included here for novelty's sake and because the meat is tasty.

GRILLED RATTLESNAKE, JAPANESE STYLE

SERVES 4

Recommended Wine: Warm sake or sherry is the most appropriate choice.

This dish is inspired by several trips to Japan and a boyhood in Arizona. To Americans, snake is viewed somewhat suspiciously. In many parts of the world, however, it is eaten readily and considered a delicacy. In America, native Indians often consumed snake. Nowadays, several areas in the Southwest organize great roundups of snakes, with the catch cooked in many different ways.

⅓ **cup soy sauce**
¼ **cup fresh lime juice**
⅓ **cup mirin (see Note), or 2 tablespoons sweet sherry**
1 pound skinned rattlesnake meat, cut into 1-inch lengths

Combine soy sauce, lime juice, and mirin. Add snake and marinate for at least 2 hours.

Prepare a fire in a charcoal grill. Remove snake from marinade, reserving marinade. Thread snake on bamboo skewers and grill over medium-hot coals, basting frequently with marinade, until tender, about 4 to 5 minutes.

NOTE: Mirin can be found in Japanese markets and well-stocked supermarkets.

Squirrel

Squirrel meat, although it sounds a bit strange, is really quite tasty. While squirrel is not farm raised, we've included a recipe because of the American tradition of cooking squirrels. Squirrels are the basis for both Brunswick stew and burgoo, two Southern classics.

BRUNSWICK SQUIRREL STEW

SERVES 6

Recommended Wine: A crisp, fruity Sauvignon Blanc plays nicely off the slightly herbal quality of this stew.

2 squirrels, dressed (about 1 pound each)
Flour for dredging
⅓ cup vegetable oil
2 cups sliced yellow onion
2 tablespoons slivered garlic
1 cup fresh or canned thinly sliced pimiento
2 bay leaves, crumbled
6 cups chicken stock or Basic Game Bird Stock (page 40)
2 cups white wine
½ pound young okra, trimmed
1 cup fresh corn kernels
1 cup fresh baby butter beans or lima beans
1 cup diced, peeled white potato
½ cup diced, peeled turnip
1 teaspoon minced fresh rosemary, or ½ teaspoon dried rosemary
Salt and freshly ground black pepper to taste
1 cup finely shredded spinach or cabbage for garnish

Cut each squirrel into 6 serving pieces. Dredge pieces in flour and shake off excess. Heat oil in a heavy-bottomed dutch oven and evenly brown squirrel pieces in batches. Set squirrel aside.

Add onion, garlic, and pimiento to pot and sauté until onion is lightly colored. Add bay leaves, stock, wine, and reserved squirrel and simmer until squirrel is very tender, about 1 hour.

Remove squirrel, cool slightly, and pull meat off bones. Discard skin and bones. Carefully skim fat from cooking liquid in pot. Add meat, okra, corn, beans, potato, turnip, and rosemary. Simmer until potato is just tender, 5 to 7 minutes. Season with salt and pepper and serve immediately, garnished with spinach.

NUTRITIONAL GUIDELINES

*T*his chart is not meant to be a definitive scientific study. The information is a compilation of many nutritional studies that have been done involving game and other meats. It is primarily derived from data published by the United States Department of Agriculture and from other institutional studies. Therefore, the information should be looked upon as broad guidelines only. Data is based on 100-gram (3.5-ounce) portions.

MEAT	CALORIES	FAT (g.)	CHOLESTEROL (mg.)	PROTEIN(g.)
Chicken without skin	140–145	3–4	80–83	26–27
Chicken with skin	200–240	7–9	82–92	25–26
Quail	160–168	6–7	56–70	23–25
Pheasant	145–151	4–5	49–62	24–25
Squab	285–297	23–25	100+	18–19
Beef (bottom round)	205–214	9–10	86–92	29–31
Beef (ground)	240–265	16–18	78–85	23–25
Beef (eye roast)	185–200	14–15	67–70	26–27
Pork (shoulder)	219–225	11–13	90–102	23–29
Rabbit	125–175	3–5	65–69	20–22
Venison (loin)	135–160	2–3	66–69	22–23
Buffalo (round)	130–140	1–3	36–45	35–36

NOTE: All game bird portions measured with skin.

SUPPLIERS AND PRODUCERS

One of the biggest impediments to cooking farm-raised game in this country is its lack of widespread availability. Many meat and poultry sections of large markets stock frozen game, but very few make the fact known to their customers. An even larger number of markets don't stock any game at all, but will almost always special order it on request. Even fewer markets stock fresh game, but the list is increasing all the time.

The following list of game suppliers in the United States, both wholesale and retail, is designed to help you find where to order game on a regular basis. We strongly urge you to contact your local supermarkets and specialty meat and poultry purveyors and ask them to carry game. At the end of each regional list of suppliers, we've included a list of primary producers of farm-raised game in the region. These producers will also often be able to help you find game more readily. Two Canadian sources are included following the regional United States listings.

West

WHOLESALE/RETAIL
Aidells Sausage Company
618 Coventry Road
Kensington, CA 94707
(415) 863-7485

Specialists in smoked game sausages.

Dale's Exotic Game Meats
214 Denargo Market
Denver, CO 80216
(303) 297-WILD

Good assortment of buffalo cuts, venison, elk, wild boar, duck, pheasant, wild turkey, and small game birds, as well as such exotics as alligator, rattlesnake, and snapping turtle. Other exotics available on request.

Durham Night Bird Game & Poultry Co.
650 San Mateo Avenue
San Bruno, CA 94066
(415) 543-6508

P.O. Box 26158
160 Sunol Street
San Jose, CA 95159
(408) 298-6404

A large supplier of furred and feathered game, as well as wild mushrooms, berries, *foie gras*, and smoked items. Retail and wholesale.

Farmworld International Foods
P.O. Box 31
Bend, OR 97709
(503) 388-2806

Wide range of products.

Frank's Fresh Foods
461 Crystal Springs Road
St. Helena, CA 94574
(707) 963-8354

Wide range of furred and feathered game.

The Game Exchange (retail)/Polarica Game
U.S.A., Inc. (wholesale)
107 Quint Street (near Army and Third streets)
San Francisco, CA 94124
(415) 282-7878
(800) GAME-USA

One of the country's largest suppliers of furred and feathered game, including many imported items, as well as wild mushrooms, truffles, caviar, *foie gras*, wild berries, and many smoked items. Home delivery in the San Francisco Bay Area with minimum order; mail order as well.

Game Sales International
P.O. Box 5314
Loveland, CO 80538
(303) 667-4090

Wide range of products.

Krabloonik Country Meat & Specialty Co.
P.O. Box 28607
El Jebel, CO 81628
(303) 963-9013

Buffalo, boar, venison, elk, pheasant, and ducks; smoked products.

Mondo's & Sons
4225 Rainier Avenue South
Seattle, WA 98118
(206) 725-5433 or 725-1565

Wide range of products.

New Zealand Farm-Raised Venison Council
70 Washington, Suite 300
Oakland, CA 94607
(800) 877-1187

The U.S. marketing wing for New Zealand venison.

New Zealand Gourmet
808 South Hindry Avenue
Inglewood, CA 90301
(213) 417-4099

Specializes in venison.

Preferred Meats of San Francisco, Inc.
2050 Galvez
San Francisco, CA 94124
(415) 285-9299
(408) 626-8836

Specializes in venison, duck, and small game birds, as well as sausages and smoked products. Home office in Dallas, Texas.

Reff. Bros. Food Co., Inc.
12650 Riverside Drive
North Hollywood, CA 91607
(818) 349-8932

Wide range of products.

Rocky Mountain Natural Meats
6911 North Washington
Denver, CO 80229
(800) 327-2706

Wide range of buffalo cuts and buffalo sausage.

Sierra Meat & Provision, Inc.
1700 East Second Street
P.O. Box 2456
Reno, NV 89505

Wide range of products.

Retail Only

Bel Air Market Place
640 North Sepulveda Boulevard
Bel Air, CA 90049

Venison.

Bristol Farms
606 Fair Oaks Boulevard
Pasadena, CA

Venison.

Consentino's
South Bascom and Union Avenue
San Jose, CA
(408) 377-6661

3521 Homestead Road
Santa Clara, CA
(408) 243-9005

Selection includes red deer, buffalo, and elk.

Draeger's Supermarket
1010 University Avenue
Palo Alto, CA
(415) 322-6129

Good supply of small game birds.

Galley Meats
610 South Arroyo
Pasadena, CA 91101

Venison.

Kinder Meats
1820 Arnold Industrial Way
Concord, CA 94520

Venison, buffalo, and game birds.

King Soopers
P.O. Box 5567 T.A.
Denver, CO 80217

Venison.

Lunardi's
720 Blossom Hill Road
Los Gatos, CA 95030

Venison.

Magnani's Poultry
6317 College Avenue
Oakland, CA
(415) 428-9496

1586 Hopkins Street
Berkeley, CA
(415) 528-6370

Large selection of game birds.

Marina Safeway
15 Marina Boulevard
San Francisco, CA
(415) 563-1378

Large selection of game birds. Occasional specials on buffalo.

Stockton Poultry
(209) 466-9503

Will ship squab, wild boar, and sheep, as well as other items.

Vic & Ken's Natural Meats (Mrs. Gooch's)
3474 Centinela Avenue
Los Angeles, CA 90066

Venison.

PRODUCERS

Adams & Friend
3022 Trenton Road
Santa Rosa, CA
(707) 887-9598

Rabbits, turkeys, geese.

Buzzard's Roost Ranch
1778 Facendini Lane
Sebastopol, CA
(707) 823-2799

Rabbits, ducks, geese.

Classic Country Rabbit Co.
Hillsboro, OR

Rabbit.

Farm Fresh Squab
(707) 938-8778

Squab.

Grimaude Farms
11665 N. Clements Rd.
Linden, CA 95236
(209) 887-3121

Fresh Muscovy ducks.

Krout's Pheasant Farms
3234 Skillman Lane
Petaluma, CA 94952
(707) 762-8613

Pheasant, wild turkeys, geese, chukar partridge, guinea hens.

Oak Crest Farm
11030 Cherry Ridge Road
Sebastopol, CA
(707) 829-5871

Game birds, Toulouse geese, Rouen ducks, New Zealand rabbits.

Phuel Farms
P.O. Box 154
Sierra Madre, CA 91024
(818) 355-6856

Game birds.

Reichardt Duck Farm
3770 Middle Two Rock Road
Petaluma, CA 94952
(707) 762-6314

Specialists in Pekin ducks.

S & B Farms
125 Lynch Road
Petaluma, CA
(707) 763-4793

Ducks, geese, guinea hens, turkeys, rabbits.

Santa Rosa Game Birds
1077 Butler Avenue
Santa Rosa, CA
(707) 546-1776

All game birds.

Matt Sikora
747 Marshall Avenue
Petaluma, CA
(707) 762-1315

Red and bronze turkeys, wild turkeys, other birds.

South and Southwest

WHOLESALE/RETAIL

Dunn Specialty Meats
1133 53rd Court
Magnolia Park, FL 33207
(305) 848-6644

Wide range of game products.

Inland International, Inc.
1083 Cobb Parkway South
Atlanta, GA 30062
(404) 426-9087
(305) 866-2204 (Miami)
(305) 859-2529 (Orlando)

Wide range of game products.

Preferred Meats, Inc.
318 Cadiz Street, Suite 217
Dallas, TX 75367
(214) 565-0243
(713) 785-6202

Wide range of game products.

Texas Wild Game Cooperative
P.O. Box 530
Ingram, TX 78025
(512) 367-5875
(800) 962-4263

Prime supplier of Texas axis venison, black buck antelope, wild boar, and smoked sausages.

PRODUCERS

Manchester Farms
P.O. Box 97
Dalzell, SC 29040
(800) 845-0421

Quail.

Plantation Quail
1940 Hwy. 15 South
Greensboro, SC 30642
(800) 843-3204

Fresh quail.

The Quail Kitchen
Route 2—Valhalla Farm
Versailles, KY 40385

Smoked game birds.

Royal International Ltd.
601 West 6th Street
Weslaco, TX 78596

Quail.

Midwest

WHOLESALE/RETAIL

Buckmaster Fallow Deer
Capoli Ranch
Lansing, IA 52151
(319) 586-2590

Fallow deer.

Czimer Foods, Inc.
13136 W. 159th St.
Lockport, IL 60441
(708) 301-7152

Wide range of game products.

Treasure Island
3460 North Broadway
Chicago, IL 60657

Eight retail stores.

Wild Game, Inc.
2315 West Huron
Chicago, IL 60612
(312) 278-1661

Wide range of game products.

Wilderness Gourmet
212 South 4th Avenue, Suite 223
Ann Arbor, MI 48104
(313) 663-6987

Wide range of game products.

Producers

The Buffalo Basin
1111 Sixth Street
Highland, IL 62249
(618) 654-2161

Buffalo.

Buffalo Gal
P.O. Box 1964
Rapid City, SD 57709
(605) 342-6434

Buffalo.

Culver Duck Co.
P.O. Box 910
Middlebury, IN 46540
(219) 825-9537

Pekin and Moulard ducks.

El-Bo Farms
Ortonville, MI
(313) 627-6288

Game birds.

Maple Leaf Farms
Milford, IN

Ducks.

National Buffalo Association
10 East Main
Fort Pierre, SD 57532
(605) 223-2829

Represents independent buffalo producers.

Oakwood Game Farms
Princeteon, MN
(800) 328-6649
(612) 389-2077

Game birds.

Peterson Ranches
Newport, NE
(402) 244-5339

Buffalo.

Prairie Farm Specialties
Route 1, Box 31
Waterman, IL 60556
(815) 264-3660

Pheasant, rabbits, suckling pigs, northern bob-white quail, small game birds.

RC Western Meats
P.O. Box 4185
Rapid City, SD 57709
(605) 342-0322

Buffalo.

Whistling Wings
Hanover, IL

Muscovy ducks.

East

WHOLESALE/RETAIL

A.M. Briggs
2130 Queens Chapell Road, N.E.
Washington, DC 20018
(202) 832-2600

Wide range of game products.

D'Artagnan, Inc.
399–419 St. Paul Avenue
Jersey City, NJ 07306
(201) 792-0748/241-4432
(800) DARTAGN

Wide range of game products, including imported European products. Sausages and smoked products, *foie gras*, gallantines, and terrines.

John Dewar
753 Beacon Street
Newton, MA 02159
(617) 442-4292

Wide range of game products.

Dole & Bailey Foodservice
P.O. Box 2405
Woburn, MA 01888
(617) 935-1234

Wide range of game products.

Evans & Van Cleef
1266 4th Street, N.E.
Washington, DC 20002
(202) 546-2150

Wide range of game products.

French Market
1632 Wisconsin, N.W.
Washington, DC 22007

Wide range of game products. Retail also.

Iron Gate Products Co.
424 West 54th Street
New York, NY 10019
(212) 757-2670

Wide range of game products.

Maison Glass
52 East 58th Street
New York, NY 10022
(212) 755-3316
(800) 822-5564

Wide range of game products.

O. Ottomanelli & Sons
281 Bleecker Street
New York, NY 10014
(212) 675-4217

Wide range of game products.

Shaffer, Clarke, & Co., Inc.
Carr's Classic Game
Three Parklands Drive
Darian, CT 06820
(800) 431-2957

Wide range of game products.

World Safari, Inc.
519 S. Larrimore Street
Arlington, VA 22204
(703) 578-0317

Wide range of game products.

PRODUCERS

Foggy Ridge Gamebird Farm
Box 88
Thomaston, ME 04861
(207) 273-2357

Pheasant, chukar partridge, bobwhite quail.

Grayledge Avian Farms
Glastonbury, CT

White Milan pheasant.

L & L Pheasantry
Box 298
Heggins, PA 17938
(717) 682-9074

Game birds.

Lucky Star Ranch
Chaumont, NY 13622
(315) 649-5519
(607) VENISON

Offers a dozen different cuts of fallow deer.

Summerfield Farm
SR 4/Box 195A
Brightwood, VA 22715
(703) 948-3100

Game birds.

Thistlewood Farm
Rt. 1/Box 448
Chantilly, VA 22021
(703) 754-4947

Buffalo.

Canada

Canada Packers—Food Service
30 St. Clair Avenue West
Toronto, Ontario, Canada M4V 3A2
(416) 926-2153

Wide range of game products.

Canwide International Inc.
World Trade Centre
60 Harbour Street
Toronto, Ontario, Canada M5J 1B7
(416) 323-0385

Wide range of game products.

BIBLIOGRAPHY

American Cooking: The Eastern Heartland. Time Life Books, 1971.

Bertolli, Paul, and Waters, Alice. *Chez Panisse Cooking.* Random House, 1988.

Bischoff, Juliet. "Exotic Game: A New Breed." *Meat Industry Magazine,* April 1986.

Bittman, Mark. "Domesticated Birds: The Newest Game in Town." *Cook's Magazine,* November 1989.

Boni, Ada. *Italian Regional Cooking.* Bonanza Books, 1969.

Bradley, Susan. *Pacific Northwest Palate.* Aris Books/Addison Wesley, 1989.

Brillat-Savarin, Jean Anthelme. *Physiology of Taste.* Translated by M. F. K. Fisher. Harvest/HGJ Books, 1949.

Brimi, Arne. *A Taste of Norway.* Norwegian University Press, 1989.

Brown, Ellen. *Cooking with the New American Chefs.* Harper and Row, 1985.

Butazzi, Grazietta. *Toscana in Bocca.* Hill and Wang, 1983.

Byrne-Dodge, Teresa. "Return to the Wild." *Spirit Magazine,* October 1987.

Caen, Herb. "Fair Means or Fowl." *San Francisco Chronicle,* November 1989.

Cameron, Angus, and Jones, Judith. *The L. L. Bean Game and Fish Cookbook.* Random House, 1983.

Camp, Raymond. *Game Cookery in America & Europe.* Wild Duck Press/HP Books, 1983.

Christian, Glynn. "Rules of the Game." *Wine,* September 1987.

Coleman, Louis. *Alexander Dumas Dictionary of Cuisine.* Simon and Schuster, 1958.

Creasy, Rosalind. *Cooking from the Garden.* Sierra Books, 1988.

Czarnecki, Joe. *Joe's Book of Mushroom Cookery.* Atheneum, 1986.

David, Elizabeth. *An Omelette and a Glass of Wine.* Elizabeth Sifton Books, 1952.

Digby, John, and Digby, Joan. *Food for Thought.* William Morrow and Co., 1987.

Drysdale, Julia. *Classic Game Cookery.* Macmillan Press/The Game Conservancy, 1975.

Egerton, John. *Southern Food.* Alfred A. Knopf, 1987.

Fearing, Dean. *The Mansion on Turtle Creek Cookbook.* Grove Weidenfeld, 1987.

Ferrary, Jeannette, and Fiszer, Louise. *Season to Taste.* Simon and Schuster, 1988.

Feniger, Susan, and Milliken, Mary Sue. *City Cuisine.* William Morrow and Co., Inc., 1989.

Fisher, M. F. K. *The Art of Eating.* Vintage Books, 1976.

Folse, John. *The Evolution of Cajun and Creole Cuisine.* Wimmer Brothers, 1989.

Graubard, Mark. *Man's Food: Its Rhyme or Reason.* Macmillan, 1943.

Grausman, Richard. *At Home with the French Classics*. Workman Publishing, 1988.

Greene, Fayal. "Invaluable Marinades." *Sports Afield*, October 1977.

————. "Sauce for the Goose, Turkey, and Quail." *Sports Afield*, December 1977.

————. "Wild Turkey: The King of Gamebirds." *Sports Afield*, November 1977.

Harris, Gladiola. *Old Trace Cooking: Native American and Pioneer Recipes*. Riverside Press, 1981.

Herman, Judith, and Herman, Margaret Shalett. *The Cornucopia*. Harper and Row, 1973.

Hom, Ken. *Ken Hom's East Meets West Cuisine*. Simon and Schuster, 1987.

————. *Fragrant Harbor Taste*. Simon and Schuster, 1989.

Hooker, Richard. *A History of Food and Drink in America*. Bobbs-Merrill, 1981.

Houser, Dave G. "Fare Game." *American Way*, November 1986.

Hughes, Mike. *The Broken Arrow Ranch Cookbook*. University of Texas Press, 1985.

Karena, Juanita Tiger. *Hopi Cooking*. University of Arizona Press, 1980.

Kreidberg, Marjorie. *Food on the Frontier*. Minnesota Historical Society, 1975.

Livingston, A. P. *Outdoor Life's Complete Fish & Game Cookbook*. Grolier Book Clubs, 1989.

Machan, Dyan. "Bambi and the Baron." *Forbes*, December 1989.

Manion, Timothy. *Game & Fish Menu Cookbook—A Country Collection*. Weidenfeld and Nicholson, 1987.

McGee, Harold. *On Food and Cooking*. Collier Books (Macmillan), 1984.

McHugh, Tom. *The Time of the Buffalo*. Alfred A. Knopf, 1972.

Oliver, Raymond. *La Cuisine*. Leon Amiel, 1969.

Robbins, Maria Polushkin. *The Cook's Quotation Book—A Literary Feast*. Pushcart Press, 1983.

Rosengarten, David, and Wesson, Joshua. *Red Wine with Fish*. Simon and Schuster, 1989.

Rombauer, Irma S., and Becker, Marion Rombauer. *Joy of Cooking*. New American Library, 1931.

Root, Waverley. *Food*. Fireside Books, 1980.

Root, Waverly, and de Rochemont, Richard. *Eating in America*. Ecco Press, 1976.

Rosso, Julee, and Lukins, Sheila. *The New Basics*. Workman Publishing, 1989.

Sax, Richard. "New Rules for Game." *Cook's Magazine*, September/October 1985.

————. "Tame Game." *Food & Wine Magazine*, January 1988.

Schneider, Elizabeth. *Uncommon Fruits & Vegetables: A Commonsense Guide*. Harper and Row, 1986.

Schwabe, Calvin. *Unmentionable Cuisine*. University of Virginia Press, 1979.

Scott, Philippa. *Gourmet Game*. Simon and Schuster, 1989.

Sokolov, Raymond. *Fading Feast*. Farrar, Straus, Giroux, 1981.

Stech-Novak, Mark. Unpublished manuscript.

Summers, Pat. "Sonoma Foie Gras." *Catering Today*, January/February 1990.

Tower, Jeremiah. *Jeremiah Tower's New American Classics*. Harper and Row, 1986.

Villas, James. *American Taste*. Arbor House, 1982.

Willoughby, John, and McCombie, T. J., "Step-by-Step to Great Smoked Food." *Cook's Magazine*, June 1990.

Wilson, C. Anne. *Food and Drink in Britain*, Harper and Row, 1974.

Wise, Naomi. *Meat & Game Cookery*. Ortho Books, 1988.

Wolfert, Paula. *The Cooking of South-West France*. Dial Press, 1983.

INDEX